Electronic
Whistle-Stops

Electronic Whistle-Stops

The Impact of the Internet on American Politics

Gary W. Selnow

Praeger Series in Political Communication

PRAEGER

Westport, Connecticut
London

Library of Congress Cataloging-in-Publication Data

Selnow, Gary W.
    Electronic whistle-stops : the impact of the Internet on American
politics / Gary W. Selnow.
        p.   cm.—(Praeger series in political communication, ISSN
1062–5623)
    Includes bibliographical references and index.
    ISBN 0–275–96163–X (alk. paper).—ISBN 0–275–96164–8 (pbk. :
alk. paper)
    1. Internet (Computer network)—Political aspects.
    2. Communication in politics—United States.   I. Title.
    II. Series.
    H61.95.S45   1998
    320.973—dc21   97–34745

British Library Cataloguing in Publication Data is available.

Library of Congress Catalog Card Number: 97–34745
ISBN: 0–275–96163–X
      0–275–96164–8 (pbk.)
ISSN: 1062–5623

First published in 1998

Praeger Publishers, 88 Post Road West, Westport, CT 06881
An imprint of Greenwood Publishing Group, Inc.

Printed in the United States of America

The paper used in this book complies with the
Permanent Paper Standard issued by the National
Information Standards Organization (Z39.48–1984).

10 9 8 7 6 5 4 3 2 1

In memory of Charles Kuralt

Contents

Series Foreword

Those of us from the discipline of communication studies have long believed that communication is prior to all other fields of inquiry. In several other forums I have argued that the essence of politics is "talk" or human interaction.[1] Such interaction may be formal or informal, verbal or nonverbal, public or private, but it is always persuasive, forcing us consciously or subconsciously to interpret, to evaluate, and to act. Communication is the vehicle for human action.

From this perspective, it is not surprising that Aristotle recognized the natural kinship of politics and communication in his writings *Politics* and *Rhetoric*. In the former, he established that humans are "political beings [who] alone of the animals [are] furnished with the faculty of language."[2] In the latter, he began his systematic analysis of discourse by proclaiming that "rhetorical study, in its strict sense, is concerned with the modes of persuasion."[3] Thus, it was recognized over 2,300 years ago that politics and communication go hand in hand because they are essential parts of human nature.

In 1981, Dan Nimmo and Keith Sanders proclaimed that political communication was an emerging field.[4] Although its origin, as noted, dates back centuries, a "self-consciously cross-disciplinary" focus began in the late 1950s. Thousands of books and articles later, colleges and universities offer a variety of graduate and undergraduate courses in the area in such diverse departments as communication, mass communication, journalism, political science, and sociology.[5] In Nimmo and Sanders's early assessment, the "key areas of inquiry" included rhetorical analysis, propaganda analysis, attitude change studies, voting studies, government and the news media, functional and systems analyses, technological changes, media technologies, campaign techniques, and research techniques.[6] In a survey of the state of the field in 1983, the same authors and Lynda Kaid found additional, more specific areas of concern, such as the presidency, political polls, public opinion, debates, and advertising.[7] Since the first study, they also noted a shift away from the rather strict behavioral approach.

Half a decade later, Dan Nimmo and David Swanson argued that "political communication has developed some identity as a more or less distinct domain of scholarly work."[8] The scope and concerns of the area have further expanded to include critical theories and cultural studies. Although there is no precise definition, method, or disciplinary home of the area of inquiry, its primary domain comprises the role, processes, and effects of communication within the context of politics broadly defined.

In 1985, the editors of *Political Communication Yearbook: 1984* noted that "more things are happening in the study, teaching, and practice of political communication than can be captured within the space limitations of the relatively few publications available."[9] In addition, they argued that the backgrounds of "those involved in the field [are] so varied and pluralist in outlook and approach, . . . it [is] a mistake to adhere slavishly to any set format in shaping the content."[10] More recently, Swanson and Nimmo have called for "ways of overcoming the unhappy consequences of fragmentation within a framework that respects, encourages, and benefits from diverse scholarly commitments, agendas, and approaches."[11]

In agreement with these assessments of the area and with gentle encouragement, in 1988 Praeger established the series Praeger Studies in Political Communication. The series is open to all qualitative and quantitative methodologies as well as contemporary and historical studies. The key to characterizing the studies in the series is the focus on communication variables or activities within a political context or dimension. As of this writing, nearly 70 volumes have been published and numerous impressive works are forthcoming. Scholars from the disciplines of communication, history, journalism, political science, and sociology have participated in the series.

I am, without shame or modesty, a fan of the series. The joy of serving as its editor is in participating in the dialogue of the field of political communication and in reading the contributors' works. I invite you to join me.

Robert E. Denton, Jr.

NOTES

1. See Robert E. Denton, Jr., *The Symbolic Dimensions of the American Presidency* (Prospect Heights, IL: Waveland Press, 1982); Robert E. Denton, Jr., and Gary

Woodward, *Political Communication in America* (New York: Praeger, 1985; 2d ed., 1990); Robert E. Denton, Jr., and Dan Hahn, *Presidential Communication* (New York: Praeger, 1986); and Robert E. Denton, Jr., *The Primetime Presidency of Ronald Reagan* (New York: Praeger, 1988).

2. *The Politics of Aristotle*, trans. Ernest Barker (New York: Oxford University Press, 1970), 5.

3. Aristotle, *Rhetoric*, trans. Rhys Roberts (New York: Modern Library, 1954), 22.

4. Dan Nimmo and Keith Sanders, "Introduction: The Emergence of Political Communication as a Field," in *Handbook of Political Communication*, ed. Dan Nimmo and Keith Sanders (Beverly Hills, CA: Sage, 1981), 11–36.

5. Ibid., 15.

6. Ibid., 17–27.

7. Keith Sanders, Lynda Kaid, and Dan Nimmo, eds., *Political Communication Yearbook: 1984* (Carbondale: Southern Illinois University Press, 1985), 283–308.

8. Dan Nimmo and David Swanson, "The Field of Political Communication: Beyond the Voter Persuasion Paradigm," in *New Directions in Political Communication*, ed. David Swanson and Dan Nimmo (Beverly Hills, CA: Sage, 1990), 8.

9. Sanders, Kaid, and Nimmo, *Political Communication Yearbook: 1984*, xiv.

10. Ibid.

11. Nimmo and Swanson, "The Field of Political Communication," 11.

Preface

In mid-1993, at the end of a cabinet meeting, Vice President Al Gore asked a department secretary to stroll with him down the long corridor, past the cabinet room to a small office that held a personal computer. The men entered the office and found displayed on the computer screen the elegant White House Website, said to be the first official government site in the world. The page offered information about the White House building, its history, and its occupants dating back to George Washington. It provided documents and press releases, E-mail connections, and a link to sites for kids. The White House page also linked to each of the 13 federal departments; this switch box to the government agencies was Al Gore's pride and joy.

The vice president showed off the site and beamed with pride, the way a young executive radiates when showing off a new Porsche. Toward the end of his three-minute cybertour, Gore scrolled to the links connecting the government departments.

Gore hesitated, then encouraged an uneasy silence as he zeroed in on the link for that cabinet member's department. The vice president clicked the mouse, and the monitor slowly resolved into a dull, gray backdrop with a vexing message saying the site was empty. Gore stared deadpan at the ashen-faced cabinet secretary, leaving no doubt about the meaning of the empty screen or the purpose of the demonstration.

This gentle but firm trip to the woodshed illustrates Gore's commitment to a federal government that is fully installed on the Internet. The insider who tells this story reports that by the next cabinet meeting, the department's site was up and running.

Two and a half years later, by the election of 1996, the Internet had grown a thousandfold since the White House first went on-line and that cabinet secretary scrambled to create his site.[1] Over a half-million sites had been installed, 40 million users had access, and more than three out of four candidates for the House and Senate had created Web pages.

Despite such rapid growth, the medium in 1996 was too young and untested to be much of a political force. Campaigns didn't know what to pack *into* their sites; voters didn't know what they wanted to pull *out* of the sites. Forecasts of the Internet's great influence on the campaigns never materialized, but the trouble was with the predictions, not the medium. The Internet was growing much faster than had radio or television in their days, but even this swiftly moving innovation needed time to mature. Users on both sides of the Websites had to experiment with ways to press this medium into useful service, the 1996 campaigns being a useful and frustrating laboratory.

From this first bench test of the Internet, several things became abundantly clear. Although it had the look and feel of the conventional media—text, pictures, audio, and video—the Internet could not use these formats as they had been used. Audiences are in firmer control of the Internet, have more to say about what information they delve into, and how they use it. The traditional relationship between the sources and recipients of information was somehow changing into something we had not seen before.

For the first time this century, the iron lock of the mainstream media was broken. The Big Three network sites, the major newspaper sites, and the heavily bankrolled political sites stood side by side with mom-and-pop sites that promoted fringe candidates, backed unfashionable ideologies, told the news as they saw it, and marshaled audiences around unorthodox points of view. This strangely populist medium defied the establishment powers that throughout this century (and back into the nineteenth century, through newspapers) had controlled the flow of information and, thereby, the political agenda. If nothing else, the test run in 1996 foreshadows a time when information control will be more broadly shared.

Most impressively, this is the first medium in history to accommodate direct voter feedback. Uplining was never seriously tested during the campaigns, but a few successful trial runs at the end of the election suggest that feedback will revolutionize the Internet and consequently alter public communication. Indeed, the fate of this medium hinges on the flow of information from the users to the Website and back again. There can be no doubt that the main force in this unfolding saga will be interactivity.

There is some evidence in the 1996 inaugural run of the Internet that it blesses with one hand and curses with the other. Ultratargeting, which allows users to track down topics of narrow personal interest, tampers

with a common agenda that has united the country around shared problems. As citizens and voters we often don't agree, but we usually argue
about the same things. The narrow channeling of individual interests
stands to fragment our delicate, pluralistic system and to deepen society's fissures.

We approach this inaugural use of the Internet in political campaigns
with the uncertainty of just where it is all going. It's like speculating on
whether a strange, green stem sprouting in the garden will fascinate us
with its blossoms or threaten us with its thorns. We can only describe
the earlier plants from which it may have issued and do our best to
speculate on its ultimate contribution to the garden.

NOTE

1. During and just after the 1996 election, the White House Website had the
following audience reach: July 1996, 1.1 percent; October 1996, 1.5 percent; November 1996, 1.5 percent; January 1997, 1.7 percent. These statistics refer to the
percentage of people using the World Wide Web who accessed the White House
site at least once during the month. Data provided by Bruce Ryan, vice president
of the Technology Division, PC Meter (subsidiary of NPD Group, Inc.), citing the
company's "Web Audience Measurement Ratings."

Acknowledgments

I am beholden to Richard Gilbert for his guidance and many suggestions for this book. His insights on American media, honed at NBC Television, were invaluable in providing a meaningful context for the Web. Thanks to the dozens of professional journalists who contributed to an understanding of what the Internet means to American news media. Special thanks to Marvin Kalb, who has been an extraordinary help in this and, over the years, in other writing projects. His knowledge of the media is truly remarkable. Charles Kuralt, who had a unique understanding of the American people, saw the Internet as a great populist medium that would become an information tool of the masses. He never tired of making that point, and it is a perspective that I have tried not to lose in this writing. Thanks to Bill Brock, once U.S. senator, secretary of labor, U.S. trade representative, and head of the Republican National Committee. His deep concern for the integrity of American politics is heartening, and his faith in the system is reassuring at a time when money fouls the electoral process and public cynicism regarding government is so high. His thoughts about the contribution of the Internet to political communication were invaluable. Finally, thanks to the many campaign staffers and Website designers who contributed so freely to the discussion in this book. These men and women are the pioneers of this new and unexplored territory, and it is they who, in the end, will have much to say about how the medium will be used in American political communication.

Introduction

THE POLITICS OF PROXIMITY

Presidential historian Theodore H. White once wrote that the completion of the coaxial cable in November 1951 nationalized American opinion.[1] The cable was symbolic and functional, shrinking the 3,000 miles that separate the coasts to the centimeters that separate split-screen images, compressing the time for information to cross the continent from days to seconds.

As a result, the media, then serving dispersed national audiences, found it necessary to weld scattered regional perspectives into singular national views, to collapse local concerns into national agendas. Media searched for the center of American audiences, and if they could not find these centers, they had to forge them and lead the country to a *nationalized* opinion.

Operating in an environment where voters are tugged toward a consensus of views, candidates faced a long-standing concern now intensified by the national media: how to demonstrate a capacity for national issues without yielding a grasp on local interests. Paraphrasing a familiar bumper sticker, politicians had to act nationally and think locally, and they had to be conspicuous doing both. Those who drift too far from the people who put them in office are soon reminded of the price.

Years ago, Senator J. William Fulbright of Arkansas, a shining star on the national stage, flickered briefly at home and faded from the Washington sky. Tom Foley, a powerful speaker of the House, was defeated in 1994 when his political horizons became broader than the vistas of Washington's Fifth Congressional district.[2] Even former electoral champs

Ted Kennedy and Bill Bradley only squeaked by when their national preoccupations distanced them from voters at home.

While running for political office, and while in possession of it, political figures have long recognized the need to be seen as one of the people. That image is fundamental to a representative form of government and essential to a successful candidacy. Office seekers pack in as many pancake breakfasts and fried chicken dinners as their arteries can stand, in order to remind voters that the candidate is just like "one of you."

Lamar Alexander, in his 1978 bid for the governorship of Tennessee, walked across the state to meet the people in the streets. In Alexander's 1996 run for the Republican presidential nomination, his device was a plebeian, red-checked shirt. Texas senatorial candidate Victor Morales crisscrossed the Longhorn State in his white pickup truck, washing down Texas dust with cafe coffee. This put him nose to nose with Texans in their own backyards.

Staying close to the people ideologically, spiritually, and physically has been endemic to American politics since our nation's beginning. George Washington, who often suffered character slams from a feisty press, was especially bruised by claims that he held receptions in "court-like levees" in "queenly drawing-rooms" to feed his own vanity.[3] Such descriptions of his presidency, true or not, were anathema to Washington's perceptions of the office and of himself, and he bitterly fought them.

The need of the officeholder to be seen with the people is a tradition perhaps best symbolized by the whistle-stop tours of Harry Truman, although they were used by other candidates. Truman used his signature whistle-stop tours for all their strategic and symbolic advantages in demonstrating that the candidate stood shoulder to shoulder with the people. In his run for office in 1948, Truman left on a 21,928-mile trip aboard a Pullman called "The Ferdinand Magellan," from which he would make more than 275 prepared speeches and some 200 off-the-cuff speeches, reaching by the end of the tour nearly 15 million people.[4] At one stop in Dexter, Iowa, Truman made an impromptu speech that leaves no doubt about his appreciation for political proximity—his need to be seen with the people. Before a crowd of farmers gathered for a national plowing contest, Truman told a story of his own labors in the field. Historian Alfred Steinberg describes the event this way: " 'I could plow a straight furrow. . . . A prejudiced witness said so—my mother.' He described how he used to seed a 160-acre wheat field 'without leaving a skip.' He went on to brag that he did all this with only four mules and a gangplow, not the tractors of the modern era. The farmers whooped and hollered."[5]

In Truman's day, the whistle-stop tour both *brought* the messages to the people and *demonstrated* that he was bringing the messages to the people, two accomplishments that furthered his goals of being identified with the muddy-booted masses. Nearly 50 years later, Bill Clinton rode the rails to the 1996 Chicago convention; his whistle-stop tour also served both goals, but now with a vastly more sophisticated communication structure in place. The clear focus of his travels across four Midwestern states was not the people gathered at the back of his train, but the cameras and microphones assembled to record it all for voters in the rest of the country. Clinton's train, of course, was less a mode of transportation than a stage prop designed to demonstrate that even the small backwater towns were not too small and their residents were not too inconsequential for the candidate, suggesting that in this era of big media, there may be greater need than ever for candidates to demonstrate their proximity to the smallest voter groups, to show that powerful officeholders and wannabees are not out of touch with the people.

The television, radio, and newspapers that have dominated the channels of political communication throughout the last half of this century are very good at *showing* the candidates among the people—shaking hands, kissing babies, eating yet another barbecued drumstick. What these media cannot do, however, is enable the candidates to *become* personal with those voters; they can only show images of it. That being the nature of the beast, candidates of late have turned to other technologies to demonstrate their kinship.

Since the late 1980s, twin engines have driven the personal components of the political information machine. The first is public opinion polls, which sound out the population and reveal pockets of like-minded voters. They disclose how voters feel, and why they feel that way. The polls illuminate the scores of tiny voter bull's-eyes at which targeted communications are aimed.

The other engine is the database. Databases isolate individual voters by age, race, income, party affiliation, and a dozen other traits. Together, the polls and the databases allow candidates to generate "personal" communications through letters and phone calls, and in some cases through face-to-face contacts by staffers or the candidates themselves. These interpersonal contacts enable the office seekers to single out specific issues, specify their messages, and personalize their appeals to voters one by one—or so it may seem to voters.

A closer look reveals that these warm, personal messages, in most cases, are generated by cold, compassionless computers. Truly personal or not, the candidates have been looking for a sure course around the wire, tube, or print, and computers can provide it.[6]

Now the Internet, a medium made in heaven for personalization, offers political candidates a tool they could only dream of a few years ago. Through E-mail, it allows the delivery of individual messages and personal appeals to voters. Through chat rooms it offers candidates direct access to virtual communities of voters. Through the Web it allows voters to seek out items of personal interest about the candidate and the campaign. Efficient and inexpensive, the Internet is becoming vastly popular among American voters—and that's good news for candidates. If it continues to grow as projected, the Internet soon will stand alongside the conventional media and become an indispensable tool in political communication.

Pioneers of cybercommunication display an unwavering optimism that has carried this medium during the early days. The Web, in particular, has been a youthful adventure, the "kids" becoming the driving forces behind the architecture and content of the earliest sites.

The establishment, however, quickly caught on to the fact that there could be gold in this mine. Afraid to be a breakthrough behind, the big players in the Fortune 500—such as GE-NBC, Disney, ABC, Westinghouse-CBS, and the national news organs—sent their claimstakers into cyberspace. Their money has had quite an effect on the evolution of the medium.

In the next few pages, we offer some context by way of an overview of the topics that weave through this book. The use of the Internet in the 1996 campaigns has a significance that transcends the political figures who set up Web sites to impress constituents. Their limited use of the medium was little more than frivolous.

But, neither frivolous nor gimmicky, the Internet is shaping up to be a serious international medium that will radically alter politics in the United States and abroad, and what's more, it will impact society on a larger level. It stands to change political and ideological alignments, the substance of news available to the population, and the relationships between political leaders and the people.

A PLACE AMONG THE MEDIA

The Internet arrives in the shadow of radio and television, twentieth-century technological wonders that brought remarkable breadth to human communication. The Internet invites immediate comparison, and on many dimensions it matches—or soon will—the broadcast media sound for sound, image for image. It also bears the text and pictures of newspapers, but is faster and publishes in living color. Roger Hurwitz, a research scientist at the Artificial Intelligence Laboratory at M.I.T., calls the Internet a huge copy machine, duplicating the formats of all the other media.[7]

But this medium is more than the sum of its parts. Unlike competing media, it allows audiences to send information back, and that changes the chemistry of communication. In Hurwitz's words, the Internet, with its two-way flow, is not a *mass medium* but a *master medium*. It is every-thing the others are, and more.

Much of the potential of the Internet was not evident during the 1996 election. E-mail and text-based delivery formats had been around for a number of years, and they had been used in campaigns since Jimmy Carter's first run at the White House.[8] It was the World Wide Web, however, that attracted major attention from voters and political cam-paigns, even if it was only a toddler at the time of the election. Few people producing sites or visiting them understood the real character of this wired-in baby. We stood rapt, like anxious parents watching eagerly for signs of talents and special skills.

Although the Internet embodies all the other media, those precedents don't help us understand it. Some observers believe the precedents may even have hurt, to the extent that programmers tried blindly to copy the formats and content of the other media. That gave their sites an uncom-fortable fit, and it probably slowed down experimentation. Audio wasn't all that good, and video was poor at best. Even as these features im-proved some through the campaign year, their old uses did not splice easily onto this new medium.

When it came to text, early audiences displayed little tolerance for lengthy copy. In the first year out, site developers (and journalists) learned to write in layers like an onion, allowing users to stay on the surface or, if they found an interest, peal down to the core of an issue.

As for content, the programmers and the audiences were still com-paring notes, still trying to find that match between what the office seek-ers wanted to say and what the voters wanted to hear. They were looking for a congruence of purpose and a union of interests, and they just didn't find it by Election Day.

The biggest slipup of the political season was the misuse of feedback. "Nonuse" may be more fitting. Hurwitz said that site developers were so mired in the broadcast model that they overlooked the extraordinary benefit of getting information *from* voters, thereby discarding the me-dium's greatest gift. They could have done so much, he said, even with the technology they had in hand, but they missed the chance. This is unlikely to happen in future elections, because in this medium it isn't what the *senders* want so much as what the *receivers* want. That old con-cept has a new urgency on the Internet. Here, it's truly a buyer's market.

POLITICAL AUDIENCES

Millions of people browsed the Web during the 1996 election, but many more millions stayed away, their absence a matter of *cost, inertia,* and *fear*. Except for the new $500 Internet boxes that began to surface late in 1996, most of the equipment was expensive and beyond the reach of large portions of the population. Even the new, low-cost hookups were too pricy for many people.

Others could have afforded the equipment, software, and connections, but these late adopters simply resist innovation. Their inertia is stong; they take time to accept the inevitability of something new, and only when they are certain of it do they make their moves. For millions, it was not yet time in 1996.

Finally, large portions of the population may have been ready, willing, and able to get into the technology, but for lack of a better term, they were frightened. The process of buying and assembling the hardware, loading the software, and completing the on-line connections was too confusing, even intimidating. Setting up the gear and logging onto a Website is demanding, especially compared to plugging in a TV and tuning in the evening news. The technical obstacles to this medium are formidable.

Andrew Glass, Cox Washington bureau chief, among the most Internet-savvy journalists in Washington, said that the Internet cannot blend fully into the family of media until its procedures become transparent. "Look at the telephone. Nobody frets about how to dial it or how to use the handset, or when they're finished talking, how to hang it up. They just pick it up and have a conversation. It's a matter of content over procedure."[9]

With the Internet, it's just the opposite. Procedure still dominates content for huge portions of the audience, and until that changes—until the medium itself becomes transparent—it cannot make a significant contribution to the information pool.

The real punch of the Internet will not be felt in politics or in any other application until the medium opens up to a broader audience. The question on the minds of many Internet advocates is how to encourage wider adoption by average people.

CENTRALIZED MEDIA

Technology, of course, has shaped the evolution and image of the conventional media, but so has the ownership structure. Throughout this century, only well-heeled individuals, powerful politicians, and large companies could buy into the major media. Radio and television stations and newspapers, with large numbers of daily readers, listeners, and viewers, cost millions to buy and operate. Today, cost restricts ownership to moneyed interests whose objectives, by necessity or charter, are to earn a profit. Heart, mind, and soul, the conventional media are businesses, governed by the natural laws of any business. This means that they must sell enough papers and generate enough programs that draw large enough audiences to pay the bills at the end of the month before turning a profit for the owners. That's the nature of the information business, and it drives media content in several ways.

First, advertisers pay by the pound, (so to speak), and media are therefore pressured to attract the largest possible audience. They call it "cost per thousand," and the multiples are in millions. The fare must have broad appeal to popular tastes, not too far left or right, not too torrid or puritan, not too assertive of anyone's perspective. Obviously, the shows that aim at "everybody" can't stray too far from mainstream norms. Get pushy, and audiences slough off at the edges, then advertisers follow the audiences to other media. The forces of conformity are strong and convincing, and inevitably they hammer conventional media into flat, common images.

Research supports this. Content analyses have revealed the homogeneity of news coverage. Media Watch content analyses, for instance, reveal that "212 TV markets, 750 stations with local TV news, 80 million people in the audience, and they're all doing the same thing."[10] Similarly, city newspapers, often drawing from the same wire services and press pools, have a common look and feel.[11]

The second effect that business incentives have on conventional media content is that they dampen experimentation with new topics and treatments. Some of this comes from the frenzy of buyouts. Gobbling up the competition does away with a principal incentive to innovate.

Then, too, programmers and editors are inclined to follow *Car Talk*'s Tom Magliozzi's caution: "If it ain't broke, don't break it."[12] If conventional story lines and formulas are drawing in ample audiences and eager advertisers, why tamper with the recipe? Maybe it's the fear of chasing off an audience, maybe it's complacency or comfort with what you know, but conventional media are loath to venture from the well-trodden path.

Innovations among television networks come largely from the rookies like Fox, which, as a start-up in the mid-1980s, had little to lose with programs like *Married with Children, A Current Affair,* and a line up of Gen X-oriented shows that pushed the conventional boundaries and challenged audiences with unconventional fare. Not all experimentation leads to exemplary programming, that's clear; but good or bad, Fox elbowed its way into the hurly-burly of network television with material that the Big Three wouldn't touch with a 10-foot pole. Fox found enough viewers to sustain itself and prosper while offering audiences new choices that weaned away 10 million a night from the big networks.

With the surge of cable television in the mid-1970s, a number of smaller, alternative cable stations and networks have evolved, each experimenting with niche programming. The likes of A&E, CNN, and MTV offer special-interest programming, although they must still attract hefty audiences to sustain production costs. Despite cable subscriber fees, television is an expensive business that requires programmers with deep pockets. Even niche programmers proceed with caution.

Radio offers an interesting addition to the media lineup because its costs are relatively low and its needs for audiences are modest; it therefore has more room for experimentation and innovation. Radio programmers can succeed with a narrow slice of the audience pie, and they can offer formats that have limited appeal. Further, if one programming attempt fails, stations can, without great expense, retool for another format and target another audience subgroup.[13] The variety of programming available on the dial is a testament to the adaptability of this medium.

A DECENTRALIZED MEDIUM

The Internet is the first truly decentralized medium with population-wide appeal and global reach. Financial constraints on conventional media are largely absent on the Internet, and since programming and ownership costs are much lower, the new medium has become a playground of experimentation and innovation, and anyone can get in the game. Still, while most Internet operators run their sites on a shoestring, a few large outfits maintain elaborate and relatively costly sites. They offer a bridge between the centralized and decentralized media. For them, one of three financial conditions must be in place.

First, following the traditional model, they must draw in enough users to attract advertisers. Sites that adopt this commercial approach must also buy into the rest of the model, which is to adopt programming material broad enough to entice an adequate audience base. In this business, it's the number of hits that matters, or more appropriately, the number of page views.[14] Here, as in newspapers, radio, and television, advertisers want large numbers; thus site owners find themselves looking for the least common denominator of programming, much as the conventional media do.

One celebrated television producer, considering a major foray into the Web, said in an interview that he was planning to adapt his standard television formulas to the new medium. He hoped his Website would replicate his past successes on television, and for him this meant big programming, big audiences, and big advertisers bankrolling the operation. He was thinking about investing in a risky experiment, testing the wisdom of creating a broad-based site in an inherently narrow-based medium.[15]

He isn't alone; a number of other programmers are attempting to reach large, heterogeneous audiences through the Web. It's like squeezing the elder sister's foot into Cinderella's shoe. Will it work? The results are still out, although no less a powerhouse than Microsoft has pulled back

from its large "network" operation.[16] There are few votes of confidence
for the concept.[17]

The second way to run a big Website is to assess user fees, usually
through a monthly charge (e.g., Electronic Library[18]). Issue a password
to eligible users and collect money through credit cards or cybercash.
Although this may become more common, it was a technique little used
during the election year.

Third, the big sites can be bankrolled by individual or organizational
owners with pockets deep enough to sustain the operation themselves.
This sounds like a big commitment, but keep in mind that development
and upkeep costs of even the most ambitious Websites pale in the face
of costs for conventional media. It doesn't take a huge bankroll to pull
off the self-financed Web site. Of course, without an expectation of outside income, the site owner is free of the need to amass large audiences
and this, in turn, opens the door to innovative content.

Most players on the Internet, though, don't establish sites with
thoughts of huge audiences and profits. Motivated by some personal
conviction to communicate, if only with themselves, they shell out the
few dollars, write their own copy, design their own layout, assemble
their own formatting code, and they're in business. That's the great attraction of a decentralized medium: almost anyone can set up his own
operation. These do-it-yourselfers often build credible sites with the technical prowess of the major players. Programming a Website is rapidly
becoming more complex, but during the campaign, when html code was
most common, it was surprisingly simple. The low technical and financial barriers to entry have become the hallmark of this medium and the
key to its rich, populist inventory.

Programmers are in it because they are committed to a point of view,
smitten by the technology, or inflated by their own presence on a global
medium. These and a driving passion for the political bustle may explain
why a lion's share of the political sites were on-line during the 1996
campaign season.

Some of those sites defy classification, but most fell into one of several
categories: sites maintained by candidates, parties, or campaign committees (e.g., the Clinton and Dole pages, the Republican and Democratic
National Committees, and the Republican and Democratic Campaign
Committees of Congress); neutral or nonprofit organizations (e.g., Project
Vote Smart, the Freedom Forum), news organizations (e.g., CBS and
NBC News, the *Chicago Tribune*, MSNBC), professional organizations
(e.g., Investigative Reporters and Editors, Radio-Television News Directors Association). Add religious groups (e.g., the Christian Coalition and
the U.S. Catholic Conference) and individuals, lots of individuals.

Never before have so many voices, singing so many tunes, been so
widely available during an election year. The contrast with all previous

elections is startling. Coming from an era when steep media entry fees kept away all but those who could affort it, political aficionados in 1996 saw that pocket change could put them in the game and keep them at the table.

Campaigns pitched candidates, news and research organizations fronted "objective" information, but the real story in 1996 was that of individuals and small groups who ran the sites as laboratories of free expression.

One prominent example is the site run by Ethel Black, a 60-year-old housewife in Los Angeles, who was upset with what she said were Clinton-bashing newspaper stories and talk shows, and anti-Clinton Websites.[19] In the spring of 1994, Black set up "Clinton, Yes!" She spent practically nothing, using a complementary Website that came with her service provider subscription. Black loaded her free page with unabashedly pro-Clinton editorials and news features. She defended Hillary, taught lobbying, told political jokes. This housewife, whose views otherwise would have never have seen the light of day, reached tens of thousands of voters nationwide.[20]

The effectiveness of such sites, their ultimate contribution to the election or defeat of a candidate, remains unanswered. That question hasn't been completely answered for television, and TV's been a campaign tool for 50 years. Research on Web effects is scant. Many of the political sites had few customers, so even if the site *could* affect voters, there often was little chance to do so en masse. For every Ethel Black who found success in a site, there were scores of little-celebrated, do-it-yourself Web operators who became their own best audience. But in that inaugural year of politics on the Internet, the central issue was access, not influence. Low thresholds of entry in this decentralized medium made ownership possible for a huge new cadre of dabblers for whom participation in traditional media was beyond reach.

THE INTERNET AND NEWS CONTENT

The conventional media were quick to get on-line with electronic versions of their print and broadcast stories. Some players, like C/Net and HotWired—creatures of the Web—have no presence in print or broadcast. They don't put a word to paper or air a remark from a human voice. The entire news product of these organizations resides in the ethereal vapors of cyberspace. That everywhere-and-nowhere concept takes some getting used to.

Several media joined hands in the creation of political megasites such as PoliticsNow and PoliticsUSA. These and other sites like them in 1996 provided a rich vein of information that was entirely new in political coverage. Never before has any medium created a purely political news product designed for the masses. It's true that these sites may slice from the voting population only a sliver of the audience attracted to politics. But the hope of developers is over time to stimulate greater interest among a broader spectrum of voters, thereby expanding the size of the slice.

Journalists reported the news on the Web, but they also gathered information from it. The Web was unmatched in its publishing of the text of speeches and position papers, of schedules and information that often were difficult to obtain from other sources. And it was a raving success—to a fault—in dispensing the results on Election Night.[21]

The Web also was brimming with poll data, financial data, and statistical facts that were not available at any price in earlier elections. This fast-delivery, always-open operation, moreover, is custom-made for professionals writing against a deadline at all hours of the day and night.

We consider several issues related to journalists and the gathering and presentation of news. For one, the Internet comes with certain costs for reporters. There's the curious fact that journalists and their audiences often get raw information at the same time. That changes the chemistry and hierarchical relationship between those who write the news and those who read it.

Then, thanks to instant posting of information, the Internet is imposing a frenetic pace on the news business. Sites can change by the minute, upstaging even the broadcast media that for 75 years have been breaking the news. Consequently, all the media will feel the hot breath of the Internet and keep a closer watch on the clock.

The Internet will unfold news stories throughout the day, so the other media must assume that some listeners, viewers, and readers already know the plotline. Just as radio replaced the newspaper's "extra editions," so the Web will change the character of reporting in print and broadcast, if only because the latter stories will seem less "newsy" to an audience that has surfed a story from its first swell. Already the Internet has affected journalistic writing practiced in some newsrooms and taught in some classrooms, and over the next few years experts say it will bring about other changes in the profession.

The instant delivery of information also increases the pressure to trim away at the edges of source verification, because verification can take time. This is a matter of great concern to many journalists, who know the dangers of skimping on documentation and failing to confirm the accuracy of a statistic or a claim. The contest increasingly will be between a story that beats the clock and a story that is checked and sourced. For now, it seems most journalists are sold on the need to run the checks, but the pressures to be first can be stressful and the long-term impact may challenge their resolve.

The validity of information on the Web raises more problems. This censor-free, umpireless medium allows everyone to set up shop in the marketplace of ideas, although much of what people peddle is nonsense. Bold, unsubstantiated claims, baseless statistics, unfounded charges from individuals and groups of every stripe fill this medium. Much of this information, so skillfully prepared, can easily deceive the unsuspecting reader. The beguiling appearance of images and text disguises fiction as fact, opinion as truth. Like the fun house at Coney Island with its wavy mirrors, this medium blurs distinctions between the real and the illusion.

For average visitors, the madcap quality of the Web is bad enough, but for reporters, the dangers are more serious. When journalists are lured into believing false information, then use it in their stories, they extend the reach and effects of the deception. Already reporters have been drawn into these misrepresentations, and the potential for others grows as more information is dumped onto the Web and deadline pressures mount.[22]

THE INTERNET AND AUDIENCE FRAGMENTATION

Throughout this century, the mass media have provided common meeting grounds for American audiences. From 1932 to 1944, FDR gathered this troubled nation around his hearth for "Fireside Chats." Network television took hold in the early 1950s and bound 230 million Americans into a single perceptual community. Each night, this medium captured "everyone"—the networks could claim that nearly every U.S. adult and most children viewed something on TV each week. These collective experiences over time unified the country around shared agendas. They implanted in the nation a common set of issues that connected the country across region, race, religion, ideology, political party, and economic class. We rarely agreed on the remedies to our national problems, but at least we were arguing about the same things—and that sometimes included how bad TV was becoming.

The Internet, however, may dismantle that model. This medium is the antithesis of network television. Where broadcast TV has a few channels, the Web has nearly a million sites. Television amasses viewers by the millions; the Internet divides the millions into tiny clusters. Network television aggregates audiences with common-denominator programming; the Internet splits audiences with special-interest attractions.

Moreover, the Internet arrives at a time when we are immersed again in a centuries-old political debate about individual vs. community rights. After all this time, we have not yet settled on the apportionment of these rights. Public sentiment runs hot and cold, and most recently—since the 1980s—a rightward pull from lawmakers has moved the population perceptibly toward the view that the unfettered pursuit of self-interests will, in the end, work to the greater good of the community.

The Internet's appeal to self-interests may play a role in this national discussion. Quite possibly it will send audiences in many directions, and by tugging at separate audience threads, fray the cloth of the national agenda. We are particularly vulnerable to such a thing. We are the most pluralistic nation on earth, and while we may look ragtag at times to the rest of the world, we have sustained a sober-minded unity that is in itself remarkable. Can the Internet challenge that? Yes, it can, given that information has been the nation's binding agent, particularly through a century of expanding diversity. Of course, it's too early to tell if this medium will have the reach and influence to bring about such effects, that being an issue we explore in the closing pages.

As it is now, there are great riches on the Net to excite and to please, new sources to draw up, new styles to be developed—and, as critic James Agee would say, "great blotches of ill-punctuated gabble." In the following pages, we'll consider the gold and the gabble that one can encounter on this fascinating medium.

NOTES

1. T. H. White, *America in Search of Itself: The Making of the President, 1956–1980* (New York: Harper & Row, 1982).

2. It is generally agreed that Thomas Foley was defeated by the gun lobby. Foley supported national gun control measures, but this was not a popular position at home. He often was portrayed as someone who had been away too long to understand the voters of Washington's Fifth Congressional District.

3. J. E. Pollard, *The Presidents and the Press* (New York: Macmillan, 1947), 20–21.

4. A. Steinberg, *The Man from Missouri: The Life and Times of Harry S. Truman* (New York: Putnam's, 1962).

5. Ibid., 323.

6. This process of political communication is described in G. Selnow, *High-Tech Campaigns: Computer Technology in Political Communication* (Westport, CT: Praeger, 1994).

7. From the author's interview with Roger Hurwitz, Artificial Intelligence Lab at MIT, on Feb. 19, 1997.

8. Robert Hobbes Zakon reports in "The Internet: A Timeline" that in 1971 Ray Tomlinson invented an E-mail program to send messages across a distributed network. He said this program was developed from an intramachine E-mail program (SNDMSG) and a file transfer program (CPYNET) that were in experimentation. Zakon's site: http://info.isoc.org/guest/zakon/Internet/History/HIT.html.

9. From the author's telephone interview with Andrew Glass, Washington bureau chief for Cox News, on Dec. 4, 1996.

10. The Media Watch study was reported in M. Booth, "Media Watch Monitors Mayhem Levels on TV," *Denver Post*, Mar. 9, 1997, p. 8.

11. Leo Bogart, "How U.S. Newspaper Content Is Changing," *Journal of Communication* 35(2) (Spring 1985): 82–90.

12. *Car Talk* is produced by National Public Radio.

13. John Selig, president of Media Monitors, Inc., in Indianapolis, estimates that of the 10,700 radio stations, approximately 885 change formats in any given year.

14. "Hits" refers to images downloaded during a site visit, and the figure can greatly exaggerate the popularity of a site. "Page views," which counts the number of times someone accesses a site, is a less impressive but more accurate measure. Nancy Maloney, senior manager of communication at Time, Inc., New Media, gave an example. She said that on Election Night the AllPolitics site received 50 million hits per hour, but 12 million page views in the 48 hours surrounding Election Day. The distinction between hits and page views is often muddled, so it's difficult to determine which statistic you're seeing. When developers are trying to impress with numbers, it's a good bet they're providing hit statistics.

15. From a face-to-face interview in Beverly Hills in July 1996. The producer has asked not to be identified.

16. Leslie Helm, "Company Town: Microsoft to Slash Internet Workers, Web Sites," *Los Angeles Times*, Feb. 27, 1997, p. D1.

17. Jeanne Dietsch, strategic analyst at ActivMedia, Inc., said, "Most Web advertisers have ignored the flattening inherent in the Web medium. Broadcasting-era market shares are out-the-window with the net. And even typical narrowcasting techniques, pooling similar target audiences, are only moderately effective on-line." This is reported in a review of "The WEB and Advertising/Media Industry Upheaval," a study released on Nov. 15, 1996, by ActivMedia. URL: http://www.activmedia.com/Advertising.html.

To answer the advertisers' need for numbers, Yankelovich, Nielsen, and others have begun measuring audience size. (A. C. Nielsen conducts polls to measure the Internet audience size and characteristics. Yankelovich Cybercitizen looks at usage patterns and other user traits. CyberAtlas reports Web use statistics from these and other sources. The CyberAtlas URL: http://www.cyberatlas.com.) The hit (and page view) count in some cases is crude, but the technology is improving. Programs are now available to record the visits, log users' identification, and track where users spend their time on the site. (Two companies marketing this software as of January 1997: Accrue, Inc., of Mountain View, California, and Andromedia, Inc., in San Francisco.) Like television ratings, Website measures figure prominently in advertising rate sheets, so accurate counts are an obvious preoccupation for programmers and advertisers.

18. Electronic Library URL: http://www3.elibrary.com.

19. Ethel Black's perceptions were confirmed by a study conducted by the Center for Media & Public Affairs: "And content analysis of television coverage of Clinton's first 18 months in office . . . shows that the Administration was hammered by the 'liberal' TV media the moment Clinton walked through the White House door." The study also discusses Clinton's rough treatment by large newspapers. This study is reviewed in B. Nussbaum, "The Myth of the Liberal Media," *Business Week* (Nov. 11, 1996), 34.

20. Ethel Black's site ran at least through the election. The URL: http://www.av.qnet.com/%7Eyes/indexo.html.

21. The rush for Election Night information jammed many of the media sites. Site operators did not anticipate the vast popularity of this information and were ill-prepared to handle the flood of traffic.

22. Pierre Salinger's run-in with Web fiction concerning TWA flight 800 is the most notable example. We look at this in Chapter 7.

Part One

Context: Lessons of the Past— Formats for the Future

The Internet arrives in a spirited media market filled with many print and broadcast options that swamp American audiences. Is there room for more? How can the Web fill a void if there is no void to fill? Like most new media, the Internet got here looking for a purpose. Here we have a wonderful multiuse gadget. Now how do we use it? Finding out was our mission in 1996, and players from all segments of the political landscape sought an answer.

The Internet is the most integrative of the media, displaying traits of each print and broadcast convention. Like the early Romans, who assimilated the gods of the nations they conquered, the Net has assimilated the original features of radio, newspapers, magazines, and television, and it even acts like a telephone! And just as the Romans not only assimilated the culture of the conquered tribes but also "Romanized" the barbarians, so the Net not only assimilates other media but also will affect and colonize visual and print media.

In the campaign of 1996, however, none of its formats was fully developed, although text and still pictures came close to print rivals. At the same time, downloading was balky, and waiting for a picture to form on the screen sometimes seemed to take forever. If stills were painfully slow, then video was excruciatingly so; but all this is changing as modem and download speeds pick up. Very soon, indeed, the Internet will have the video qualities of television, the audio of radio, the text and pictures of fine magazines. It will isolate each format, or integrate them all into what is a true multimedia display.

Apart from the pictures, text, and sound that we have come to know and love, the Internet has interactivity, about which we know very little. We know it in person-to-person interactions, but we're not sure about it when interactivity involves person-to-machine-and-back-again communications. This is new for us, and quite misunderstood, as the political sites demonstrated in 1996. Some tinkered with them, but according to most experts, the sites didn't use the power of audience feedback to the users' or their own advantage.

If a lesson is to be learned from the campaign, it is that the Internet is remarkably different from its predecessors despite initial appearances and assimilated features. Its capacity to soak up user information and respond to users individually is a revolution in public communication that will occupy our attention for years to come.

No one knows how the Internet will develop over time—or what miracle will replace it. The only sure thing is that when we look back on the campaign of 1996, we'll marvel with amusement at the primitive sites and silly applications, the way visitors to the Smithsonian marvel at the old crystal sets and iconoscopes that were the early versions of radio and television, respectively.

Primitive or not, the Internet has been preceded by other media with which we *are* familiar, which we *do* understand, if somewhat belatedly. We may know where the Internet is going if we look at where the other media have been, and that's the job of this section.

Chapter 1 begins with the leading theories about media and group influences on voting behavior. We examine the old "hypodermic needle" model of communication, which credited the media with powers far beyond anything they could actually bring to bear on an audience. Over time, more moderate expectations have formed, each in its time explaining something about how media influence voters.

Voters do not live by media alone, but naturally reside in social groups that impact their outlooks on political matters and how they vote. Accordingly, threaded among the media theories are explanations of interpersonal and group influences. All of these are woven together to form an explanation of what it takes to make an electoral choice. The theories, one at a time or in concert, help explain some of the research findings, some of the observations, some of the patterns evident among the voting populations.

The real challenge, to understanding the Internet, however, is feedback. None of the theories account for this phenomenon because it is unique to the Web. Print and broadcast media have nothing like it, and with no precedent, it is something of an enigma. We just don't know how feedback—or interaction—can foster personal communication with a mass medium. That's the key to another intriguing feature.

As soon as you raise the issue of interaction, you slip from the realm of media communication to interpersonal communication, and interaction becomes a curiosity when it takes place on a machine. After all, for thousands of years people have interacted with people, not with machines—at least not at the level possible on the Internet. It is likely that very soon visitors can send information to the site computer, in either text or voice, and hold a kind of conversation. However Orwellian this sounds, it deserves attention. Even if purists wince at the comparison, consider the possibility that from the user's viewpoint, interacting with a computer may be like interacting with another person.

Finally, some experts argue convincingly that feedback has already become the distinguishing feature of the Internet. If so, it is a huge step in media evolution, separating the Internet about as far from print and broadcast as we are from our prehistoric ancestors. That makes feedback more than a gimmick.

At the close of the chapter, we tweak a basic voter influence model with the addition of Internet feedback. This amounts to the emergence of the Web as the tabula rasa of mass communication—the first time anything got "personal" and "mass" at the same time.

Chapter 2 looks briefly at media history, with particular attention to the relationship between format and content. As each new medium came into being, the formats—print, sound, visual—provided new content possibilities. Radio lifted the silent words from the newspaper page and gave them real voice, so audiences could listen to their president, rather than just read what he had to say. Television, with its visual format, has virtually become political communication. Despite early predictions that television would never serve as a potent political tool, the audiovisual medium clearly is the most powerful political weapon in campaign arsenals today. Its power is so alluring that campaigns risk the voters' wrath and legal sanctions in their efforts to raise money to finance its use. Television in recent years has become a political opiate so potent and so pricey that some observers believe it has poisoned electoral politics.

Chapter 2 also examines more directly the relationship between format and content laid out years ago in an essay by media theorist Percy Tannenbaum. He treats the interplay between what is said and how it is said, shown, or printed, and offers some insight into the communication possibilities of the Internet's multiple formats.

The two chapters in this section describe the media forebears of the Internet in order to better understand this enfant terrible. Doffing our hats to media and persuasion theorists, we will spotlight their insights upon this interactive marvel unfolding before us.

Chapter One

Theory: Mass Communication and Its Lessons for the Internet

We're like kids going into the zoo. So far, we've just seen the monkey cages and already we're excited. Just wait until you see the rest. We'll have more fun, it'll be more interesting and more frustrating than anything we can imagine now.

—William Brock

THEORY AND PRACTICE

Potentially, the Internet is the most effective organizational tool to hit politics since the telephone. But its power to sway votes is still an open question not likely to be answered anytime soon. The medium is changing too rapidly. Its look and feel early in 1996 had changed by Election Day into something new and better, and its evolution continues. Even empirical research at this early stage would tell little about the Internet when it is fully matured.

Thus, conclusive answers to the really important questions must wait. Can the Internet become as pervasive a political tool as television or as compelling as interpersonal persuasion? Will it shrink the roles of conventional media? Will it put political communication into the hands of fringe candidates who in the past have run campaigns that were a day late and a dollar short? No one knows, even though everyone, it seems, has an opinion.

The Internet in 1996 was a bud about to open. No one fully understood its powers to target voters or its capacities to link one voter with another. No one knew what combination of elements on a Website would make the strongest case or leave the deepest impression. We didn't know how to get people back again after a visit or two, although Web designers tried every trick they knew, from interactive games to chats with the candidates.

At a distance now from the campaign, our questions deal mostly with matters of effectiveness. During the campaign, however, the preoccupations were with something else. Candidates and campaigns spoke mostly about the appearance and popularity of their Websites. Those were their measures of success at the time, and that's understandable. This medium appeared so suddenly that there was little time to think about the most important underlying questions.

In a matter of months, we went from hearing hardly a whisper about the Internet to being tossed headlong into a bazaar where everyone was selling access and hardware, and promoting sites.[1] We couldn't integrate this medium easily into our understanding of what a medium has always been.

The Internet, we were told, is part computer, part newspaper, part radio, part television, part library, and more. The failure of similes didn't help. The confusion was in the streets, where voters mingle, but it also was in the campaigns, where professionals mint strategies. Indeed, political communicators themselves weren't certain just how they should measure the success of a medium that looked so familiar and yet was so different from the media they had known.

In the final analysis, most campaigns in 1996 gauged audience impact by the number of visits, not the changing of minds. The influence of the messages went unnoticed because bragging rights went to the teams whose tents attracted the largest crowds. Who cared if voters left those tents converted—or alienated? 1996 was a year to ring the bells and toot the whistles, to put the barkers at the door, drawing in as many people as possible by cramming each Website with every attraction technology would allow.

Uncertainty about media contributions to voting decisions is nothing new. The perennial debate about the many influences on voters is particularly difficult to resolve when voters are seldom able to nail down just what leads them to support one candidate over another. The media, face-to-face encounters, pressures from interest groups—all have been seen by theorists, since the late 1940s, as affecting voting decisions. The trouble is, no one knows for sure where the influence of one leaves off and another begins.

Unfazed by the doubts, social psychologists, communication specialists, and political scientists have tried to peel away influences to understand how voters settle on one candidate over another. We ask: Does a newspaper advertisement or broadcast commercial do the job, even part of the job? How about coffee shop discussions, speeches, and labor union endorsements? How do these and other information sources convince a voter to make a decision?

The shelves hold an inventory of theories and models, each claiming to account for the influences on voting behavior. The prize is huge for the ones that work. Implicit in the choice is power: the campaign consultant who understands the calculus of forces in political persuasion, it is thought, can manipulate the variables with predictable outcomes. In practice, however, those outcomes have been less than satisfying.

Still, the descriptions—the models and theories—offer a starting point from which to get a sense of how voters may be affected by the information sources and the political persuaders.

Media Effects on Voter Decisions

One of the earliest metaphors used to explain the impact of media on their audiences is the hypodermic needle. The "hypodermic needle" model describes audiences as passive recipients of media messages, effectively moved by whatever is syringed into their minds by the press, other print, and electronic sources. It proposes that what you see, hear, and read is what you do.[2] Arising in parallel with stimulus–response thinking popular among learning theorists during the early part of this century, the model had a surprisingly long run even though its claims were never convincingly demonstrated by empirical research.

That "hypo" assumption of a defenseless audience, all-powerful media, and a one-step decision process by the voter was ill-conceived and soundly laid to rest in the early 1940s by Paul Lazarsfeld's voting studies.

Lazarsfeld, a social psychologist at Columbia University, examined how people voted and how they used the media. Try as he might, he found no support for the conditioning effects of media exposure on voting decisions predicted by this model.

Although the Columbia team could lay its hands on no evidence for significant, direct media effects on voters, it found a strong influence of interpersonal relationships.[3] Lazarsfeld did not deny the obvious fact that media played a role; he simply found no *direct* influence.

In a work published in 1963, Lazarsfeld and Menzel looked back at their early research: "This study went to great lengths to determine how the mass media brought about such changes. To our surprise we found the effect to be rather small. . . . People appeared to be much more influenced in their political decisions by face-to-face contact with other people . . . than by the mass media directly."[4]

The media were only the means to an eventual end, they said, and the effects were felt only through the secondhand influences of "opinion leaders," who, in face-to-face encounters, persuaded others how to vote. Lazarsfeld called this the "two-step flow" model of communication: step one involved the media influencing opinion leaders; step two, the opinion leaders influencing the voters. According to the theory, the crucial role of opinion leaders worked as follows:

1. Voters who changed their minds during the campaign or who decided late in the campaign were more likely than others to cite personal (opinion leader) influence as having figured in their decisions.
2. Opinion leaders were found at every social level and were presumed to have values very much like the people they influenced.
3. Opinion leaders were heavier users of the mass media than those who were not.[5]

Obviously, opinion leaders were the dominant factor in voter persuasion. If the media played a role, it was as reinforcer, not persuader. Persuasion was forged in the heated alchemy of social relationships; the media served only to cool the metal, hardening judgments already made by average voters.

Lazarsfeld and other supporters of the two-step flow model continued research through the next two decades and refined the notion of interpersonal influence in general and of opinion leadership specifically.[6]

Naturally, that put opinion leaders at center stage. Since they were key to the decision process, much of the early research centered on their qualities and their pivotal roles. Several characteristics emerged. The affected voters, as you would guess, found their opinion leaders highly competent, that is, knowledgeable and skilled in their judgments. They were seen as capable of evaluating the evidence and drawing correct conclusions.

Second, the persuaded ones trusted their opinion leaders because they shared the values and the goals of the group. Unions call this solidarity; at least they did before leaders began earning corporate-size salaries.

Third, those who were persuaded valued physical contact with the persuaders in group activity. Staying in touch meant that the opinion leader experiences the group's pains and pleasures. Even if supporting a local candidate produced a negative outcome—say the candidate failed to come through on promises—members knew their woes would be felt personally by the opinion leader who led them down this path.

The competence, solidarity, and presence of leaders bring to mind a social tenet called "source credibility." Political consultants know that the credibility of an information source—political candidates, union and trade association leaders—is measured by "trust" and "expertise." Followers must trust information sources in order to put credence in their good efforts to advise and direct,[7] and they also must believe the information sources know what they're talking about—that they have the necessary information and the ability to apply it to reach a correct decision.

Opinion leadership has a lot in common with source credibility. No matter what campaign tinkering over the years may do to alter influences on voting decisions, credibility doesn't change. Voters must trust the competence and character of opinion leaders, who are sources of political information, whether it's face-to-face, on television, or on the Internet.

Striking another hard blow to direct media influence, Lazarsfeld's studies put political campaigns in a frustrating double bind. Not only did media hold little sway with an audience, but they had little opportunity to do so. Why?

The answer is paradoxical: Voters *least likely* to be influenced by the media had the *greatest media exposure*, and voters *most likely* to be influenced by the media had the *least media exposure*.

Consider the two groups. First, voters most interested in politics are usually committed partisans who come to an election with well-entrenched views about the candidates and issues. True, their interests stimulate a hunger for political information, but, at the same time, their selective appetites drive them toward media that support views they already hold; they load the plate with their favorites and don't sample the full menu. The partisans seldom examine alternative viewpoints and therefore are unaffected by them.

The second group—people less interested in politics—hold few political positions strongly and therefore show little interest in sifting through the claims and counterclaims of politicians. Since politics is low on their personal agendas, they avoid political information in print and broadcast, and most likely in their personal discussions as well.

Today, 65 percent of Americans can't name their member of Congress and 51 percent do not vote in presidential elections.[8] Americans have among the worst voting records in the developed world. How can TV or radio or newspapers influence citizens who choose to ignore politics and sit out the campaigns? Even if media have the capacity to persuade, there is little they can do when half the voting population is uninterested.

During World War II, learning theorists, most notably Carl Hovland, came to pretty much the same conclusions about the media's power to persuade, arguing that film propaganda rarely fulfilled the expectations of its advocates or justified the fears of its critics. The films might increase viewers' knowledge but rarely affected their attitudes.[9] This early research led to the conventional view that the media may supply information but do not alter viewpoints—that job is left to one-on-one communications, particularly through opinion leaders.

Another influential researcher, Joseph Klapper, added his voice to the debate on the capability of media to reinforce attitudes engendered by personal contacts.[10] In 1960, he published the enormously influential *Ef-*

fects of Mass Communication, which was based on an exhaustive literature review. This work convinced many scholars of the "minimal effects" of the media; consequently, for several years it all but shut down serious examination of media influence in political decision making. Klapper said:

1. Mass communication ordinarily does not serve as a primary cause of audience effects, but functions through a nexus of mediating factors.

2. Thus, mass communication contributes to but does not create commitment, certainly not as a sole cause of voter decision making. In short, it affirms original agents of change, but is not *the* agent of change.[11]

By Klapper's account, the media may spice the broth, but they don't add much meat. Klapper's book was so convincing that scholars over the next few years focused exclusively on the primary persuaders—personal and group influences—virtually to the exclusion of media impact. So much for the "hypodermic needle" model.

The two-step flow model changed thinking about direct media effects, but eventually trouble arose for this model as well. In the decades after its introduction in the early 1940s, this model met a number of challenges.

First, the notion of two steps was too rigid. Everett Rogers countered that sometimes the persuasion process actually consisted of only a single step (direct media effects), but sometimes it involved many steps (going through several opinion leaders, blending with media influences).[12]

Next, not only was the model too rigid, but it also failed to describe the on-again, off-again role of opinion leadership. In the hierarchical thinking of Lazarsfeld and Klapper, you were an opinion leader or you were not. That didn't square with some observers. Rogers argued that sometimes people are opinion leaders and sometimes they're opinion followers, depending on the topic and their personal relationships with others.[13] Lazarsfeld notwithstanding, opinion leaders aren't always active users of media and followers aren't always media avoiders. Each, at different times, may use or steer clear of the media. Further, in Rogers's opinion, media and interpersonal influences can weave in and out at different times, so decision-making can follow many paths. None of this is adequately charted by the two-step flow model.

These early studies and writings leave us without a clear explanation of the process by which the media affect political decision-making—if at all; whether it is direct or buffered by social influences. The hypodermic needle model says that the media directly and significantly persuade. Lazarsfeld's studies, reinforced by Hovland and Klapper, say the media do not influence directly, and even when they do, not significantly. Who's right?

Addressing that question has been recurrent, something like the wide ties and double-breasted suits that come and go. Out of style during the Eisenhower 1950s, media effects thinking returned in the late 1960s. Communication researchers McCombs and Shaw, studying television use in the 1968 presidential election, dealt with the issue, but put the case differently: whether or not TV persuades or conditions voters, you can be sure it "sets the agenda."[14]

Suddenly, "agenda-setting" became the favored explanation because it seemed obvious that media put certain issues on the voters' plates (and leave other issues off), even if they don't persuade directly. Press coverage of political news and speeches, position papers, commentaries, 30-second political commercials, and other conspicuous media messages obviously elevate certain topics to public attention while subordinating others. Agenda-setting says that the media may not convince voters of anything more than that the topic is important. But, as salesman, preachers, and college professors know, that's a critical first step.

By 1972, the politics of persuasion took another twist. Patterson and McClure reported that in the presidential campaign of that year, television not only set the voters' agendas but also influenced decisions by means of commercials.[15]

Contrary to what most pundits were saying, Patterson and McClure found that the primary source of influence on voters was not network news but the new pariahs of the airwaves—the political campaign commercials. Arguably, viewers learned more from the partisan 30-second spots than from television newscasts. If true, this theory debunked the conventional thinking about the persuasive power of the Cronkites and Brinkleys.[16]

Not only did Patterson and McClure surmise the minimal effects of television news, but their content analysis uncovered a surprising lack of substance in network newscasts. They saw that political stories on national television lacked depth, and that the thin, superficial coverage lowered the public's sense of political campaigns. In an effort to be smooth, brief and balanced, the networks came off as superficial, vacuous, and trivial. By contrast, Patterson and McClure found that the political ads, however trifling and partisan, stood as beacons of information.

Notwithstanding the lessons for network newsrooms (and lost on them, it would seem, since they still specialize in balanced superficiality), the findings demonstrate that through advertising, television and radio can do more than reinforce or set agendas. Broadcasters can materially influence audience thinking on political matters and, to some extent, affect voting decisions.

So the progression has gone from the hypodermic fix to reinforcement to agenda-setting to another fix—the political ad, often negative in nature. Michigan State University's Peter Troldahl put forth a theory that explains these media effects while tempering the direct influences proposed by the hypodermic model. Troldahl's "one-step flow model" says: "Mass media channels communicate directly to the mass audience, without the message passing through opinion leaders; however, the message does not reach all receivers equally, nor does it have the same effect on each."[17]

Troldahl acknowledges the obvious: that the media reach audiences directly. But he adds that the effects of messages are seldom the same for all individual voters. This is so because messages are filtered at three stages: at reception, at processing, and at recall. Each of these had been identified in earlier research to account for audience resistance to media-borne messages.[18]

At the stage of reception, there is selective exposure: not everyone gets to see or hear the message. Some may miss the ad; others may channel-surf over it. You can't very well be directly influenced by political spots if you don't watch television, or cut away from the ads.

In the late 1960s, selective exposure was not the same as it is today. Back then, TV touched "everybody," as the three networks put it, and they were right. They reached big audiences with general material, a little something for everyone. So as long as you turned on CBS, or picked up *Look* magazine, or dialed your radio to WNBC, you couldn't avoid a broad range of information.

Today, with four networks, public broadcasting, CNN, and dozens of cable channels specializing in narrow programming genres, you stand a much better chance of dodging unwanted information. Thanks to today's targeted and parochial media, it is easier to find information sanctuaries that preach only sectarian views. In the late 1960s, information delivery was more ecumenical. Today, you can bunker yourself deep into your choice issues—in short, selective exposure.

Selective perception is the processing of information at the second stage of filtering. People perceive messages consistent with their experiences and predispositions. If they meet an inconsistent message nose-to-nose, they often interpret it to reinforce preexisting beliefs.

For instance, you may be drawn to a policy proposal from the other political party—say universal health insurance—but since they are for it and your candidate is against it, you perceive it as a crass attempt to snatch votes from your candidate. You may not avoid alternative viewpoints, but when you stumble onto one, selective perception says that you are likely to bend it to serve your own biases. Accordingly, the same message may have different impacts on different voters, depending on starting positions.

The third stage is selective retention. Obviously, we don't remember everything we see or hear. Like a computer hard drive, the human brain is a few messages short of storing everything. Eventually, you need to make space for new files. When that happens, we selectively retain information with the greatest personal relevance, interest, and utility.

Unlike the hypodermic needle model that overstates media influence, unlike the reinforcement thinking that understates it, unlike agenda-setting that finesses influence, the one-step flow model explains how one message can have different effects on different audience members. This has reemphasized the importance of media in a political campaign and contributed to a revival of interest in the value of media in voting decisions.

Media researcher Steven Chaffee's summary of this thinking: "The weight of evidence indicates that direct flow from the media is the rule for most people, more often than not."[19] It's a direct flow, however, that attenuates through filters of exposure, perception, and retention.

Interpersonal and Group Effects

Most voters form political decisions in the context of networks and groups. Apartment buildings, neighborhoods, offices, congregations, and classrooms assemble people into groups embedded with norms, informal rules of behavior, standards of beliefs, and patterns of interaction, all of which impose pressures that stimulate conformity. Without a doubt, mass media and the personal influences of family, friends, and respected leaders impact voters along with larger group forces that are also in play.

Communication scholar Alfred Smith said groups provide not only a context for individual behaviors and judgments but also serve as a repository for values. Here he explains why group values temper media influences: "Mass communication does not make individuals change their ideas easily because ideas are not held by individuals. Instead, ideas are held by individuals in groups—in groups of friends, family groups, professional groups. In groups, individuals reinforce each other's ideas and maintain a consensus of the group as a whole."[20]

Few individuals act alone. We are influenced by groups that impede quick and radical changes of attitudes and behaviors. By their very nature, groups demand the observance of common goals.[21]

Where does this leave us? Despite earlier research, we see that the media and opinion leaders don't take on voters one by one, but en masse, which is to say that social networks intervene between would-be influencers and their targets. Given the malignancy of negative ads, this may be a saving grace. At the same time, this research, accumulating since the early 1930s, explains the ineffectiveness of many media and interpersonal strategies that ignore the organizing pressures within groups. What do we know about group pressures on individual decision-making?

For one thing, people look to other people for guidance and group standards. In tight-knit, long-standing groups such as neighborhoods, clubs, Army units, and close families, these norms are clear and well defined. Members hold reasonably consistent views on ideologies, values, and customs. They often have set views about politics and policies on specific issues such as race relations, taxation, and economics.

In 1936 social psychologist, Muzafer Sherif demonstrated that people change personal judgments in light of opinions expressed by others in a group.[22] He even saw how these judgments persisted in the group's absence, demonstrating that people internalized changes, rather than merely expressing them to gain approval. Sherif also found that the more uncertain the situation, the more people rely on the group for guidance. For instance, voters faced with a choice between two similar candidates, or voters deciding on a complex referendum, are likely to turn to others. Political matters, with all their uncertainty, complexity, and ambiguity, are ripe for group intervention.

The power of groups to influence individuals was demonstrated by Solomon Asch in the mid-1950s.[23] Asch put subjects in a room with a half-dozen confederates, and asked each to match the length of a line drawn on a sheet of paper with three comparison lines. All of the confederates offered similar answers, all obviously incorrect. Even so, Asch found that his subjects, knowing the rest were wrong, offered the same estimate as the group. The interpretation of this research has been challenged, but at one level it demonstrates that people will forsake their own judgment in the face of group consensus. If they do this when judging the length of a line, a task not all that ambiguous, how quickly would they give up weak support for a candidate if their reference group is wholeheartedly behind another candidate?

Kurt Lewin, who discussed group cohesion in the late 1940s, theorized that the greater the collective concern and attraction, the stronger the group cohesion and the more powerful group influences would be over individual members.[24] Members look to the group for security, accomplishment of goals, personal satisfaction, friendship, and other personal needs; and the more the group satisfies those needs, the more the individual becomes dependent on the group.

Highly cohesive groups—where members become increasingly dependent on one another for needs satisfaction—exert greater force on members to conform. How are those forces applied? As carrots and sticks. The group offers support to members who adhere to its norms and continue positive reinforcement for the "correct" beliefs and behaviors. Essentially, the positive rewards of a group continue as long as the member remains within the acceptable norms.

Backsliders feel the sticks—the cracks and jibes and censures. "Disconfirmation," where the group ignores the member, is among the strongest sanctions. Withholding group rewards—companionship, support, and approval—punishes and ultimately drives away the apostate. Even the anticipation of such sanctions may be enough to keep a would-be dissident in line. Religious groups ostracize nonconformists. Primitive tribes banish wrongdoers, who have been known to die as a result. The Amish "shun" deviant members by ignoring them. Catholics and others excommunicate the seriously deviant.

You would expect politicians to see the efficacy. The importance of groups has not been lost on political parties. Formal groups may have been strongest in the old ward and precinct system, where parties made a point of marshaling the natural forces of neighborhoods in support of a candidate. Precinct captains were the nominal leaders whose job it was to keep the voters behind a candidate by offering small rewards, stressing solidarity, and issuing threats to members who might defect and take others with them. The Chicago political machine was notorious for its exploitation of the precinct system, remarkably massing its group forces for lucky candidates, sometimes bringing home more votes than there were voters in the district! As Mayor Richard Daley of Chicago is said to have remarked, "Vote early, vote often."

Contemporary groups that form around other focal points are often no less powerful than the precinct groups. Unions, for example, are perennial political organizers, supporting union-friendly candidates and propositions. They use union money, organization, and member pressures to deliver votes, and even though membership is down and labor union ideology is more diverse than it used to be, unions continue as a force in national and state politics. Bill Clinton was the beneficiary of union support in 1992 and 1996, and that may have been on his mind when he backed minimum wage hikes, health care legislation, job safety, and other issues of interest to labor.

Among the fastest-growing groups to surface in American politics since the late 1980s are the religious Fundamentalists,[25] or, as the Christian Coalition prefers to be called, the Evangelicals. There is a remarkable degree of uniformity among these conservative religionists who became a considerable force in local and national politics for presidents Reagan and Bush, for the "Gingrich Revolution" in 1994, and again in 1996, when they constituted one-third of the delegates to the Republican National Convention.[26] Ralph Reed, Pat Robertson, and company held consistent views on abortion and homosexuality, as well as on taxes, states' rights, and gun control. According to the polls, Fundamentalists overwhelmingly supported Republican candidates.[27]

Christian conservatives, spread throughout thousands of congregations, are textbook examples of group cohesion as they manifest the power of group pressure. Their churches serve as the organizing force in people's lives, providing all the benefits that a group can confer on its members. The believers center their social lives in the church, form friendships with other members, volunteer time, give money, find comfort, discover purpose. Families join churches, the churches have home Bible study groups, so the influence of the church is extensive—neighbors attend together, the congregation forms throughout the week as well as on Sundays mornings and Wednesday evenings. As Fundamentalists have witnessed new political powers arising from their solidarity with like-minded churches around the country and from the deft political skills of their prominent national leaders, their cohesion has grown even stronger. This, of course, implies a greater pressure toward conformity within and across the groups, and this makes Evangelical groups more intimidating and gives them more political power. This power became evident at the 1996 Republican National convention and in the party platform, which reflected the strong views of the Christian Coalition.

Group support in politics is a blessing and a curse for the candidate. The blessing is the ease of one-stop shopping. Once you've made the case with the group, internal pressures generate and sustain member support. And not only will candidates receive the backing of group members, they will benefit from other voters whom group members recruit. Support comes in votes and money, and in volunteer envelope-stuffers, call-makers, and chauffeurs on Election Day. Harvesting group support is wholesale politicking and, on a vote-for-vote basis, it can be a real bargain.

However, group support can be costly. Step on the toes of the wrong group members, and you stand to lose the whole group. No Republican candidate would care to offend leaders prominent in the Christian Coalition. The result could be an Evangelical defection that the candidate would be powerless to reverse. Not only do political campaigns court groups but, once recruited, they tiptoe carefully around them.

President Clinton, in an attempt to neutralize his image as a tax-and-spend liberal, alienated many homosexuals and advocates for the poor, but reasoned, as Dole did vis-à-vis the Christian Coalition, that his constituencies had no other place to go. That thinking can be risky; group members can always stay home on Election Day.

The bigger the group, the heavier the pressure on candidates to bend to the group's will. Earning friendship may not be enough. In return for their support, groups may press for legislation or other political favors that may set off troubles elsewhere in a campaign, and even come back to haunt the successful candidate.

An interesting exception to the "bigger the group, the greater its political impact" was noted by the author when he was consulting with NBC-TV during the Grant Tinker era of the 1980s. This network put in the hands of its policy resources director, Dr. Richard Gilbert, a series of annual three-day seminars for interest group leaders. Forty to fifty religious, political, educational, fraternal, sexual, "hyphenated-American," and other organizations voiced their complaints about TV—especially how they were treated dramatically and depicted socially. Gilbert noted, after several years of directing these seminars, that some of the broadest-based groups had the least clout.

The Roman Catholic Church, with 50 million members, was less successful in realizing its goals in TV than say, the Gay and Lesbian Anti-defamation League, the number of whose card-carrying members was minuscule. Why? Because the Catholics were pushing a broad agenda—everything from "save the safety net" (liberal) to anti-abortion (conservative), from anti-violence (liberal) to tuition vouchers for private schools (conservative)—so broad that church members were scattered on all sides. The gays, by contrast (and the gun lobby, the Hispanic-, the Italian-, and the Arab-Americans), had a narrow agenda and represented almost everyone in their constituency. The lesson: If a group is too big or too broad to represent its members, it loses its power to say "We speak for all our members, so you'd better take our complaints seriously."

Look at the anti-abortion plank in the 1996 Republican platform. It was crafted by the Fundamentalist delegates to the convention, but it did not support the views of the larger Republican constituency, and certainly not those of the electorate at large, which endorsed a pro-choice position.[28] Dole could do little to modify this stance without throwing the convention into chaos, so he worked quietly behind the scenes to salve the wounds of pro-choice Republicans, with whom he pleaded for peace. He succeeded in downplaying the Christian right by featuring minority women speakers, some of whom were pro-choice. Dole's best hope was to minimize the issue in public by saying that he didn't read the platform and didn't know much about its contents. That he got away with it is a testament to his political skills.

Another concern about group support even more noteworthy in the age of the Internet—when groups can easily assemble without formal structure—is the "anti-group."

A funny thing about some groups: people can make as much a point of being *out* of a group as others make about being *in* it, and that musters up a countergroup of outsiders. As topsy-turvy as it sounds, this can have real political consequences.

Consider the National Rifle Association, a vocal group whose members take visible positions on a range of controversial issues. The NRA opposes nearly all gun control, and in the past has advocated such policies as unfettered rights to possess concealed weapons, semiautomatic rifles, undetectable plastic guns, armor-piercing bullets, and some explosives. NRA members unite aggressively behind the group's positions, and become a formidable source of funds and votes.

But the anti-NRA group—people outside the organization—often are equally vociferous, aggressively opposing positions advocated by the gun group. They scope out the NRA position, ridicule it, then take the opposite side of the issue. They see whom the NRA supports, then back the other candidate. In some television commercials, candidates have hung the NRA support around their opponent's neck like a noose. And some conservative politicians regret the "gunners" as a political tar baby, not the kind of thing you want to get stuck with.

The concept was vividly demonstrated in the 1996 primary when the Log Cabin Republicans sent Bob Dole's campaign a $1,000 check. Nice support. What politician wouldn't welcome the donation? Except, the Log Cabin's members are homosexuals. Say what? Even though pols rarely turn down contributions, the anti-group horror hit the campaign hard. Fearing that Dole's identification with gays would drive away support from the right, and maybe even mainstream voters, the staff quietly returned the check, whispering, "Thanks, but no thanks."

The rejection didn't stay very quiet, though; the press and the Democrats had a field day. Finally, Dole accepted the money and the endorsement, although he all but ignored the group throughout the campaign.

How does the anti-group affect candidates' decisions to seek group support? Apart from the financial implications of such a decision—special interest groups are, after all, the source of so much campaign money—a candidate must weigh the size, coherence, and commitment of givers in both groups. No mainstream candidate seeks the support of the Ku Klux Klan, the militias, or the Communists. It's a cost–benefit calculation; most extremist organizations are small in numbers, whereas the size of the anti-group can be substantial and its members readily motivated against the endorsements of fringe organizations.

PROBLEMS WITH THE OLD MODELS IN THE NEW ENVIRONMENT

Researchers sometimes view individual and group influences apart from media influence, although today most recognize that in political decision-making, there is nearly always a blend of all three. Clearly, even Lazarsfeld was aware that no single influence is all-powerful at political persuasion, although in his day, the distinctions among the media and lines of interpersonal influence may have been clearer than they are today. In the 1990s, we have integrated the media more fully into our daily routines, and we are faced with a greater range of media choices. Investigations of voters today must embrace a larger assortment and a more complex blend of influences. Radio, television, video, cable, newspapers, magazines, phones, newsletters, and indirect mail are on the information buffet. Now we add the Web, E-mail, list servers, chat rooms, news groups, and other items to the table.

The information age is marked by an extraordinary richness of sources that makes analysis increasingly difficult. If theorists ever thought they had a handle on the lines of influence to public persuasion, the Internet will give them new worries. How do you classify this hybrid? It's part mass medium, part targeted medium, part interpersonal medium. It blurs all our previous distinctions and evaluations of media and person-to-person shaping of voters.

Academics, like politicians, have always been intrigued by the paths of influence on electoral decisions. But somehow the old hypodermic needle model, the two-step flow, the one-step flow, and other more current, but no less convincing, explanations, each in its time assessing the blend of media and back fence contributions to voting decisions, shed little light on the vagaries of new forums. The growing variety of these paths of influence thwarts simple explanations.

There is also a startling public apathy toward politics today that make it even harder to understand how voters make electoral choices. Decisions are often capricious, millions of voters doing little more than flipping a coin before entering the voting booth. So much randomness in the process confounds the analysis. The experts, who breathe the air of politics, occasionally need to remind themselves that half the eligible adults don't bother stopping by the polling place, and in nonpresidential election years, the no-shows go as high as 70 percent.[29]

This is hard for political enthusiasts to swallow, but for millions of Americans, politics is little more than a passing annoyance. Although Americans may never have approached politics with great fervor, they were more committed during the years when much of the media research was done.[30] That made analysis easier and more insightful because the voting act itself was more purposeful. Voter turnout around midcentury reached well into the 60 percent range.[31]

Another blurring factor goes straight to the heart of any campaign. Try to sort out the political characteristics of a candidate's personality, party, voting record, incumbency, opposition, interest group support, money, and region. All these affect the candidate's messages and means of communication. There is no ideal, one-size-fits-all approach to political communication. The blend of campaign strategies—grassroots support, organizational backing, media applications—is determined by factors that don't easily fit simple descriptive models, or that require so many caveats and footnotes that they lose predictive value.

Finally, neither the media nor the voters' use of media remains static. Think about media innovations since the 1920s. Early in this century, newspapers and radio dominated, with content prepared for broad audiences whose members shared common interests. Not for long. Riding on the power of network radio from the 1920s through the 1940s, television seized control of the population's time and attention, siphoning off huge audience blocks and soon replacing newspapers as the nation's primary source of news and radio as a mainstay of home entertainment.

Now, the Internet has arrived before the gates of the variable, targeted, and mass media. Undeniably the most audience-specific medium on the planet, the Internet has its biggest success among its smallest audiences. Once again, we will have to retool our thinking and alter the models that explain the blend of influences on political decision-making.

In sum, media use and the media themselves have changed dramatically. The media environment in the late twentieth century is nothing like the media environments that prevailed during the years when much research examined information impact on voting behaviors of the American electorate. Earlier models, in their time, may have explained some of the impact on decision processes, but the conditions today render them less valid.

Moreover, you have to take into account the changing society and political structures. The public regard for politics has changed over time, and the campaign climates have changed with different financing mechanisms and party roles—resulting in a different constellation of influences. These affect the way candidates approach the issues and the voters, and weaken the previous explanations of political persuasion.

While all of these changes have had a significant impact on political decision-making, it's possible that the influences of the Internet will be even greater. To understand its potential significance, we look now at some of its unique qualities.

THE INTERNET

Through the past 60-odd years of voting decision analyses, researchers have disagreed over many issues, but they have not had much need to debate the definitions of a mass medium or interpersonal communication. Media were media—newspapers, radio, television, magazines—and that was that. Interpersonal communication was people talking with people, one-on-one, in groups, face-to-face, or maybe on the phone, and that's all there was to that. Paul Deutschman presented an intuitive, and at the time complete, model that set apart media and face-to-face categories, and within each, public and private communications. There was little ambiguity in his typology.[32]

But, more recently, communications have been blurring the line, and the Internet promises to give us real trouble because it will not conform to conventional classifications. This new medium is a hybrid; part mass medium, part interpersonal medium, and, as strange as it may sound, in time, an Internet site will eventually hold one-on-one conversations.

To understand how the Internet may affect the political information flow, we examine its three characters and communication roles. The first two—mass medium and personal medium—simply build on the past. The third, the Internet's capacity for one-on-one conversations, will take more getting used to.

Mass Medium

The traditional mass media aim at audience groups, not individual audience members. Their content is for collectives; sometimes for general audiences like those who watch network television, sometimes for targeted audiences of like-minded souls, such as audiences for radio and magazines. Whatever the scope, mass media make messages for groups, that is, for statistical averages of an audience and not for specific individuals. Announcers long ago may have said at the end of radio programs, "This is for you, and for you, and especially for you," but everyone knew it was for all-of-you, and not especially for any-of-you.

Two, the traditional media deliver information; they don't receive information from their audiences. Read a paper, listen to a radio, watch a television set—the medium holds all the cards. Your only real options are to respond with letters to the editor and phone calls to the station, and that's about as blunt an audience response instrument as you'll find. The process does not constitute a genuine, two-way flow of information seen in face-to-face exchanges. The result is a sender-dominated communication with pre-formatted messages that may anticipate general audience reaction but cannot adequately accommodate the responses of individual audience members. The mass media are not in the business of the free exchange of ideas, even though radio call-in shows give that impression. After more than 70 years, readers, listeners, and viewers have come to accept the top-down flow to huge audiences because that's the format we know.

Many of the large Websites, although still a far cry from the beefy television networks, have the appearance of general audience media. The major papers (e.g., *USA Today*, the *Washington Post*, the *Los Angeles Times*[33]) stock their sites with much of the same material found in their print versions, all calculated for general audiences. Similarly, many political sites operating during the 1996 campaign (e.g., Project Vote Smart, PoliticsUSA[34]) offered general information for voters with shared interests.

Many sites are more focused. The Heritage Foundation site,[35] for instance, aims at right-of-center voters and not many others. Only a firearms advocate could love the Oregon Gun Page.[36] Most sites press the audience-focusing advantages of the Web with material narrow in scope, targeted in design.

Whether the scope is broad or narrow, most Websites share at least this characteristic with traditional mass media: they shoot for statistical averages and audience clusters rather than individual recipients, and that information travels downline to receivers.

Personal Medium

The Internet also functions as a medium for interpersonal exchanges—as a tool for individuals to send and receive personal information. E-mail is now widely used to exchange text-based and graphics information. Once a luxury but now a virtual necessity, E-mail has become a fixture in business, government, the media, and universities. It is indispensable to political campaigns, which use E-mail's two-way flow to organize volunteers and keep the troops in the field up to date and in touch.

In mid-1996, Netscape Navigator and Microsoft Internet Explorer outfitted the Net with telephone-like features allowing users to interact by voice in real time.[37] The quality is a bit lacking, but the very idea of free voice communication is a real find for people who, mindful of stiff phone company charges, have grown accustomed to timing long-distance calls with an egg timer. A cheap microphone and speakers, some giveaway software, and an Internet hookup allow users to reach out and touch other users. Free voice communication is nothing short of extraordinary during a time when people are budgeting monthly communication expenses for TV and Internet hookups, cellular phones, and pagers.

Free real-time, point-to-point voice communication, along with E-mail and graphics file transmissions, have made the Internet a popular carrier of interpersonal communications. In Paul Deutschman's typology, these features qualify the Internet as an important carrier of "interposed, interpersonal communication."

Mass media characteristics give the Internet an immediate relevance in public communication, and the interpersonal features give it instant utility for interpersonal exchanges. The last feature, though, is the one to watch.

One-on-One Interaction

The other part of the medium, the capacity for feedback, integrating its mass and one-on-one communication features, makes the Internet a stunning addition to twentieth-century media. The audience can send information back to the source, which has never before been possible on a large scale.

On the early political sites, upline communication was applied mostly to games and gimmicks, treating the process as a parlor trick. Bob Dole's first sites allowed visitors to create personalized wall posters, bumper stickers, and screen savers. Such trivial applications of this extraordinary, interactive technology, although appealing to new, wide-eyed audiences, cloak the most significant applications of two-way information.

In addition to Website interactions, upline information gives site operators a hot line to visitors through E-mail. Sadly, few of the major political sites in 1996 established routine procedures to read and evaluate messages sent upline from site visitors.[38]

Used to its fullest, feedback will help campaigns, but it also will give users a piece of the action. Before the Internet, you could shout at your television or toss an offending newspaper in the fire, and while such acts may have eased your frustration, they did little to address your concerns. The Internet satisfies the need to take action. Sending a message gives a sense of involvement and peace of mind; after all, you didn't just *sit* there, you *did* something. Action sometimes is its own reward.

Although the Web prepares messages for audience groups, it can also target a mass audience person by person through "customizing" information for individual users. As crude as some of this early evidence may be, it points clearly to a path we have never taken. Consider the new speech software from IBM that lets users talk to Website computers.[39] Earlier generations required slow, halting speech, but this IBM update, and parallel developments from other companies, allow normal, conversational language, and even let users with heavy accents "train" the software to recognize their speech anomalies. "This is the first step toward the holy grail of speech recognition," according to David Nahamoo, IBM's senior manager of human language technologies.[40]

How might this be used on the Web? Writer David Einstein suggests that a visitor to a travel agent's site could say something like "I want to fly from San Francisco to Philadelphia tomorrow, and I want the cheapest ticket."[41] The Web computer may come back with a table of options or, with a humanlike voice, ask about seat preferences, departure points, and other choices. Sound like an interpersonal exchange? That's where the technology is going.

Increasingly, computer-to-person exchanges will come to approximate person-to-person exchanges, a thought that may not sit well with some obervers. In a few pages, we will examine more closely the nature of human–computer interaction, but it is important first to set up that discussion with several examples of what we mean by the oxymoronic notion "interpersonal–computer communication."

In order to personalize the message successfully, it stands to reason that Website computers must have access to information about the visitors. They can come by this information in several ways. First, they can ask visitors a series of questions. How visitors answer will determine the course of the subsequent interaction.

Website computers also can dip into your cookie jar, a neat but scary trick. Here's how it works. Whenever you visit a site, the URL (Universal Resource Locator or address of that site) is stored on your computer in a file called a cookie jar. This happens automatically; most people aren't aware of it. Now, any properly equipped site can search those files—reach into that cookie jar—to check out your recent stopping-off points. It's like reading a log of your journey on the Web. The cookie jar file clearly marks each place where you stopped along the way. Did you visit the sites of Greenpeace, Save the Whales, Ozone Action, and Wildlife Conservation? It looks like you have an interest in environmental topics, so expect a political site to feed you the candidate's environmental line. The sample of cookies may not always match your interests perfectly, but it's a good start—and a technique that many sites will be using more frequently.[42]

Third, Andrew Conru, CEO and founder of W3.com, an interactive Website development firm, said designers can use "site tracking," where the Website computers follow you from place to place and within a site. They will interpret your meanderings as clues to your interests.[43] Suppose a visitor to a candidate's site looks at discussions of Social Security and welfare, then links to another site for more detail. In the background, unbeknownst to the user, a computer on the candidate's site has been noting these movements.[44] It also has noted the user's identification (IP address). So now it knows who you are and what drew your interest. "From now on," said Conru, "users must assume that everything they do on the Web is being recorded and may be put to use." How can site operators use the information gathered from questions, cookie jars, and site tracking?

One application is called "issue modeling." When users later return to the site, the computer will detect their IP addresses and recall their previous activity on the site—their answers to questions, where else they have visited, what they looked at, where they linked to. The computer then will alter the Web page information it assembles for each user. Now, rather than serving up the standard page designed for first-timers, the computer will customize a page that reflects topics of apparent interest to a particular user: in our example, Social Security and welfare. It's a small step toward the delivery of personal information based on the apparent interests of an individual rather than on the statistical average of a demographic group. This is an asset for people who want tailored information, but the background monitoring techniques raise ethical questions about privacy and disclosure little discussed in our rush into this new medium. The user isn't let in on the game. None of the Web specialists interviewed about this matter suggested that visitors are likely to be alerted to the computer's watchful eye.

Kent Godfrey, CEO of Andromedia, a developer of tracking software, sees his programs as a tool to improve the focus of Website content. "Most of the content is just repackaged broadcast content. It's not really taking advantage of the on-line capabilities."[45] With his software, he hopes to customize messages, using visitor feedback to gratify visitor appetites.

Michael Lynch, Webmaster at *New Media* magazine, said the programs are largely an aid to advertisers interested in keeping track of message exposure. "Mostly we want advertisers to know who has clicked on their ad."[46]

Apply this personalized information to the next generation of issue modeling. In response to user feedback, campaigns will be able to use stock digital clips of the candidate to assemble, on the fly, video messages that appear to be aimed directly at the recipient. The digitized candidate will talk to voters about the issues they have identified or are likely to find of interest. This personalized message will appear as a seamless clip, direct from the candidate to the voter.

Andrew Conru says, "It will be easy to project such personalization through a video clip just as today we can weave together a personal message instantly in a few paragraphs of text. With digital, the process is much the same."

The problem right now, according to Conru, is the bandwidth limitation. The speeds are too slow today, and the stream-down video is not smooth enough to be convincing. A number of technologies in the wings, however, will speed information between the user and the site, and when that happens, personalized, digital video will become a fixture on the Web. Several designers of political sites speaking with the author said they are eager to press this feature into use.

Hi-tech surveillance and high-target communication are bound to raise hackles and preoccupy honorable theorists. Privacy issues aside for now, how will voters perceive the "serendipitous" matchup of information? In what light will users regard something like a give-and-take with Website computers? How will they size up this clever medium when the voice recognition is refined, digital video improves, visitor analysis-on-the-fly becomes more intuitive?

From the user's point of view, these Internet exchanges might be taken as a kind of personal exchange. Political figures, always seeking ways to get closer to voters, may push the opportunities of this feedback-rich medium, and take the politics of proximity to the next level.

The messages on this medium clearly can be more elaborate than a message on any traditional mass medium. The digital clip—not being a real person—does not qualify as a traditional interpersonal exchange, yet the appearance, from the visitor's viewpoint, may not be much different. Not fully a personal communication, not fully a mass communication, what is it? Well, it's breaking the mold and requires some rethinking on how we size up both mass and interpersonal communication.

Notes on Interpersonal Communication and Computers

Where does the Internet fit into the catalog of communication media? How will the medium likely be seen by its audiences in the first decade of the twenty-first century as Internet technology advances? Can the Internet actually engage a user in an information exchange—or at least appear to? Can it explain and instruct as another person might?

The time is rapidly approaching when Internet site designers will need to confront the evolution of their tools and examine the paradoxes revealed by their successes. As technology grows more sophisticated with intuitive software, and as faster, better hardware adapts to human senses, the mass media nature of this tool will fade as the one-on-one communication character takes shape. The technology within the next decade may become so refined that users at times may lose sight of the fact that they are interacting with a computer and not with another person.

This may occur because the better technology becomes, the less it looks like technology and the more it looks like the humans it serves. The ultimate goal of artificial intelligence, after all, is to model human learning and reasoning. When that happens, the naive user asking about the cheapest fares to Philly won't be sure whether he's talking with the travel agent or with the agent's computer.

Some time in the twenty-first century, the interactive sophistication of Hal, the computer-gone-amok in Stanley Kubrick's *2001*, will become evident in computers on a desktop and on the Internet.[47] As we approach such sophistication, we can expect computers to simulate the give-and-take of interpersonal exchanges, which communication theorist Dean Barnlund says display several familiar characteristics. To begin, they involve two or more people who perceive the presence of one another and respond to one another. Then, he says, messages must be exchanged, and third, the interaction must be relatively unstructured.[48]

Add several other features. Messages must be receiver-specific, that is, tailored to each receiver individually. They must be interdependent (a true give-and-take). In other words, a message must respond to the one preceding it and perhaps anticipate messages to follow. Finally, there must be a two-way flow of information between sender and receiver and back again.

Clearly, feedback lies at the core of interpersonal communication. It's the personal "stuff" that sets off a true exchange from generic mass communications. In mass communication, one message fits all. In interpersonal communication, by contrast, feedback is responsive and alters the course of interaction.

To be meaningful in human communication, feedback must provide explanation. Whether you interact with a person or a computer, you need to know if your responses are correct or appropriate, and why. This is especially true in a learning environment. Consider the differences between a simple acknowledgment of correct responses (knowledge of results) and real feedback.[49]

First, knowledge of results (e.g., "NO, B is the wrong answer.") does not improve a person's chances of doing better next time. He or she needs to know *why* B is wrong in order to improve future performance.

Second, the information must be clear and the receiver must know what is relevant. Some information will help in future performance, and some will not, but the person must recognize the difference.

Third, the feedback must be sufficient. Ask a blindfolded person to draw a five-inch line. After each try, shout, "Inaccurate." The information may be true, but it is hardly sufficient.

Finally, feedback is aimed at future actions rather than offering a commentary on past performance.

At the end, knowledge of results confirms a response ("Right. What a good boy."). Feedback provides an explanation that can be used later in new situations ("Right. Good boy. See, you crossed the street after looking in both directions.").

As we look at interpersonal communication, the obvious question becomes "Can the computer provide real feedback, or is the computer limited to offering simple "yes" or "no," "correct" or "incorrect" responses? Can it explain? Rephrased more appropriately, "As the user sees things, from the human point of view, can the computer explain?"[50]

At one level, the answer is an easy "Yes." The computer can ask different questions contingent on your answers. It can be programmed to provide explanation to say "why" you are right or wrong. It can branch. For instance, if you said your age was 68, it could be programmed to ask you about Medicare. If you said you were 22, it could ask about your prospects for work after graduation.

Can the human partner sense that the computer is engaging in a personal exchange? It's tough to make this case now because computers aren't up to it yet. But it's not unthinkable for the future, when computers have more humanlike facades, such as better voice recognition and voice generation, and when they can go well beyond what interactive computer expert Andrew Conru calls "focused domains," which refers to a limited set of issues. So, yes, today there can be narrow and standardized exchanges, and the day of almost unlimited exchanges may arrive.

In sum, computers will likely be able to satisfy many characteristics of interpersonal exchanges. Messages between users and the computer move in both directions. Through on-screen text, pictures, and voice information, the computer can deliver a message and users can send one back through keyboard, mouse, voice, or other input device. The exchanges will be specific and interactive.

Go back to the voice exchange with a travel agent's computer. Here, unique messages are created spontaneously in response to the user's feedback, through the novelty of digital audio. The system is still primitive but, as Conru reminds us, it's evolving quickly.

But are we overdoing it? How far can we personify computers? After all, the person really communicating is the programmer who originated the messages. If it's the programmer, then we must conclude that the computer is more like the newspaper or television set, but that doesn't fit either. Isn't each message contingent on feedback? Isn't each participant active, providing responsive information to the other? Isn't a give-and-take occurring? Although each message on the computer side may have been preprogrammed, from the user's viewpoint this scenario looks a lot more like an interpersonal exchange than watching a television program ever could.

Stepping back from the nuts and bolts of feedback and interaction, it would be foolish to propose that computer and human partners are the same. The origin of information is not the same, and although both are products of rational thinking, one is extemporaneous and the other is not, no matter how much it may appear to be so to the user. Even though the range of responses may be restrained in both cases, there obviously is greater adaptability and pliancy between human interactants. The modes of interaction usually are different, although people are becoming more comfortable communicating in real time through E-mail and in chat rooms. These, of course, have real people at the other end, and so they are different in kind and quality from computer interactions, but the front end is the same, and it is comfort with format that will help visitors interact more freely in this new medium. Before long, interactive voice communication over the Internet will become a communication staple and make it even simpler to exchange messages with the computer.

There soon will be a remarkable similarity between human–human interactions and human–computer interactions in reasonably structured environments. The experts agree that will happen in the first decade of the twenty-first century.

For political communicators, a truly interactive Website will be an extraordinary extension of voter outreach. In its grandest form, with voice and video and the give-and-take between a visitor and the campaign, the candidates will focus their messages to address the needs of voters one by one. This beats print and broadcast communications and gets closer to stump speeches and door-to-door campaigning. A fully developed Internet by the second decade of the twenty-first century will put political figures closer to the voters and add a new dimension to the politics of proximity.

For the theorist, however, the Internet is a headache. Its three characters—mass medium, carrier of personal messages, interpersonal interactant—cloud the working models and confuse our understanding of how information plays in the decisions of voters. As information content and format change, so will the influences on electoral judgments.

SUMMARY: A PRE-INTERNET MODEL

Over the years, voting decisions were seen to be influenced disproportionately, at one time or another, by the media, interpersonal relations, and group pressures. As noted, however, most observers today agree that voters are motivated by a blend of all these influences. Were that not so, if voters were swayed by only a single influence, we probably would have discovered it, dropped the useless efforts, and put the matter to rest. But there isn't a magic bullet, and we haven't put the matter to rest, and it's improbable that we'll ever lay our hands on a single force that sways the vote.

The process of decision-making changes along with evolution of the media and their public use. Since the late 1960s we have seen major shifts in the use of print and television, and now we are poised for another revolution in the way audiences obtain and respond to information.

In an interview, Dan Boltz, political reporter for the *Washington Post*, said that information changes society, and information delivery systems alter the way societies operate. It happened, he said, with the telegraph, which linked distant places in real time for the first time ever. That may be humdrum today, but at the time it was nothing short of wizardry. The telephone reduced the abstraction of dots and dashes and put instant communication in the hands of average people. The mass media have their own significant effects on us personally and on society, and one of these effects is that they join us into groups and split us into factions. Change the information flow in a society, and you change the society itself.[51]

Society changes, yes, but in what ways is not always so clear. At best we can hope to lay out the array of likely influences, recognizing that at any given time, for any given voter, this composition and proportion of influences may not be valid. Measuring influence is far from a precise science. Path analyses that have sought to quantify the pattern of influence have met with little success in prescribing winning communication strategies. Moreover, the data are limited by the peculiarities of the studied groups, and beyond that, the data are statistical averages, around which there is great variance among individuals.

Figure 1
Influences on Voting Decisions (Pre-Internet)

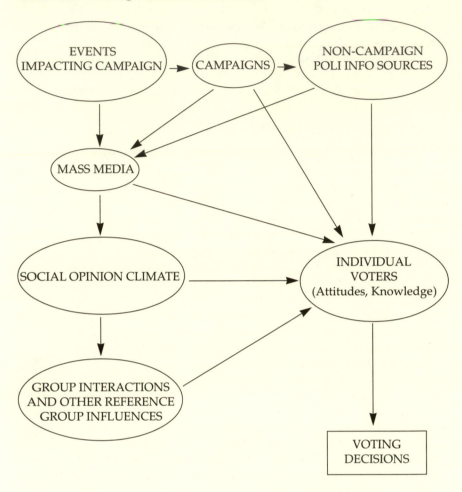

So, at the end of the day, we must accept that any model attempting to characterize voting decisions can offer only a simple structure built on a foundation of caveats. With this in mind, we turn briefly to a model depicting the items that have demonstrated some influence on voters (see Figure 1).

In this model, the voter is impacted by information from campaigns and noncampaign sources—for instance, political parties, labor unions, and other interest groups. These communications may be sent through the mass media or through direct channels, such as direct mail and phone banks, and even face-to-face visits. The mass media, primarily through news reports and commentary, provide information directly to individuals, and much of this finds its way into the social interactions that, by some accounts, play so heavily into individual decisions. Here is the cluster of influences said to affect individual knowledge and attitudes, and ultimately voting behavior.

This is a stripped-down model, to be sure. Other writers have included additional features that chart a more elaborate process. Those descriptions reveal additional influences on voting decisions subsumed in this abbreviated model. Lenart, for instance, provides a more complete matrix of elements at the interpersonal level involving social opinion climate, individual discussion, group interaction, and local opinion climate.[52]

Add the Internet

To the model we now add a few simple but significant changes that account for Internet communications. We replace the one-way flow arrows—from the media to individuals—with two-way flow arrows showing that now information can flow upline as well (see Figure 2).

The action takes place in the upper-right portion of the model, showing that individuals can now interact with campaigns and noncampaign sources, and in new ways with each other—for instance, in chat rooms and news groups. This simple addition stands to change political communication in several ways.

First, the two-way flow of information gives users an active communication role. They can provide instant feedback that wise Website operators will recognize as a rich source of information and an integral component of this interactive medium. The old top-down, one-way information flow from campaigns to voters will not work in this new environment.

Why? Competition is fierce. Barriers to entry are low, maintenance costs are low, and thus sources are plentiful and unfulfilled audience interests can quickly be met by more accommodating information providers.[53]

Another implication of two-way communication is the highly personalized messages that can flow from the campaigns. Powerful new Website computers can use voter information to tailor messages. Bob Dole's wall posters and bumper stickers offer a crude example of a personal response. For something more interesting, look to issue modeling with text and later with video. Compared with conventional media, it's a step closer to the touch and feel of a personal message. Just as one person in a conversation shapes his or her message to match the other person's interests, so computers on Websites will configure information to match the user's interests. They will answer questions and ask them, explain

Figure 2
Influences on Voting Decisions (with the Internet)

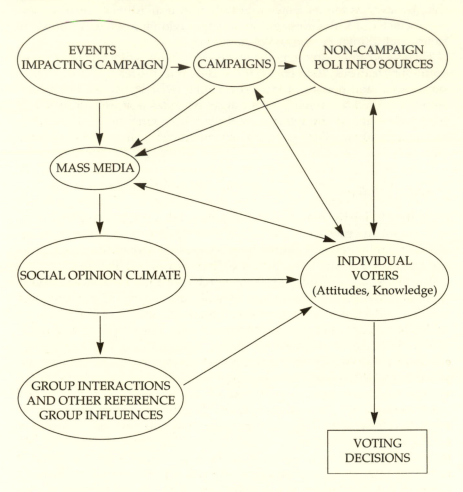

issues, then confirm that the user has understood them. These interactions will smudge the traditional line between mass and interpersonal communications.

The model shows that the two-way flow expands voters' communications with each other, using a new assortment of E-mail, news groups, and chat rooms. These redefine the social environment in which voters interact and make political decisions. Before the Internet, it was not possible for strangers scattered around the country to form ad hoc groups and talk politics with each other. Today such interactions are commonplace, and their popularity is growing.

Several questions arise when examining the effects of Internet groups. Will on-line discussions expand the range of topics and perspectives, thus broadening the bases for political judgments, or will they narrow the focus among like-minded voters, and tighten electoral decisions around a single point of view? In other words, will the expanded range of contacts expand the range of views, or expand only the number of people who feed on ever-narrowing views?

Probably each occurs, but which scenario dominates and for which voters? It's hard to say, in the absence of convincing empirical data, but with conformity so strong a force in groups, there's a good chance that on-line groups will reinforce similar viewpoints, doing little to expand discussion to a broader range of issues.

Two-way Internet communications can influence the evolving definition of reference group and community. Most people think of community in geographic terms, but that may be changing as the Internet expands a person's reach beyond the next-door neighbor. Chat rooms and news groups were busy places during the election. The formation of such "virtual" groups alarms some people, who are quick to see trouble for the society built largely around geographic clusters. They may be right. Still, in light of the fact that few urbanites know their neighbors, and most people find community in work and play groups, the loss of geographical fellowship may not be all that serious.

Meanwhile, Internet group affiliations are likely to influence participants' voting behaviors, and we should be curious about the possible effects of these groups as they involve more people more fully in the years ahead. These novel little groups will surely change society in many ways, only one of which is political decision-making.

The potential for virtual groups, along with many other Internet forums, to influence voting decisions calls for flexible models to account for the new environmental factors. Like any descriptive model, the configuration of influences displayed in Figure 2 offers a snapshot of a dynamic process but, at best, catalogs only some of the items likely to play a role in political judgments. But whatever else this model may reveal, it's clear that upline communication changes the complex of influences.

NOTES

1. Robert Zakon reports The Internet: A Timeline that demonstrates the rapid development of the Net. He provides these statistics:

	July 1992	July 1996
Hosts	992,000	12,881,000
Networks	6,569	134,365
Domains	16,300	488,000

Source URL: http://www.info.isoc.org/guest/zakon/Internet/History/HIT.html.

2. Sometimes the concept is referred to as the "magic bullet" theory of communication.

3. P. F. Lazarsfeld, "The Election Is Over," *Public Opinion Quarterly* 8, (1944): 317–330; C. I. Hovland, A. A. Lumsdaine, and F. D. Sheffield, *Experiments in Mass Communication* (Princeton: Princeton University Press, 1949).

4. P. F. Lazarsfeld, and H. Menzel, "Mass Media and Personal Influence," in W. Schramm, ed., *The Science of Human Communication* (New York: Basic Books, 1963), 96.

5. E. Katz, "The Two-Step Flow of Communication: An Up-to-Date Report of a Hypothesis," *Public Opinion Quarterly* 21 (1957): 61–78.

6. This research was reported in R. K. Merton, "Patterns of Influence: A Study of Interpersonal Influence and Communication Behavior in a Local Community," in P. F. Lazarsfeld and F. Standon eds., *Communication Research* (New York: Harper and Brothers, 1948); D. Katz, and P. Lazarsfeld, *Personal Influence: The Part Played by People in the Flow of Mass Communications* (New York: The Free Press, 1955); J., Coleman, et al., *Medical Innovation: A Diffusion Study* (New York: Bobbs-Merrill, 1966).

7. "Trust," in this application, is generally considered to mean that the source has no personal vested interest in the outcome.

8. People can't name their member of Congress: W. Williams, "Good Citizenship in the Information Age," *Seattle Times*, May 27, 1996, p. B5. The turnout for the 1996 election was 49 percent. Reported on the Federal Election Commission (FEC) Website: http://www.fec.gov/pubrec/summ.htm.

9. Hovland, Lumsdaine, and Sheffield, *Experiments in Mass Communication*.

10. For instance, see J. T. Klapper, "What We Know About the Effects of Mass Communication: The Brink of Hope," *Public Opinion Quarterly* 21 (1957–1958): 453–474.

11. Ibid., p. 459.

12. E. M. Rogers and F. F. Shoemaker, *Communication of Innovations: A Cross-Cultural Approach*, 2nd ed. (New York: Free Press, 1971).

13. E. M. Rogers, "Mass Media and Interpersonal Communication," in I. de Sola Pool and W. Schramm, eds., *Communication Yearbook*, vol. 11 (Beverly Hills, CA: Sage, 1973), 555–594.

14. Maxwell G. McCombs and Donald L. Shaw, *The Emergence of American Political Issues: The Agenda-Setting Function of the Press* (St. Paul, MN: West Publishing Co., 1977).

15. T. E. Patterson, and R. D. McClure, *The Unseeing Eye: The Myth of Television Power in National Political News* (New York: G. P. Putnam's Sons, 1976).

16. For news consumption patterns, see the Pew Research Center for the People & the Press Website. http://www.people-press.org.

17. Peter Troldahl, quoted in Rogers, *Communication of Innovations*, p. 208.

18. See W. J. Severin, and J. W. Tankard, Jr., *Communication Theories* (New York: Longman's, 1988).

19. S. H. Chaffee, "The Interpersonal Context of Mass Communication," in F. G. Kline and P. J. Tichenor, eds., *Current Perspectives in Mass Communication Research*, vol. 1 (Beverly Hills, CA: Sage, 1972), 107.

20. A. Smith, *Communication and Culture* (New York: Holt, Rinehart and Winston, 1966), 520.

21. Silvo Lenart, *Shaping Political Attitudes: The Impact of Interpersonal Communication and Mass Media* (Thousand Oaks, CA: Sage, 1994), 21.

22. M. Sherif, *The Psychology of Social Norms* (New York: Harper & Brothers, 1936).

23. S. E. Asch, "Studies of Independence and Conformity: A Minority of One Against a Unanimous Majority," *Psychological Monographs* 70(9) (1956): 1–70.

24. K. Lewin, *Resolving Social Conflicts: Selected Papers on Group Dynamics* (New York: Harper, 1948).

25. There is much confusion over the meaning of "Fundamentalist." In America, religious historians generally see a distinction between Fundamentalists and Evangelicals. "Fundies" are radical Evangelicals in both doctrine (biblical literalness) and behavior (mean-spirited, can't affirm their way without denying yours). As a percentage of Evangelicals, maybe 30 percent, they share the need for born-again conversion. Think of Falwell as a Fundamentalist and Billy Graham as an Evangelical who is not a Fundamentalist. It's really more attitude than belief. Graham is sweet-tempered and ecumenical, whereas Falwell is nasty, icy, and intolerant.

26. J. Bennett, "The Delegates: Where Image Meets Reality," *New York Times*, Aug. 12, 1996, p. A1.

27. G. Kessler, "The Evolution of Where GOP Finds Its Voters." *Newsday*, Nov. 11, 1996, p. A6.

28. This viewpoint has been expressed in many polls, the strength of response depending on the question wording. For instance, in a July 1996 Gallup News Service Poll, 53 percent of respondents identified themselves as "pro-choice." In a CNN/USA Today poll by the Gallup Organization, 69 percent did not oppose abortion, saying it should be legal "under all circumstances" (17 percent) or "only under certain circumstances" (52 percent). In that same poll, 24 percent said that abortion should not be legal "under any circumstances." Poll information was obtained by fax from the Gallup Organization.

29. Voting information taken from the FEC Website. http://www.fec.gov/pages/htmlto5.htm.

30. Average turnout rates for presidential elections in the 1940s (57.1 percent), 1950s (61.8 percent), and 1960s (62.1 percent) were higher than they have been in recent times. Turnout rates through the century are as follows: 1900—73.2 percent; 1904—65.2 percent; 1908—65.4 percent; 1912—58.8 percent; 1916—61.6 percent; 1920—49.2 percent; 1924—48.9 percent; 1928—56.9 percent; 1932—56.9 percent; 1936—61.0 percent; 1940—62.5 percent; 1944—55.9 percent; 1948—53.0 percent; 1952—63.3 percent; 1956—60.6 percent; 1960—64.0 percent; 1964—61.7 percent; 1968—60.6 percent; 1972—55.2 percent; 1976—53.6 percent; 1980—52.6 percent; 1984—53.1 percent; 1988—50.1 percent; 1992—55.1 percent; 1996—49.1 percent. Statistics for 1900–1968 are reported in *Historical Statistics of the United States, Colonial Times to 1970*, pt. 2 (Washington, DC: U.S. Department of Commerce, Bureau of the Census, 1975), 107. Statistics from 1972 to 1996 reported on the FEC Website, http://www.fecigov/pages/htmlto5.htm.

31. Turnout rates for presidential elections in the 1940s (57.1 percent) and

1950s (61.8 percent). Statistics reported in *Historical Statistics of the United States, Colonial, Times to 1970*, p. 1071.

32. P. Deutschman, "The Sign-Situation Classification of Human Communication," *Journal of Communication* 7 (Summer 1957): 63–73.

33. *USA Today*, http://www.usatoday.com; *Washington Post*, http://www.washingtonpost.com; *Los Angeles Times*, http://www.latimes.com.

34. Project Vote Smart, http://www.vote-smart.org.; PoliticsUSA, http://www.politicsusa.com.

35. Heritage Foundation Site, http://www.heritage.org.

36. Oregon Gun Page, http://www.telepot.com/~stane/gunpage.html.

37. Described by Rebecca Buckman of the Dow Jones News Service: R. Buckman, "Internet Phone Providers Going the (Long) Distance," *San Francisco Examiner*, Sept. 15, 1996, p. B5.

38. Evans Witt, former director of PoliticsNow, a premier political Website in operation during the campaign, said that E-mail feedback is a rich source of information from precisely the audience that the campaigns try to reach. And yet, he said, most campaigns, even the major national ones, ignored their E-mail. Why? "[They] didn't have a clue about this new medium. Like everyone else in the game in '96, they didn't know how to use the rich information available to them." Witt added that the learning curve is steep and that next time campaigns are unlikely to stand like deer in the headlights. In future campaigns, voter feedback will become a prized commodity (from the author's telephone interview with Witt on Feb. 4, 1997).

39. Other language software developers, working on similar programs, include Dragon Systems of Newton, MA, and Kurzwell Applied Intelligence of Waltham, MA. See David Einstein, "New Era in Speech Software," *San Francisco Chronicle*, Sept. 12, 1996, B1, B9. IBM was promoting its VoiceType Simply Speaking dictation software early in 1997 for $99. This included software and a headset mike. This information was contained in a quarter-page ad in the *San Francisco Chronicle*, Feb. 2, 1997.

40. Einstein, "New Era in Speech Software."

41. Ibid.

42. The *San Francisco Chronicle* has identified several of the many sites that use cookies: Software.net, Infoseek.com, Netscape.com, Hotwired.com, Yahoo.com, Firefly.com, Microsoft.com, msn.com, Wired.com, MSNBC.com. J. Answin, "Got Cookies?" *San Francisco Chronicle*, Mar. 11, 1997, p. C4.

43. From a telephone interview on Feb. 12, 1997.

44. Several companies are selling software that enables site developers to track visitor movements. The *San Francisco Chronicle* reports that Accrue Inc. of Mountain View, CA, is selling a program for $15,000 per copy. Andromedia Inc. in San Francisco sells its tracking software in a price range of $1,800–$5,000. Julia, Angwin, "Web Site Software Tracks Visitors," *San Francisco Chronicle*, Oct. 8, 1996, p. C4.

45. Quoted in ibid.

46. Quoted in Ibid. Author's note: The information obtained by these programs is overkill, however, if the only concern is advertiser curiosity about audience profiles. It's one thing to obtain a demographic image of those exposed and quite another to acquire specific information about individual users. This is

a striking escalation in audience measurement. Historically, advertisers have been satisfied to know the general audience makeup. In fact, most legitimate polls remind respondents that their answers will be blended with the answers of all others taking the poll and that nothing they say will be linked to them personally. Tracking software, by contrast, racks up detailed accounts, building a personal database on each visitor.

47. If Microsoft's Bill Gates is right, the operations of desktop and on-line computers will merge and users may not know or care if they are working on computers at arm's length or a continent away.

48. D. Barnlund, *Interpersonal Communication: Survey and Studies* (Boston: Houghton Mifflin, 1968).

49. K. U. Smith, "Cybernetic Principles of Human Behavior," in G. Whiting, ed., *Toward a Theory of Communication* (Madison, WI: College Printing and Publishing, 1972), 42–45.

50. This often is referred to as the phenomenological view.

51. Interviewed on Feb. 11, 1997.

52. Lenart, *Shaping Political Attitudes*.

53. As Evans Witt said, most political site developers haven't a clue to the special features of this medium, least of all the feedback from visitors. This Gutenberg thinking in a Bill Gates environment is not likely to last much beyond the 1996 campaign. The Internet will not tolerate communication that fails to understand, empathize with, and involve the user.

Chapter Two

Media History and Evolution: New Formats, New Content

To cite the hazards and shortcomings of television as a political instrument is simply to suggest that, in spite of its enthusiasts, it is
neither qualified, nor destined to replace the traditional forms of
American electioneering and its active reporting by a vigilant press.
                                                        —Robert Bendiner
                                New York Times Magazine, Nov. 2, 1952[1]

INTRODUCTION

Ever since the ancient Sumerians put their cuneiform messages on clay
tablets around 7,000 years ago, the flow of communication has moved
in one direction only: from sender to receiver. Those at the top sent down
the news and information to quiescent consumers. Those in the know
SENT, and those needing to know RECEIVED. It's true that in more
recent times, the market-driven media survive by their audience appeal,
but still they are controlled from the centers of power that dictate what
is delivered and what is suppressed. Markets only guide; the owners,
producers, and publishers direct.

Receivers, those variously called readers since Gutenberg, hearers
since Marconi, and viewers since Zworykin, have never been able to
dislodge the senders from their thrones. What about exceptions like the
underground press? Or ham radio? In a national context they mean nothing. Mass communication means mass audiences and mass power.
Which is why Hammurabi kept his thumb on the cuneiform, Stalin controlled the airwaves, and Castro runs the presses.

Now, for the first time in human history, a medium has been created over which the power elite cannot exercise control. Suddenly, the plebeian souls at the other end of the whip have activated their PCs to obtain information based on *their* needs, *their* interests, *their* pleasures—in simple disregard of the media sovereigns.

This includes some communications that are trivial and entertaining and some that are deadly serious. Already, heroic stories of the Internet are making their way into the history books. Hours after Serbian dictator Slobodan Milosevic shut down the radio stations and newspapers in 1996, students, professors, and journalists by the thousands logged onto the Internet and instantly connected to the rest of the world. They did an end run around the central media that are so vulnerable to the whims of a despot. They told their story to the rest of the world and received assurances from people and governments beyond their borders. Ten thousand Lilliputians would not tolerate the tyrant's grip and used their computers to pry open his fist. Milosevic, a creature of the Iron Curtain, faced the new realities of the Iron Sieve and felt the power of decentralized communication.

What can we call the revolution in cyberspace? New ideas demand a new vocabulary. Is "interactive" good enough to describe the oscillations of send-and-receive, give-and-take? What about the metaphors? Does the "two-way street" of continuous traffic fill the bill? Not quite, but the transformation of a society wrought by automobiles is analogous to what is happening with the PC and its drivers. What about "interpersonal"? No doubt that will rile purists who fight to preserve the human quality of "I-Thou" relationships. But the hard truth is, a person on the Net can "talk" to a machine, ask questions that the machine will answer individually, and inform the machine conversationally about what is on the user's mind. Until we find better words, we can see that such activity is interactive, it's two-way for sure, and it's at least interpersonal in the barest sense of that word. Adequate vocabulary or not, the watershed nature of Internet communication has us clicking "thesaurus" to find the right adjectives.

However, before we get carried away by the uniqueness of cyberspace, we ought to bear in mind that on the surface the Internet is mostly a composite of print, radio, film, and television. As such, it bears many of their familiar features; that's the "multimedia" nature of the medium.

This is hardly surprising when you remember the ways conventional media developed. Traditionally, the engineers invented new forms of media and the programmers then put them into service, using the print and broadcast formats to carry information content for audiences to consume in the commotion of the marketplace. Indeed, some of the questions we ask of the Internet, its predecessors were asking (and are still asking) of their channels of communication: What should our newspaper say and how should we say it and picture it? How should our radio stations use sound to shape a program, to inform and entertain? What information load should our TV network carry in this audiovisual world and how should it sound, what should it look like? And above all, how can we get the response we want from audiences?

Comedian Bob Newhart, portraying an early Madison Avenue executive, had some recording fun with early inventors. In one scene, Gutenberg enters his agency office, carrying a press. The inventor demonstrates his new thing called "type," cast in metal, that prints on homemade paper. A paraphrased version of Newhart's script goes something like this:

Bob: Okay, now what does it do?

Gutenberg: Well, it doesn't do anything, but it saves thousands of hours spent by monks copying manuscripts by hand.

Bob: (laughing): What ELSE have they got to do, Mr. Gutenberg? I mean, how can we make a buck out of saving time for a bunch of monks?

Gutenberg: Don't you see? We can turn out books by the millions and people all over the world can read for themselves.

Bob: Johannes, sweetheart, do you know how many people in the world can read? It's maybe 17 outside the monasteries. You've got some nice pieces of metal there, but, trust me, there's no market for it. I'll tell you what. You figure out how to turn that metal into gold, and you got a deal!

A manufacturer's agent would have had the same trouble with Marconi. What was it, a way to call all the ships at sea? Big deal! As for Zworykin's iconoscope, invented in the 1920s, the big boys of GE and RCA hardly thought his television worth much attention until the early 1940s. Nobody knew the answers then because standards had to evolve as engineers, producers, and audiences sampled formats and contents in order to settle on conventions over time.

The Internet is experiencing the same growing pains. Appearance, content, and usage, to say nothing of the hardware, changing week by week, are up for grabs. And the 40 million users could be 160 million by the end of the 1990s.[2] All anybody knows, Bob Newhart, is that there is alchemy afoot, and whoever gets the chemistry right will glean riches like Bill Gates, and whoever gets it wrong will die as penniless as Gutenberg.

THE INTERNET'S PLACE IN THE MEDIA EVOLUTION

Today the Internet is evolving and, like radio in the early 1920s, its ultimate appearance and content will not be settled quickly, nor will its look be as uniform as it is for the conventional media one television station looks pretty much like another, newspapers everywhere have similar appearances. This is so for several reasons.

To begin with, the Internet displays all the formats of the traditional media—text like a newspaper, audio like radio, and audiovisual something like TV or movies, and it can do them all at one time. This increases the combinations and permutations possible with Website communications. (Note: Throughout this chapter we refer to the modes of communication—for instance, video, sound, and text—as *formats*. Some broadcasters use "formats" to mean program types, such as sitcoms, dramas, and news shows. That is not our meaning here.)

The political sites of 1996 were among the best bench tests found on the Internet. Programmers tried all the formats: the audio, the visual, the text. They offered all the content possibilities: speeches, testimonials, schedules, biographies, games, whatever they could think of. The short lives of the campaigns—ending abruptly on November 5—provided the focus, the urgency, and the freedom to experiment, and it is likely that these political experiments will help shape how, in time, millions of other sites will use the medium.

The Internet also does not need large audiences to survive, and this will allow programmers to appeal to individual audience tastes. Sites can accommodate huge audiences, of course, but, unlike the broadcast channels, most don't need them. This medium operates by a different calculus, not on the economies of audience scale but on the loyalty and consistency of audience patronage. The Internet needs devoted audiences, not necessarily large ones, and so it can appeal to isolated interests.

This medium allows audience feedback—we never tire of making this point—which means that, unlike all the other media, which send but do not receive, the Internet can interact with its users as individuals, so the better Websites will be personal. As a result, not only will one site be different from another site, but individual interactions on the same site also may be quite different.

But that gets ahead of the story. To understand the interplay between content and format on the Internet, it will help to know something about the early histories of the traditional media, to see how they used their new formats to present news and political information.

MEDIA START-UPS

Newspapers, the First Days

Not without dispute, Johannes Gutenberg is generally credited with inventing the press with movable type.[3] As Bob Newhart observed, there weren't a lot of newspapers circulating at the castle, so Bibles and other religious texts seemed the best bet. Printing Bibles and "cradle books" wasn't necessarily Gutenberg's choice as much as it was the demand of the times in which he forged his press. The Roman Catholic Church, which touched all of German life in 1455, was not convinced that common people should read—period. The Protestants, led by Luther, made sensational gains during the next 100 years, because they wanted everyone biblically literate. Teaching the masses to read was a re-formation of human society, one that Gutenberg triggered.

At the time of the first movable type, literacy was a rationed commodity, possessed only by the clergy and government officials. Their literary appetites, on the surface at least, tended toward the religious. If Gutenberg wished to prosper, valued his freedom, and hoped for an audience, his book list would remain short, parochial, and religious.

By 1700, other publishers would work the presses, aiming at secular readers. Nobody knows exactly where and when the first newspaper appeared on the North American continent, but many look to Boston in the early colonial period, around the late seventeenth century.[4] To call the journals of that day newspapers would be a stretch, but they did contain news about commerce and politics, and much of their material consisted of reprinted pamphlets, letters, sermons, and essays. It was more the *Utne Reader* than the *New York Times*, but this was the period when publishers experimented with audiences and the concept of journalism.

In 1729, Benjamin Franklin hit the streets with *The Pennsylvania Gazette*, a paper he touted as offering the "Freshest Advices Foreign and Domestick."[5] It didn't much resemble today's daily paper, but by standards of the time, its advice was fresh, and its appearance was distinctly newspaper-like. Franklin, always the innovator, tinkered with the appearance and story content of the *Gazette*. His legacy was twofold: the *Gazette* set the standard for today's publishers, who aim both to make money and to stimulate political debate.

As for the moneymaking, Franklin wore not only a newspaperman's green eyeshade but also a merchant's apron. From the start, he packed advertisements into his paper, many for his own goods, including the stationery, ink, and pens in his shop. When Franklin advertised, he established the side-by-side placement of advertising and editorial content, which planted deep in American newspaper history the roots of advertiser support. This reinforced a commercial funding mechanism that kept the cost of news relatively low and affordable to the masses, even though, at times, it raised eyebrows about journalistic objectivity, particularly toward coverage of those who placed the ads. He who pays the piper calls the tunes—or, just as powerfully, bans certain tunes. Happily, for many years, starting a competing paper was quick and inexpensive, as it is today for starting up a Website.

Franklin's inclinations toward the commercial affected his philosophy of a journalism of editorial objectivity. It was his view that anything interfering with the reader's enjoyment of his advertising was anathema to proper newspapermanship. And since political or ideological tilts in reporting would inevitably offend some, driving them away from the paper and away from its commercial income, a prudent editor would stick to the facts and avoid controversy.

Feeding this instinct for survival was the fact that other professions served all quarters of the market. Why should newspaper publishers be any different? Franklin's rule: Serve everyone, displease no one. "The Smith, the Shoemaker, the Carpenter . . . work indifferently for People of all Persuasions, without offending any of them . . . or suffering the least Censure of ill will on the Account from any Man whatever."[6]

In all fairness, Franklin's objectivity was not simply self-serving or commercial. He argued passionately for balance, with the reasoning that all sides of an argument deserved public exposure, and that from the airing of all views, the truth would emerge. In the same article, Franklin wrote:

Printers are educated in the Belief, that when Men differ in Opinion, both Sides ought equally to have the Advantage of being heard by the Publick; and that when Truth and Error have fair Play, the former is always an overmatch for the latter: Hence they cheerfully serve all contending Writers that pay them well, without regarding on which side they are of the Question in Dispute.[7]

With that in mind, politics entered the lists. Unsurprisingly, newspapers did not always observe Franklin's call for evenhandedness in their coverage of political issues. As relations between the colonies and England grew more contentious during the mid-1700s, papers took decidedly partisan positions, often at the behest of their readers. The *Journal of Occurrences* and the *Boston Gazette*, for instance, took firm stands against British control, advocating a range of public responses to the increasing economic demands on the colonies from abroad.[8]

In the decades between the Puritan sermons of Cotton Mather and the Republican papers of Franklin's time, one can see the transition from pamphlet to newspaper, from elite to masses, from the academic to advertising, and above all from the religious to the secular. It was only a small step from these values to political persuasion. Publishers found that, indeed, their role in society was very different from those of the smith, the shoemaker, and the carpenter. Newspaper publishers were not just the chroniclers of political events; through the power granted by the format of print and the information content it bore, they became part of the political process itself.

Radio, the Early Days

For 200 years, newspapers went unchallenged as the most popular—and political—of the media. There was theater, of course, and novels emerged in the nineteenth century, but they served a different audience—those seeking entertainment, not news.

Then came a sea change. What a leap it must have been for audiences during the early 1920s! So accustomed to getting news and information from the pages of a newspaper, they were suddenly treated to sound through the audio of radio. First came talk. Then commercial programmers quickly expanded the audio format to include music, sound effects, and voice-over. Joined with the spoken word, radio reduced the abstraction of mass communication, opened windows to nonreaders, and revealed unheard-of wonders to the human imagination.

With radio, you could hear the president speak. You formed a mental picture of the man, potentially far more powerful and memorable than static words on a page. On radio, you could hear the crowds, listen to the bands, sense the excitement of a political gathering with an immediacy that print could never offer.

But perhaps more compelling was the aliveness of the radio experience. Radio could take ten million listeners to a convention, or a congressional hearing, or the signing of an armistice. At best, a paper, even with its speedy "extra," could only retell these events and only later touch readers never assembled as one. Radio delivered a sense of community—the brand-new feeling that you were sharing a moment with "everybody else," and could talk about it later.

These were history's first wired-in events. The medium delivered not only news and entertainment, but presence and involvement, demonstrating that a mass medium could be more than a simple vehicle for information. By this time, radio and movies had borrowed their entertainment values from the dramatic art of theater and the literary art of the novel. Neither displaced stage and book, although both went far beyond the "old" media in their enlistment of mass audiences.

In the sense of borrowed skills, radio was no exception to the uncertainties that confront all emerging media: how the givens of a format affect the content of programming. Writing for the ear was different from writing for the eye (theater) or the mind's eye (print). And predicting audience reaction was chancy, since no audiences' ears had ever been attuned to a faceless sound. Those uncertainties of early radio copywriters are not unlike the uncertainties of copywriters for Internet audiences in 1996. How do you present information in an unfamiliar format—or combination of formats? Trial and error, it would seem, trial and error.

Development of Radio

After serving as little more than a ship-to-shore convenience during the 1910s, radio emerged as a commercial medium in 1920, by most accounts, in the garage of Pittsburgh resident Dr. Frank Conrad.[9] Conrad was clowning around with the radio novelty, airing tunes from the horn of his Victrola and doing schtick for a close-knit fraternity of ham operators, when he caught the eye—or at least the ear—of Westinghouse executives.

Westinghouse, at the time, was manufacturing small numbers of radio receivers, mostly for the hams and harbor masters, but the company saw in Conrad's antics a pretext to promote radio to a much wider customer base. In this earliest commercial concept, the format and content of radio primarily served the ends of hardware production. If programming, which promoted the sale of receivers, informed and entertained the audiences, that was a bonus. It just wasn't necessary.

On November 2, 1920, KDKA went on the air, and in a burst of prescience, the first program it broadcast was the election results of the presidential race between Warren G. Harding and James M. Cox.[10] Commercial radio was only minutes old, and already politics was involved in broadcasting. The transmission quality was poor and the audience small, but radio preempted every newspaper in the country, and it did it on a shoestring budget.

The number of receivers sold and the number of stations logging on the air expanded rapidly during the next few years as audiences seized on the audio format and on the instant, "real-time" delivery of information. Programmers experimented with reckless abandon, testing format options, audience preferences, and the tolerance of government, guilds, and the powerful newspapers unwilling to sacrifice their dominance in the business of information. Entertainment, news, and public affairs quickly became staples of the new medium.

Radio was a natural vehicle for political information. The medium could deliver breaking news and provide periodic updates on stories unfolding at home and abroad. Moreover, the public's ability to hear the political figures promoted a personal relationship between pols and the people and demonstrated that politicking could be personal even as the population was expanding. And it put a top premium on "voice," the kind of resonant, sincere, trust-inspiring voice that first surfaced with FDR.

Radio's entry into the information marketplace sparked a few battles, one of them with newspaper publishers, who didn't much like the intrusion of broadcasters into their news business. Papers had always been first at the breakfast table, first on the newsstands, first at the train stations and bus stops. Now radio was skimming the cream—the breaking issues—leaving the rest for print.[11]

First to fall to radio were the "extras" hawked on street corners. Editors agonized over the laws of physics that gave radio a time advantage over print. A radio reporter could air his story nationwide before a newspaper reporter could spool copy paper into his typewriter, much less wait for type set by hand. Nothing could change that advantage, although the publishers of newspapers tried.

After radio did in the special editions, it continued to nibble away at newspaper audiences. In 1933, newspaper publishers said enough was enough. Early in that year, the major papers pressured the three wire services—the United Press, the Associated Press, the International News Service—to refuse news distribution to the radio networks, in hopes of starving broadcasters while keeping newspaper larders well stocked.

It didn't work—worse, it backfired. Left without a major news source, the networks set up their own news-gathering operations. At first, cutting the wire service umbilical cord was painful, but in the long run, it freed the networks from a dependency on outside news sources. In the long run, the newspapermen's actions designed to weaken radio competition actually strengthened it.

Truces of one kind or another were arranged to resolve differences between the radio networks and the papers, but most attempts were short-lived. Among them were restrictions imposed on radio stations to impede the delivery of fast-breaking information and the establishment of the Press-Radio Bureau to allow broadcasters to air only certain kinds of news.

The quick fixes didn't work in most cases, and they didn't work for long in any case. Many stations didn't sign the agreements, other news sources emerged, and then even the wire services, which had refused to dispense news to radio, caved in at the loss of a lucrative market, eventually dropping efforts to hamstring the broadcasters. But the damage was done. The networks now had well-developed news-gathering operations with stringers calling in live from every major city around the globe. Where the wires once had a virtual monopoly, they now faced competition that they had a hand in creating. Of course, the major broadcasters used the wires after this, but largely as a well-written supplement. In actual practice, news editors used AP, UP, and Reuters mostly to cover the run-of-the-mill stories and features, the fillers around live, on-the-scene reports so popular with listeners.

At the start of World War II, the radio and newspaper battles had pretty much ended. The Press-Radio Bureau shut its doors, the broadcasters had their own news bureaus, and the wire services were making money selling news to all takers. In the wake of radio's entry into the news and information market, newspapers changed, but they didn't lose, at least not very much. Radio captured their market for fast-breaking news and special editions, so, yes, that was the newspapers' loss. But the public grew more interested in news, perhaps as a result of radio coverage, and this strengthened the market for information in general. This fell to newspapers as a gain.

Thus, attempts to restrict radio—an economic censorship—failed because audience demand was unwavering and newspapers could do nothing to change it. The market, and the dollars that chase the market, will ensure that a medium unleashed cannot be suppressed.

We note the struggles of news organizations in early radio because they offer such a stunning contrast to the experiences of news outlets that have joined the Internet. As we describe later, not only did the existing media impose no impediments to the rise of information sources on the Web, but many created their own sites and were among the first to put up pages.

Television, the Early Days

Given the public's lust for TV today, it's amusing to go back a half-centruy and read how some experts were denouncing the budding medium. In 10 short years (1950 to 1960), television took the world by storm, its popularity unmatched by any other innovation in the twentieth century. Today, the average American spends more than four hours a day watching TV, and the average family set is on for seven hours each day.[12] Academic studies confirm that kids spend more time watching television than doing anything else except sleeping, and that includes sitting in the classroom. In scholarly journals and the popular press, television has been credited, if that's the word, as one of the greatest single influences on political judgment, consumer habits, and social development, not to mention personal behavior. The affinity for television is so strong that even in many rural settings, here and abroad, people without refrigeration or phone service or indoor plumbing somehow have managed to wire up a television set. Antennas sprouting from thatched-roof huts have become a symbol for the ubiquity of the medium.

Development of Television

Why, then, did the early pundits see television mostly as an interesting novelty? Well, as Darryl Zanuck, head of 20th Century-Fox, reasoned in 1946, "[Television] won't be able to hold on to any market it captures after the first six months. People will soon get tired of staring at a plywood box every night."[13] Why watch a 10-by-12-inch screen in puritan black and white when movies were in Technicolor and on a wide screen? The critics may be forgiven. The earliest televisions, such as those shown at the 1939 Worlds Fair, were curiosities only, displaying little of their audiovisual potential. Anyone might have missed it. These Model-T televisions, now on permanent display at the Smithsonian Institution, demonstrate nothing remarkable about the early incarnation of a medium that later would be called the "window to the world" and "a replica of reality."[14] At the time they were dirty windows indeed, and reality never looked so awful.

More than primitive technology kept television from its eventual place at the center of American households. A handful of stations were on the air in the early 1940s, but their efforts were disrupted when the war siphoned off resources and creative talent, and drew away the attention of the nation. And, as if the market-driven resource drain were not enough, in 1942 the government imposed a wartime halt on the construction of stations and television sets, stopping the industry dead. Only six stations operated during the war, and these reached barely 7,000 receivers with programming that aired just four hours per week.[15]

Nevertheless, technology was on the march. Audiovisual science benefited from wartime research, and after V-J Day, the industry found itself in possession of impressive new tools, to say nothing of a hungry market of consumers who had done without for five years. The wartime freeze on television was lifted in 1945, and immediately applications for station licenses began pouring in. That created a gridlock at the Federal Communications Commission (FCC) that was to last five years. To be sure, television at this moment was poised to explode on the consumer, but it was not to be. Not yet. Several battles had yet to be fought.

The first arose over the format of color television. The Radio Corporation of America (RCA) and the Columbia Broadcasting System (CBS) sought FCC approval for their competing color technologies. CBS proposed a mechanical system (the field sequential system) that offered superior images but was incompatible with existing black-and-white sets. In effect, it came down to a better picture versus a more economical transition to color. RCA offered an electronic design (the dot sequential system) that, while it was compatible with existing television sets, produced an inferior image. Receiver sales halted pending a decision, which came down in 1950, in favor of CBS.

But that was not the end of it. Before the decision could be implemented, RCA and a cabal of set manufacturers filed suit, again putting the decision on ice. Then, in the spring of 1951, the Supreme Court upheld the FCC's decision. That should have ended it, since Supreme Court decisions usually prevail. But not this time. In the epilogue, the National Television System Committee (NTSC), an industry group of engineers, studied the options further and, after much analysis, pronounced the superiority of RCA's electronic system. Finally, in 1953, with strong

NTSC support, RCA convinced the FCC to approve its dot sequential system.[16] That marked the end—at least of *that* problem.

Meanwhile, the second industry delay was tied to the avalanche of TV station applications. From 1945 to 1952, the FCC ordered a freeze on new applications in order to study interference problems. Moving with glacial speed, the government experts reviewed technical studies, encouraged industry negotiations, and held public hearings. It's not clear if the FCC staff studying color technology was speaking to staff on the license application front, but at just about the same time in 1952, the FCC lifted the freeze and let the industry get on with its business.

The battles over color transmission and station licenses bottled up the industry like a champagne cork. Now freed of impediments, the industry exploded during the 1950s. In 1950, researchers reported that approximately 10 percent of American households owned television sets. That number leaped to nearly 60 percent by 1955, and to 90 percent by 1964. Moreover, reflecting the medium's popularity and advertisers' thirst for large audiences, television station revenue increased dramatically from $6.2 million in 1948 to $372.2 million in 1955.[17]

Early Television Content

Waiting in the wings during this moratorium like prima donnas patting their feet while orchestra instruments tuned their A's, the creative community of producers and writers was dreaming up *The Honeymooners*, *I Love Lucy*, and *Playhouse 90*. From scientists, who over many years painstakingly developed the transmission of images through the vapor, to technicians who figured out the electronics, it now became the job of programmers and audiences to arrive at how to use new formats to carry the news and entertainment content.

The programmers tried it all: movies, song and dance, comedy. They adopted hit radio programs like *Amos 'n' Andy* and *Gunsmoke*, and recycled talent like George Burns and Gracie Allen, Jack Benny, and Bob Hope. They shanghaied audiences with live dramas direct from Broadway and created new concepts like *Tonight with Steve Allen*.

Entertainment has always been the mainstay of television, although during the "golden years," news and public affairs found their way into programming logs. Still, news was not the staple you might expect it to be for a medium that could take audiences to an event live, with sight and sound. In the early 1950s, each of the three networks, led by CBS, aired 15-minute daily newscasts. Thirty-minute newscasts wouldn't debut for another decade. They would start on CBS in 1963, and then the National Broadcasting Company (NBC) and the American Broadcasting Company (ABC) in 1967. But even before the longer newscasts were instituted, polls showed that television became the most relied-upon and the most believable medium for news, a distinction it enjoys to this day.[18]

Early network newscasts were shoestring operations that often used visuals purchased from newsreel companies, which sometimes staged events to support the story. Thus early network news sometimes looked like clumsy docudramas, but this changed once the networks beefed up their news operations, adding staff and video units on which it could impose tighter journalistic standards, including a halt to reenactments.

Politics became an early favorite of the medium, providing the focus for shows such as *Pick the Winner, Meet the Press,* and *Keep Posted.* Other information-based programs emerged. For instance, Edward R. Murrow and Fred Friendly developed *See It Now,* an investigative news show that became the benchmark for televised documentaries. In one of the most celebrated episodes, they took on the powerful Senator Joe McCarthy, whose self-appointed mission to root Communists from the government and other American institutions was based on rumor, innuendo, guilt by association, and flat-out deceptions. McCarthy's destruction of lives and reputations made him a perilous but appealing target for journalists.[19]

Politicians were among the earliest users to scramble onto the World Wide Web in the mid-1990s, but their quick interest in a new medium broke precedent. In 1948, political candidates did not jump at television. The Truman–Dewey race was the first that could have used television, but both candidates rejected the opportunity. Truman, a no-frills, down-to-earth pragmatist, didn't much like television, which he thought had "sold out to the special interests." Perhaps realizing that he looked and sounded like a bumpkin, he avoided television in his campaign, relying on print, radio, and, of course, his whistle-stops—face-to-face speeches from the back of a train. Not that he was that much better on radio.

Thomas Dewey, rejecting the advice of his advertising agency, also spurned television.[20] Nor did he use his "radio voice" to his advantage. In contrast to Truman's whiny twang, Dewey spoke with the round tones and the rhythms of a radio announcer. Maybe the technology was too new, maybe Truman's rejection of television played a part, or maybe Dewey put too much credence in his glowing poll numbers. Would Dewey's use of television have made a difference in Truman's razor-thin victory? Probably not, given the small number of sets in use. Either way, Dewey was the last Republican presidential candidate to take the chance.

Television was used more actively in the election of 1952, when Dwight Eisenhower, who also distrusted and disliked television, accepted the advice that Dewey rejected; at the urging of consultants, he aired a series of 20-second spots extolling his distinguished war record.[21] Despite Eisenhower's comfortable lead in the polls, the Citizens for Eisenhower blitzed television audiences during the closing weeks of the campaign, at a cost of $2 million.

The Democratic contender, Adlai Stevenson, who felt that television packaged a candidate the way it packaged breakfast cereal, wanted no part of it. An orator of world stature and a wordsmith born for the era of newspapers, Stevenson relied solely on radio to broadcast his speeches. He was the last presidential candidate to turn a cold shoulder to television.

Four years later, in his unsuccessful rerun against Eisenhower, Stevenson reluctantly gave in to the medium, although he never looked good on it. Eisenhower, by this time, was so far ahead, it is doubtful any strategy—involving television or not—could have reversed the outcome.

Although the short spot quickly became a political advertising staple, candidates, resorting to the radio model, occasionally used larger blocks of time. The best-known example was vice presidential candidate Richard Nixon's Checkers speech. During the 1952 election, in the face of accusations that Nixon misused campaign funds, the Republican National Committee bought a half-hour on network prime time so he could defend himself. Nixon denied all wrongdoing, then ended with a saccharine account about a cocker spaniel puppy he received as a gift during the campaign: "And our little girl—Tricia, the six-year old—named it Checkers. And you know the kids love that dog, and I just want to say this right now, that regardless of what they say about it, we're going to keep it."

New York Times political affairs writer Robert Bendiner wrote, "Television must be rated as a major factor in the remarkable comeback of Richard Nixon after revelations concerning his finances seriously threatened to force him off the Republican ticket." Bendiner reported that Nixon's handlers were convinced that the medium counted "very heavily in his rescue from impending disaster."[22]

The 1948 national party conventions—both held in Philadelphia— were the first to be covered by television, although the whole production involved little more than a stationary camera fixed on the speaker's platform. No more was possible or necessary. The audiences were too small to justify more effort for an event already well covered by newspapers and radio. The 1948 conventions were content experiments and little else, not unlike the Internet's trial run in 1996.

The campaign of 1952 was the first to be covered thoroughly by television. The medium ran live coverage of the nominating conventions, election returns, and inauguration ceremony. Corporations spent $8 million on network coverage during the convention and on Election Night returns. Both parties allocated considerable money for TV, although the expenditures were lopsided in favor of the Republicans.[23] As noted above, the Citizens for Eisenhower spent nearly $2 million on television ads during the final weeks of the campaign. The Democrats spent $77,000 on spots, mostly condemning Republicans for the depression of 1929.[24]

Sadly, politicians didn't wait long to go negative on the new medium.

Bendiner attributes three major campaign events to television in 1952. First, although Stevenson did not advertise on television, he received a lot of coverage in the conventions and other political forums, and this helped to elevate this "Great Unknown" of American politics to national stature. Second, television pulled Richard Nixon from the fire. Third, television was likely responsible for increasing voter registration and stimulating turnout at the polls.[25]

Much of the attraction of television had to do with the improvements in coverage of political events. The television lockdown during the late 1940s and early 1950s didn't stop engineers from advancing new audiovisual technologies, many of which debuted at the 1952 conventions. Battery-powered cameras, for instance, followed roving reporters who now were free to interview delegates live on the convention floor.[26] Innovations in floor interconnections allowed smoother handoffs among correspondents scattered throughout the convention hall. New editing and display technologies created split-screen images and vote tallies that could be superimposed over other scenes. This expanded visual possibilities and added depth to convention coverage.[27] These and other developments in cameras, sound technology, and staging provided convention coverage with a presence and spontaneity that gave audiences not only a sense of being there but also of active participation.

It became evident early in the development of the medium that television did more than just give a visual image to the sound of radio. Television's integrated formats of sight and sound could effectively alter audience perceptions of events in subtle and sometimes dramatic ways. William Schlamm tells an interesting story that reveals the impact of the audiovisual format on the perception of content. While watching network coverage of a political convention in 1952 (he doesn't say which convention), he observed how a camera shot changed the audience impression of an incident. Schlamm's own words tell it best.

A minister was giving the nightly invocation, and the TV camera was conveying the sudden hush of reverence even ward captains sense when the Lord is invoked. But then, just as ceremonial mention was made of Love, the cameraman took the cue and, whoosh, switched to a young lady in the aisle who was indeed a peach. . . .

The incident . . . identified with an almost disarming frankness, the inherent nature of the medium. TV has unlimited means of reference, but its formative instinct is "entertainment"; and so it cannot help being vulgar. It must vulgarize what it touches.[28]

Newspapers and radio could not have had such an effect. We will see later how the visual format is a powerful conveyor of content, often changing the meaning of spoken words beyond recognition.

In addition to the political firsts and lasts marking this watershed year of televised campaigns,[29] the conventions of 1952 introduced American audiences to Walter Cronkite, who, more than any other figure in television history, came to represent average viewers on the national stage. NBC's team of Chet Huntley and David Brinkley ruled the 1950s, but come 1960 the news venue belonged to "Uncle Walter"—a moniker bestowed with great respect. His convention debut demonstrated the personal and professional skills that later would establish him as a trusted American icon. Cronkite interpreted and explained the political significance of events, but he did much more through his shoulder-to-shoulder interviews with national leaders in which he demonstrated that the live television format, put to proper use, could project a personal authority that newspapers and radio could not.

In later years, Cronkite's public trust, unmatched even by political and religious leaders, positioned him between the real world faced by viewers every day and the mythical world presented on television. While Eisenhower was busy putting a human face on politics, Cronkite was busy putting a human face on television. And that, as much as anything else that took place in these early years, demonstrated that television would become for the nation much more than radio with a view.

The Relationship between Format and Content

The interplay between format and content resurfaces as each new medium adds another format and expands the opportunity to provide different content. Formats—print, audio, and video—are like vehicles, and content—articles, music, dramas, comedy—are like cargo. Some cargo is better suited to some vehicles: the question is how to make the match.

In 1955 media researcher Percy Tannenbaum discussed the subject in a short essay on the "indexing" process of communication.[30] Essentially, Tannenbaum looked at how the elements of a communication—the visuals, sounds, text—contributed to the information (the content) packed into a message. For our purposes, the elements are building blocks of formats. For instance, the audio format can comprise voice, music, and sound effects. Print can include text, photos, and line art.

Tannenbaum was concerned not only with objective content or "message content," but also with the emotional or evaluative portions, which he called "affective content." You come away from a political speech or a 30-second spot with knowledge of the facts and figures, but also with an *evaluation* of the information and of the person who presented it. Tannenbaum saw communication as a composite of the objective and the evaluative. He said that communication conveys these through elements that make up the message.

Tannenbaum proposed that the combination of elements affects your perceptions of the message. The speaker's voice, words, facial expressions; the crowd response; balloon drops; brass bands; and everything else in the communication, taken together, add up to impressions. Change the elements—say from audiovisual to text—and impressions are bound to change. Reading a speech just isn't the same as hearing one. Remember how the solemn impression of the invocation at the convention changed when the camera zoomed in on the "young lady . . . who was indeed a peach"?

A televised political speech before a flag-waving crowd will have a different effect than the same speech made in the silence of a sound stage. This was never more clear than in 1996, when Bill Clinton delivered his State of the Union speech in the crowded House Chamber before a joint session of Congress, and afterward Bob Dole gave the Republican response in an empty room. Clinton was awash in warm waves of applause. Dole sat stiff in cold silence. Whatever words these men uttered were affected by the total impact of the setting.

Radio listeners may hear things television audiences do not. They may listen more carefully to the text, and maybe to the vocal characteristics—the hesitations, strains, and other cues made less conspicuous on television by the other elements that preoccupy audiences. The weight of each element shifts in the presence or absence of other elements. Tannenbaum said we should look at the blend; it is more than the sum of its parts.

This point is demonstrated by the 1960 Kennedy–Nixon debates. No less an authority than humorist Russell Baker of the *New York Times* said that he caught the debate on his car radio. As a lifelong liberal, he went home discouraged, for obviously Nixon had bested JFK. He was dumbfounded, he said, to hear colleagues who had seen the debate on TV say that Kennedy had won hands down.

The handsome, tanned, television-savvy Kennedy knew how to work the camera. Nixon, on the other hand, was uncomfortable with TV, and he looked dreadful. Every bristle in his heavy beard was magnified. He was pale and drawn from a recent bout with the flu, and his eyes' rapid movement between two cameras made him look shifty. Then, with the heat of the lights and the lingering effects of the flu, Nixon perspired heavily, and his sweaty brow led audiences to believe that the vice president was not convinced of his own answers.

Voters who heard the debate on radio, however, said Nixon won. His voice was steady and reassuring, and his information-filled answers demonstrated that the candidate was knowledgeable and articulate. Kennedy's New England accent and thin voice—laid bare on radio—hurt him. True, these vocal qualities were present on television, but on radio they were unblended with other elements. The relative weight of each element shifted with the different blend in each medium

Which format is more accurate? Wrong question. Tannenbaum, for one, says it isn't relevant to his thinking about format and content.[31] The issue isn't truth but perception, and while truth may rest with the source of information, perception rests with the receiver, and Tannenbaum is concerned about the receiver. In communication, he argues, the receiver's viewpoint matters most, and any format, any content, must be measured by what the receiver takes away from the communication.

How, then, do the elements of the communication, the cues—the images, sounds—affect the communication? Tannenbaum says they do so in two ways. First, they attract attention to the message—some elements have particular audience appeal. Attractive people, brass bands, and throngs of flag-wavers conspicuously hold audience attention. But any element that forms a message can invite attention.

Second, an element helps receivers decode—or interpret—a message. It helps them understand what the sender means, but it also helps them make sense of what the message means to them personally. In the Kennedy–Nixon debates, receivers analyzed the meaning of the candidates' messages, and they also figured out what these message meant to their lives. Would it change their vote, alter their view of democracy, affect their perceptions of Republicans and Democrats? The receiver interprets messages from his or her own frame of reference, and always with an eye toward personal relevance.

Accordingly, the sender cannot fully determine what is and what is not meaningful in a communication (which is why great writers, directors, and actors can sometimes make box office disasters. It also explains why Hollywood has become a major consumer of audience research, live-testing every frame before a movie is released.). Interpretation is the receiver's job. The receiver must integrate the personal meaning of each element into the total configuration of elements contained in the communication. For some receivers, an element will be revealing, and for others it will not.

You may recall Trodahl's thinking about selective perception discussed in Chapter 1: Communication impact is specific to the individual. Thus, Nixon's appearance may have had no effect on a dyed-in-the-wool Republican, while it may have swayed the fence-sitters looking for any sign to help them make up their minds.

This strikes at the matter of individual meanings within an element. A sweaty brow for some voters may signify a nervous, unsettled speaker, while for others it may show a candidate unfairly put upon by a mean-spirited moderator. In the first case, audiences conclude the speaker is deceitful; in the second, the speaker is a victim.

A multimedia environment with text, visuals, and sound may offer more *available* information, but not necessarily more *usable* information. Why? Recall that each element contributes to the package of cues in a communication, and that the importance of some cues increases or decreases in the presence of other cues. The communication elements are like ingredients in a stew. With the addition of each seasoning, the flavor of the stew changes. Moreover, when blended, seasonings yield their individual flavors to the total mix.

FORMAT DECISIONS

Each new medium that came on-line through the twentieth century handed public communicators a new bundle of formats with which to tell their stories. As we have seen, each format held promise for political candidates, but it also issued threats as office seekers determined how the sound of their voices or the appearance of their images would affect the impact of their messages. Today, most candidates have learned to adapt to all formats. In this section, we look at some of the issues that figure in the thinking about media and format decisions.

Source Characteristics

A political candidate's communication strengths are soon identified and exploited. Ronald Reagan had terrific camera appeal and was unmatched when speaking from a prepared script. He was so good that most people thought his TelePrompTed talks were extemporaneous. He did not do well, however, in true extemporaneous situations that required a familiarity with the facts and quick responses.

Bill Clinton, too, is good on camera, with scripts or shooting from the hip—but his voice quality isn't good for radio. Bob Dole's voice is not bad on radio, but his uncomfortable appearance is too stiff for television.

How campaigns market their candidate is determined in large part by the physical characteristics and communication strengths of the candidate. Staffers look for media formats that spotlight the assets and black out the liabilities.

The problem with current campaigning is that television, the medium from which most voters get their political information, demands an attractive candidate, or at least one comfortable in the lights. Ever noticed how few of the new congressional winners are, well, unattractive? Lincoln would be an unlikely candidate today.

Jimmy Carter did not do well in front of a camera, and Michael Dukakis was worse. Dukakis's helmeted head was a hilarious sight embarrassingly immortalized in an Army tank. Reagan would have looked as natural as George Patton, but for Dukakis, the scene was ludicrous, a huge mistake played over and over on evening newscasts.

It's too early to nail down how the Internet will play these strengths and weaknesses in political communication. It has multiformat possibil-

ities, so it's a good bet that video will continue as the dominant element—perhaps merging in some way with television. Whatever the
political significance of the Web, it will likely be kind to attractive candidates.

Message Characteristics

Some messages demand a particular format. It's tough to describe a
Picasso without a photograph or to get across the sound of a tenor sax-
ophone or a blues harp without a recording. Yes, it can be done, but not
efficiently or as effectively as showing the image or playing the tape.

The presentation of numbers is another example of content driving
format selection. A rule of thumb among public speakers is that visuals
are needed for lists that have more than three entries. Large numbers
require visual backup, and so do trend statistics. Obviously, details and
"fine print" are best displayed in text formats, such as in newspapers
and magazines, and now on the Internet.

Television, much less radio, is not the best venue for the presentation
of complicated statistics even if the visuals supporting the presentation
can be simplified. Ronald Reagan was known for using oversimplified
charts to support his television addresses. To make a point of economic
growth over several years, he would show a chart with two bars. The
short bar would represent economic growth during the Carter years and
the towering bar would, of course, depict economic growth during his
own administration. The intended conclusions were obvious even if they
weren't entirely accurate, but for many voters, the bar charts made Reagan's point. Interestingly, Ross Perot used graphics extensively in 1992
but was ridiculed for his efforts, proving once again that the image of
the messenger in politics is often more determinative than the message
itself.

Sometimes it's not just efficiency, but a desired impact, that compels
a format choice. The famous "revolving door" spots during the 1992
campaign used visuals to do what never could be done with other formats.[32]

These 30-second spots showed inmates going around in a prison turn-
stile, the most prominent prisoner being black. This image was linked to
Willie Horton, a black prisoner who committed rape and assault after
being allowed to participate in a weekend release program signed into
law by Michael Dukakis, then governor of Massachusetts. The images,
text, and voice-overs of these ads created the impression that Dukakis
was responsible for 268 "escapes" of convicted murderers who, on parole, committed other horrible crimes.

You would think that the backlash from this infamous spot would
shame the practitioners of attack ads, but no, 1996 exploded with "Hor-

ton-type" TV ads, such as the one accusing Governor Jim Hunt of North Carolina of personally turning the key to liberate dangerous criminals.

The clever use of television images can lead some viewers to incorrect conclusions. In the Dukakis and Hunt cases, what voters believed about the numbers of prisoners involved, the seriousness of their crimes, the frequency with which they escaped, was shamefully exaggerated. Nor was the full picture ever presented, showing that similar bills had been signed by Republican governors in other states, as part of a parole process that boasted good results. According to the polls, few voters knew this at the time. And the fact that the "soft on crime" attack backfired (Hunt was reelected) is cause for some rejoicing.

A classic example of the unabashed use of emotive appeals in political advertising is the "Morning in America" spots developed for Ronald Reagan's reelection in 1984. One of the memorable spots opened with warm rural scenes shot in the glow of dawn, through a frosted lens that softened everything it depicted. Serene music played under the honeyed voice of an announcer who poetically described a Norman Rockwell America.

The spot depicted a country that never really was and never could be, this side of heaven, and attributed it all to Ronald Reagan. In Tannenbaum's terms, this was probably the purest form of "effective content" ever to be captured in a political spot. Critics castigated the series for its misleading images, but the spots were effective among voting audiences who over four years had come to exult in Reagan's endless optimism. Indeed, for many observers, the "Morning in America" series was a video metaphor for the Reagan presidency.[33]

Only television could have delivered the goods for the producers of this spot. There was little interest in "message content," little concern for issues raging in the greater political debate. Emotions and feelings mattered here. Only the warm visuals and soothing audio could have brought about the desired effect.

Finally, evidence in the psychological literature demonstrates that the strength of an argument can also suggest a format. Festinger and Macoby were first to look at the issue in a series of "distraction" studies.[34] This is where one element—say, the visual—draws the receiver's attention away from the real message presented through another element—say, the verbal. In 1976, Petty, Wells, and Brock refined this work and reported that some messages, namely those with strong, well-reasoned arguments, benefit from a simple, uncluttered presentation.[35]

For instance, if an officeholder's policies have produced positive results, readily demonstrated through statistics, the theory proposes that he or she would benefit from a simple message in print, radio, television, or on the Internet. No matter which medium, the message must be clear, the information free from distractions that might weaken the impact of the content.

Why is this so? Because rational voters will recognize the strength of well-reasoned claims that the candidate's policies have been effective. You can improve the chances that reasonable people will see the logic in your evidence if you keep your message simple and clean.

What about weak messages? In this case, Petty, Wells, and Brock apply the same logic to reach the opposite conclusion. When the facts and arguments are *not* on your side, when policies may have failed, apply distraction. Candidates with weak arguments can exhibit their grandchildren, show home movies, wave flags. These are not only powerful political symbols, but they distract the viewers from unpopular or indefensible positions.

Can distraction render a weak message as convincing as a strong message? Maybe not, but it's a matter of making the best of a bad draw. If you must present a weak message, wave Old Glory and talk family values.

Channel Characteristics

The 1960s guru Marshall McLuhan caused a sensation with his "the medium is the message"—or, as he put it more accurately in later writing, "the medium is the massage." He meant, of course, that the very act of sitting in front of the television set for thousands of hours defines you more lastingly than the ideas and events you are experiencing, program by program. This is an exaggeration, of course. We know how each element packs its perceptual punch—the sender's personality, the message's freshness, the viewer's values or moods, and the mysterious chemistry of sight and sound, music and images.

Politicians, like entertainers, never forget that the channel can be as important as the content information. Channels are not neutral conduits of information, because they endow the message with tangible qualities. We looked earlier at how television and radio audiences can come away with different perceptions of a political speech. A news story in the *New York Times* is seen differently from the same story carried by the *National Inquirer*. The selection of media and the choices of outlets can affect the message.

Another channel consideration pits journalism against advertising. Candidates unable to get their messages out through news stories can circumvent the papers and buy direct access. And the information voters get from bought TV and independent papers is as different as propaganda from reportage.

Larry Grossman, former president of NBC News, discussed the effects of television advertising and press reports on public perceptions. "People think they are getting a better view of the issues if they see the candidates for themselves. They have come to believe there is no need for interpretation and explanation of events if they can see the candidate with their own eyes."[36]

In short, seeing is believing, and television leads its viewers into believing that they have just seen the "real candidate." Viewers will put more weight on their own snap judgment of a seven-second clip on the evening news or on an advertisement than on a journalist's analysis, and this reduces the information base on which voting decisions are made. Television advertising allows candidates to skirt the analytic process and present their own versions of reality. The medium affects the message.

To one degree or another, the same may be said of all media. Think about the name brands such as the *New York Times*, the *Wall Street Journal*, and National Public Radio.

If the *Times* doesn't cover a story, for some loyalists the story doesn't exist. A statistic reported in the *Times* takes on biblical proportions; it cannot be questioned. Where is the greater authority? Still, as Archie Bunker reminded us in the 1970s, many readers put their faith and trust in the supermarket tabloids, not the *New York Times*.

One interesting exception to the declining impact of all media except TV for politicking is the recent surge of public radio, which since the 1970s has cultivated a sizable and influential audience with programs such as *Morning Edition*, *All Things Considered*, *Marketplace*, and *Talk of the Nation*. These public affairs programs have amassed dedicated audiences of mostly upper-income, educated listeners who, like audiences for the *New York Times*, give credence to the events that are covered by a medium they trust. The lesson? Since public broadcasting has extended its reach beyond academics, liberals, and news fans, political figures might well give National Public Radio a second look. They can't buy time on it, but they can become assessible to its news staff.

Then there is the need for speed. Just how quickly must a campaign get out its information? Can it wait for the morning paper, or must it hit the next newscast? No doubt about it, since the late 1980s we have seen more rapid responses, and with the rise of the Internet, we're likely to see that getting on the next newscast is just too slow. *Expectations* for speedy delivery expand along with the *capacity* to move information quickly.

For Internet enthusiasts, it's E-mail or no mail; snail mail won't do. The pokiness of regular U.S. mail inspired a robust overnight delivery business, but increasingly, even overnight and cross-town messenger delivery are just too slow.[37]

Will the rush for instant information through the Internet threaten the news hegemony of TV just as radio displaced printed news? The need to move information with electric speed may compel political figures to rethink media formatting. Over 30 years ago, the name of the political game changed from stump talks to sound bites, from huge crowds to photo ops. Now the Internet is further ratcheting up expectations for rapid-fire delivery of campaign information, and this will further propel politicking into a pace measured by a stopwatch. There is little doubt that the Internet can become a major player in political communication, competing with and maybe even displacing the conventional media for significant portions of the voting public.[38]

Receiver Considerations

Entertainers are forever complaining that academics worry so much about message content that they forget the payoff element—audiences. Media researchers may sometimes forget the audience, but successful political campaigns have almost always kept it in mind. Pinpointing audiences was at the core of Harry Truman's whistle-stopping, which took him to the tiny towns, where he met the voters one by one, giving speeches tailored for greatest local appeal. Audience-targeting has always been a matching game that obliges campaigns to figure out what information the voters want and what media or means are best suited to deliver it.

Many campaigns have used twin engines to power their targeted political information machines. First, specially designed public opinion polls sound out a population and reveal pockets of like-minded voters. They disclose how voters feel and why they feel that way, and they identify the most productive means—the best formats—of contacting individuals in small voter groups at which the targeted communications are aimed.

The other engine of targeted political information machines today is the computer database. Databases single out voters by age, race, income, education, gender, party affiliation, and other traits. They hold the names, addresses, phone numbers, and, increasingly, E-mail addresses. They amass huge quantities of information, store it, order it, and sort it, enabling campaigns to single out voters. Thanks to inexpensive, off-the-shelf computers, even the smallest campaign can manipulate sophisticated databases that feed the targeted strategies.[39]

Guided by the polls, campaign staffs sort through the databases to match individual voters with the topics, treatments, and media that hold the greatest promise of a successful outcome. The polls chart the strategy by which to deliver the pitch with the greatest punch; the databases put it into action at the individual level. Since 1985, this approach has been successful.

Does the Web, however, demand fresh thinking about the old maxims of targeting message and format to specific audiences? Two unique features we have attributed to the Internet will inevitably affect audience targeting. For one, compared with TV's passive viewers, Internet audiences actively select a site and interact with it. Almost anyone can surf TV channels or twirl a radio dial. A remote requires a thumb; a mouse demands an active mind because landing on a site involves choice, sometimes a bevy of choices. Visitors must *do* something, and if a site doesn't serve the right information in the right format, users will leave.

The Internet's other striking feature is its inventory of every conventional format—text, pictures, video, audio—along with the facility of user choice. This remarkable medium is a four-ring circus where the crowd under the big top plays along with the performers.

The activity and choice are evident in a story appearing in the *New York Times* that described the action on the Web for the 1996 Republican National Convention.

The volunteers with the party's electronic gear will join a brigade of on-line journalists who plan to feed Web sites with delegate diaries, real-time vote counts, speech texts, state rosters and news releases. . . . [MSNBC] has an Internet booth . . . so delegates, news makers and commentators can stop in for on-line chats . . . the CBS site plans to carry live audio and video from the proceedings, gavel to gavel . . . a closed-caption transcript of the convention will be stored on the site and can be searched and printed. . . . The Media Research Center plans to post a "Convention Watch" each morning [that will] . . . include "alerts" the group will E-mail to talk-show hosts. . . . Politics Now . . . features a Virtual Convention where users can vote . . . and it will carry the full text of The Hotline.[40]

The political party home pages also indulged the users. The Republican National Committee page asked users to choose among Event Guide, Multimedia, Search Engine, Live Video, Live Audio, Floor Phone, and Forum Rooms. The Democrats let visitors select from many of the same options.

Compared with television, radio, or print, where a package of formats is preselected, the Internet can let the users choose. It's a buyer's market, and that imposes a significantly more active role on the receiver. The old questions about which formats users would find most attractive and which formats are likely to attract and hold them become less critical because of what many sites are doing. The message is presented in several formats and the users are allowed to decide for themselves. Receivers in this medium are much more likely to *meet the information sender halfway in the targeting process*.

This concept is exploited further with onboard search engines that allow visitors to dig for information of personal interest. Something like a research library where electronic retrieval tools help patrons single out the volume or the statistic they need, many Websites provide tools for users to unearth just the information that interests them.

Consider a few examples. The U.S. Bureau of the Census churns out huge quantities of data that, for years, were printed in heavy volumes that sagged library shelves. Now, in an act of mercy, the Census Bureau has installed large portions of its database on the Web with search engines that allow users to sort through a mass of data to isolate the information they want. The process personalizes information mined from a generic mass and delivers data specific to the interests of each receiver.

Similarly, Internet posting of campaign finance data provides receiver-specific information.[41] Some cities and states are experimenting with posting campaign financial statements on the Internet to facilitate public scrutiny of the money flow. This offers a way to deliver just the data that voters, watch groups, and the press find of particular interest. Here, too, the receiver participates actively in the targeting process.[42]

The old questions about receivers ("Exactly what does each group want?" "How can we best deliver it?") are less relevant today because Web audiences don't wait passively for information. The traditional notion of "targets" doesn't fit. Visitors are active in selecting items and formats on a site, and in configuring data to match their interests. A new partnership is forming between source and receiver, shifting the obligation for message-matching more equitably between the interactants. "Passive recipient" over the years has been a redundant expression; what could a recipient be but passive? Until now.

CONCLUSION

In our examination of the handshake between format and content, it has became clear that the Internet is capable of hosting the formats, and therefore the content, of all the other media. This is impressive. Far more exciting, however, is the addition of upline communications, which recasts the receiver as an active participant, a great change in the reckoning of mediated communication. On a mature, multimedia Website, receivers can select their format and content. They can interact with others in real time, and fire back their opinions upline to the message source. They are treated to tailored communications from site-based computers that respond instantly and precisely. Furthermore, receivers can command the Website computer to retrieve specific data from large information pools.

All of this—recipient initiatives and source response—is new. Far from just another mass medium with a few bells and whistles, the Internet is wholly a new medium that elevates the receiver's status in public communication.

NOTES

1. In all fairness, Bendiner did say, "As an adjunct to those, however, it is already extremely valuable and will doubtless become more so."

2. Measures of on-line users vary considerably among research firms. Yankelovich in August 1996 counted 42 million U.S. users 18+ years of age who have been on-line within the previous 12 months. Nielsen found, in a study conducted during the same month, that 48 million people age 16+ in the United States and Canada had access. IntellQuest found 35 million people 16+ years of age who used an on-line service or the Internet in the first three months of 1996. These statistics are reported by CyberAtlas on the company's site downloaded on Feb. 25, 1997. URL, http://www.cyberatlas.com/market.html.

The projection statistics are as follows: International Data Corp. predicts 163 million Internet users by the end of the 1990s. Morgan Stanley predicts that 152 million will use the Internet by the year 2000. These statistics were reported on the CyberAtlas site, same date, same address as above.

3. E. Emery, *The Press and America: An Interpretive History of the Mass Media*, 3rd ed. (Englewood Cliffs, NJ: Prentice-Hall, 1972).

4. The first newspaper really depends on the definition of "newspaper." According to John Tebbel, *"The Present State of the New-English Affairs*, published in Boston in 1689, [was] the first attempt to print a domestic news report in America." He argues that the phrases "This is published to prevent false reports" and "published by authority" were the essence of U.S. newspaper history. Emery places the first newspaper in New England in 1704. He says that the *Boston News-Letter* was the first to have all the qualifications of a newspaper. Emery acknowledges that the other publications—newspaper-like—were published well before this. J. Tebbel, *The Compact History of the American Newspaper* (New York: Hawthorn Books, 1963); Emery, *The Press and America*.

5. On October 2, 1729, Benjamin Franklin and Hugh Meridith assumed control of *The Universal Instructor in All Arts and Sciences; and Pennsylvania Gazette* from Samuel Keimer. The new publishers immediately shortened the title to *The Pennsylvania Gazette*. Franklin and Meridith dissolved their partnership on July 14, 1730, and Franklin continued as sole publisher until 1748 when he teamed up with David Hall. In February 1766, Franklin left the paper, and Hall became the sole proprietor until May 1766, when he took in William Sellers. Information from J. M. Lee, *History of American Journalism*, 2d. ed. (Boston: Houghton Mifflin Company, 1923).

6. Benjamin Franklin, "An Apology for Printers," published in *The Pennsylvania Gazette*, June 10, 1731; cited in J. Folkerts and D. L. Teeter, Jr., *Voices of a Nation* (New York: Macmillan, 1989), 36.

7. Ibid., 35–36.

8. See Tebbel, *Compact History of the American Newspaper*.

9. L. F. Smith, *Perspectives on Radio and Television: Telecommunications in the United States*, 2nd ed. (New York: Harper & Row, 1985).

10. KDKA's "first on the air" claim is not without challenge. KCBS in San Francisco (formerly KQW in San Jose), WHA in Madison, Wisconsin, and WWJ

in Detroit hold some claim to the distinction. For a discussion, see Smith, *Perspectives on Radio and Television*.

11. Not two years after KDKA went on the air, the first volley in a 20-year content struggle was launched when the American Society of Composers, Authors and Publishers (ASCAP) challenged the radio stations' use of copyrighted music. (This is the same ASCAP that, in mid-1996, faced a public relations disaster when it assessed copyright fees on Girl Scouts and Brownies for singing "God Bless America" around the campfire. There was no way ASCAP could have come out of this fight unbloodied, just as there was little chance it could have won a quick and early battle with radio stations in the 1920s.) Back in 1922, ASCAP, drawing on pretty much the same argument it later used against the Scouts, claimed that radio programmers were violating a 1909 copyright law that prohibited the public presentation of music without permission of the copyright holder. Radio stations contested ASCAP's demands, the sides were drawn up, and the 20-year battle of attrition was on. Some readers may remember an ASCAP boycott in 1941 that withdrew all popular music from the airwaves, a period in which the repetitions of Stephen Foster's "Jeannie with the Light Brown Hair" and "Beautiful Dreamer" drove the public crazy.

12. Weekly viewing: 29 hours per person, on average; 52 hours per household, on average. *National Audience Demographics* (New York: Nielsen Media Research, Feb. 1997), 10, 11. Data provided by Karen Kratz, manager of communication for Nielsen.

13. Quoted in *Newsweek* (Jan. 27, 1997), 86.

14. These terms have been attributed to George Gerbner, former dean of the Annenberg School of Communication at the University of Pennsylvania. Gerbner used these descriptions in many of his writings.

15. Smith, *Perspectives on Radio and Television*, 70.

16. As though the FCC delays, federal suits, and industry complaints weren't enough, scandal marked this case. Just months after the FCC issued its final decision in favor of RCA, the chairman of the FCC quit to accept a position as senior vice president and general counsel at RCA.

17. Adoption statistics provided by Arbitron, NBC, and A. C. Nielsen. These and revenue figures are reported in Smith, *Perspectives on Radio and Television*, 71, 78.

18. Smith, *Perspectives on Radio and Television*.

19. Murrow and Friendly's show, mostly using McCarthy's own words, made the senator look like a loose cannon. In a sense, Joe McCarthy presaged a later TV event, the Nixon–Kennedy debates. McCarthy had a radio voice—deep, resonant, and persuasive—but not a face for TV. He had a swarthy look and the worst five o'clock shadow before Nixon. Had the hearings been on radio, McCarthyism might have carried the day. As it was, the TV broadcast of the hearings and the Murrow show are credited with turning public opinion against McCarthy.

About a month after the first CBS program, the networks aired McCarthy's blistering response, which attacked Murrow rather than clarifying the issues raised in the original piece. The volatile image was reinforced, and public opinion hardened against McCarthy and his hearings.

Television producers found in the McCarthy stories a passion that drew in audiences, and McCarthy, who loved the spotlight, obliged them. On national television, McCarthy became his own worst enemy who faced growing public anger. In 1954 the Senate censured McCarthy and shut down his inquisition. Newspapers and radio covered the hearings, but television put faces and voices to the characters and brought the story to life. No doubt it hastened his demise.

20. Dewey's advertising agency, Batten, Barton, Durstine & Osborne, urged him to invest in short spots. Four years later, the same agency recommended television advertising to Eisenhower, who took the advice.

21. In 1950, 20-second spots on network television cost around $600 each. In the late 1990s, the cost is often well into the hundreds of thousands of dollars. Of course, audiences today are larger, but the per capita cost then was still much lower. The $600 figure is cited in R. Bendiner, "How Much Has TV Changed Campaigning?" *New York Times Magazine*, Nov. 2, 1952, repr. in H. Marx, ed., *Television and Radio in American Life* (New York: H. W. Wilson, 1953).

22. Ibid.

23. Statistics reported in this paragraph were reported in ibid.

24. E. Chester, *Radio, Television and American Politics* (New York: Sheed and Ward, 1969).

25. Bendiner, "How Much Has TV Changed Campaigning?"

26. T. H. White, *America in Search of Itself* (New York: Harper & Row, 1982), 167–168.

27. The split screen was more dramatically demonstrated in November 1951 by Edward R. Murrow. In a live national broadcast, Murrow showed off a transcontinental coaxial cable and split-screen technology by airing side-by-side pictures of San Francisco's Golden Gate Bridge and New York's Brooklyn Bridge. See T. White, *Breach of Faith* (New York: Atheneum/Reader's Digest Press, 1975), 37–40.

28. W. S. Schramm, "TV Coverage of National Conventions," *Freeman* 2(810) (Aug. 25, 1952), repr. in H. I. Marx, ed., *Television and Radio in American Life* (New York: H. W. Wilson, 1953), 38–40.

29. The campaign of 1952 will forever be remembered for a first and a last. Eisenhower was the first to run a nationally televised advertising campaign, and Stevenson was the last to reject the medium. Eisenhower was the first office seeker to announce his candidacy on television and the first to use campaign spot announcements. Stevenson didn't recognize, until it was too late, that he was opposing not only a beloved war hero but also a man who understood the tactical advantages of using all the weapons in his arsenal. Political candidates and audiences already felt television's considerable powers to distribute information and project images in this young medium just freed from government restraints. In 1952, one candidate saw that and the other did not. That would not happen again.

30. P. H. Tannenbaum, "The Indexing Process in Communications," *Public Opinion Quarterly* 19 (1955): 292–302.

31. Ibid.

32. For an excellent analysis of the revolving door spots, see K. H. Jamieson, *Dirty Tricks: Deception, Distraction, and Democracy* (New York: Oxford University Press, 1972).

33. Harold Evans, a British journalist, remarked on PBS's *Television in Politics* (Oct. 1988) that "[Ronald Reagan] turned the White House into a soft-focus TV studio."

34. L. Festinger, and N. Macoby, "On Resistance to Persuasive Communication," *Journal of Abnormal and Social Psychology* 68 (1964): 375–388.

35. R. W. Petty, G. I. Wells, and T. C. Brock, "Distraction Can Enhance or Reduce Yielding to Propaganda: Thought Disruption Versus Effort Justification," *Journal of Personality and Social Psychology* 34(1976): 874–884.

36. Larry Grossman, quoted in G. Selnow, *High Tech Campaigns: Computer Technology in Political Communication* (Westport, CT: Praeger, 1994), 142.

37. The need for speed was not lost on the Clinton campaign, which learned valuable lessons from Michael Dukakis's bid for the presidency in 1988. Dukakis—always a day late and a dollar short in response to Republican attacks—was hurt badly by GOP ads and speeches that assaulted his policies and attacked him personally. The Bush campaign seemed to be at the starting gate a little earlier than the Dukakis team, and this gave the Republicans a real advantage in getting the word out first.

Clinton vowed never to be upstaged or preempted, never to let the sun set on a Republican charge, and never to let a Republican initiative be issued without issuing a fast and forceful response. His "rapid response team" monitored Republican troop movements like Patton scoping Rommel's line of tanks. The tactics: respond immediately to GOP threats and proposals with quick and decisive media strikes.

The rapid response team was ready when Dole announced Jack Kemp as his vice presidential running mate. Several days before the decision was official, the Democrats handed out miniature footballs printed with the words "Hail Mary Pass," referring to Dole's desperate efforts to save his campaign by enlisting the former Buffalo Bills quarterback. Just to nail it down, the Democrats included a nine-page memo reviewing the long-standing policy disagreements between Dole and his new running mate and pointing out political differences on a range of issues, including the gold standard, budget balancing, and welfare. Although reporters did not admit that the memo influenced them, their stories covering the Kemp announcement were quick to point out the many policy disagreements specified by the rapid response team. (This is from an Associated Press story: "Democrats Snap Back at Dole Pick," *San Francisco Chronicle*, Aug. 10, 1996, p. A4.)

38. The problem now is the size of the Internet audience. Not enough of the public is on-line, and more important, those now on-line are the early adopters, the easy sells. The second wave will be more difficult to coax into this technology, and it will require a lot more coddling. See audience acceptance of the Web in Appendix A.

39. For a complete description of these techniques, see Selnow, *High-Tech Campaigns*.

40. M. Allen, "Taking in the Sites: On-Line Access to G.O.P. Convention," *New York Times*, Aug. 12, 1996, p. D4.

41. A good deal of controversy surrounds use of the Internet for campaign financial statements. Candidates complain that the process is too difficult and

that it would overburden campaign staffers. Some opponents have complained that the voters would misunderstand the numbers. A few cities have tried electronic filing, San Francisco generally credited with being the first. After a successful start, however, San Francisco's new mayor, Willie Brown, showed little support for the effort, funding eroded, and the site fell hopelessly out of date.

42. How does electronic filing work? Candidates, using free, in-the-box software, submit the same data they now provide on paper forms. Preparation involves the same amount of typing—maybe less—and it can be completed on any standard computer. The registrar then assembles the data into a standard database and posts it on an interactive Website. Users can search for the desired information—by candidate, contribution amount, donor, party, or any combination—and have the data in seconds. Users also can run on-line comparisons—for example, how much money did Candidate A and Candidate B each receive from all construction companies? The statistics will be posted side by side. Such an analysis with paper forms would take hundreds of hours—if it could be done at all. The interactive format offers an accessible and efficient way to deliver campaign information quickly. (In 1997, the Federal Election Commission is taking a voluntary approach. Candidates can file on-line if they wish. This toothless strategy, reflecting the FEC cave-in to political pressures, is unlikely to be effective.)

Part Two

Political Communication on the Internet

Until early in the twentieth century, office seekers pounded the pavement in search of personal contacts with the electorate. Newspapers carried stories and endorsements, candidates produced brochures to spread the campaign gospel, but nobody ran for office without "pressing the flesh."

As we saw in Chapter 2, political campaigns since World War I have been conducted through centralized media, with most voters obtaining campaign information through the press or paid advertisements. Wholesale campaigning through the media has supplied more voters with more political information, but it also has virtually eliminated pressing the flesh from American politicking.

One result has been political candidates who are distanced from the voters. In the absence of regular contact with a broad spectrum of the electorate—either personally or through campaign workers—candidates have relied increasingly on scientific polls to reveal public attitudes and interests. True, survey research offers valuable information about populationwide views, but it falls short as a sole measure of the public mind. There really is no substitute for pressing the flesh.

Not even the Internet can stand in for face-to-face campaigning. Arguably, the Web can close the gap some between candidates and voters because it pinpoints political messages and gives voters a direct line to candidates. But no one knows the effectiveness of such targeting and feedback, or whether it's possible to reestablish a fresh means of one-on-one communication.

It's apparent that most candidates (along with most scholars and media practitioners) didn't realize the full potential of the Internet during its trial run in 1996; nonetheless, they were not hesitant to use it. Chapter 3 looks at why the political campaigns eagerly put up Web pages and embraced E-mail communications. Through interviews with campaign staffers and Web designers, we examine how the campaigns used the Internet.

Chapter 4 reminds us that the Internet arrived at a time when the population was rediscovering the spirit of individualism. Thousands of individuals, small organizations, and disorganized coalitions took to the Web like pioneers staking out homesteads. The huge and impressive array of participants from across the political and ideological spectrum demonstrated the success of a decentralized, open-to-the-public medium. At the same time, however, the glut of participants reminds us of nagging issues that this country has yet to resolve.

Since the nation's founding, Americans have wrestled with issues of power and rights. Should we focus power in Washington or devolve it to the states (centralization vs. decentralization)? Should the balance of rights rest more fully with the individual or with the community? Rising and falling in prominence over the years, these issues became more conspicuous through the 1980s. With an early push from Ronald Reagan and a steady pull from conservative lawmakers, we have moved perceptibly toward the view that the pursuit of individual interests will, in the end, work to the greater good of the community. That was the clear subtext of the Republican "Contract with America," and it has been the spirit behind much social policy enacted through the 1990s. Clinton's shift rightward and the retention of Republican majorities in both House and Senate have provided visible markers for the flow of these political currents running deeply through the country.

Into this environment of political decentralization came the decentralized Internet. What timing! Nobody owns it, nobody keeps its gates, nobody controls it, nobody regulates it, and therefore it suffers no limitations on who can access it or who can stock it with information. And, if there were early doubts about freedom of speech on the Internet, they were soundly put to rest by the Rehnquist Court in mid-1997 when it ruled that the government had no business censoring the Web.[1]

So, in a sense, Chapter 4 examines a national celebration of individualism, decentralization, freedom to speak your mind, freedom from government restraint. The mainstreamers operated next to the sidestreamers, the big and powerful voices sang beside the small and frail voices. Never before in an American election had political expression been so open or had participation been so much of a free-for-all.

The question is, Open and free to do what? To speak your mind, yes. To express your point of view, defend your candidate, attack the other candidate, proclaim some dimwitted philosophy, yes. Participants did all these and more, but it was evident from a casual glance that few operators had a good idea of what they expected to accomplish or how they expected to accomplish it. The medium was new and untested, and the rough-and-tumble on the Web was a reminder that 1996 was as much an experimental period for the Internet as the early 1920s were for radio and the late 1940s were for television.

Chapter 5 looks at the activities on the range of political sites. Many developers posted a few pictures and personal essays, then walked away from their sites. These unimaginative souls did not use the Web's best features. Happily, many other designers were more creative, their efforts instructing us on the Web's special features.

Hundreds of adventurous Web innovators let visitors play on their sites. These sites were linked to other sites, allowing users to track down personal interests. The link concept is simple, and it exploits the Web's distinctive feature—interconnectedness—that gave the Web its name.

Many sites bench-tested interactivity. They allowed visitors to play games, answer quizzes, talk to the site operators and to each other. Several developers provided rich databases derived from public opinion polls, candidate surveys, and other research activities. They encouraged visitors to pursue their own concerns and isolate specific information. Visitors, therefore, could create unique communication experiences, another example of individualism on the Web.

Finally, some larger Websites covered routine campaign events with a new flair. At least they *tried* to punch up coverage of the conventions and debates with a bevy of format choices and interactive displays. Sadly, no matter what they tried, traffic was light and public interest quite low. Only the coverage of Election Night results drew much of a crowd. Use of the Web on that occasion was different from its use at all other times during the campaign.

The Web on Election Night allowed people to select coverage of just the races that concerned them, skipping over the rest. The sites delivering the results were fast, their information rich and specific to individual users. These traits made the Web unique among media.

While the speed and specificity of election results released on the Web are virtues, such a luxury may come with a price tag. The problem is the darker side of individualism. Curtis Gans, director of the Committee for the Study of the Electorate, said, "One function of voting is to bring people together. The more activities in the electoral process that we accomplish in isolation, the more it atomizes society."[2] Any activity that undermines the sense of community in politics is dangerous to the body politic, and the Web may well become the great fragmenter.

For all television's faults, it at least encourages Election Night gatherings around the set, everyone watching and waiting together for the outcomes of races. During the wait, the networks discuss national trends and offer perspectives on the apparent meaning of the returns. For a few hours the analysts discuss how voters around the country are sizing up the national problems and evaluating the leaders who would solve them.

Tracking election results on television may be the last real community event associated with voting (given that voting by mail is so common), and now it is challenged by a medium that splits audiences by encouraging participants to examine only the outcomes that interest them. With each voter picking out the threads of choice, the tapestry may come undone.

In Part II we spotlight the candidates and the other players who reveled in their newfound, decentralized resource for political expression.

NOTES

1. *Reno v. American Civil Liberties Union*, No. 96–511, June 1997. Chances are, a decision otherwise would have made little difference. With nearly 50 percent of the Websites run from foreign countries, there isn't much that promoters of regulation could do about questionable material. People sometimes lose sight of the fact that this is a global medium not easily controlled by any one government or even a consortium of governments. We are reminded by Ralph Daniels, former senior vice president for standards at NBC, that attempts at legislation are doomed. "The whole regulatory mechanism for the industry—decency, intellectual property, commercial standards—can't work on the Internet," Daniels said. "The regulatory system is outmoded for this medium."

2. From an interview on May 28, 1996.

Chapter Three

Mainstream Candidates on the Internet

The major campaigns didn't have a clue about this new medium. Like everyone else in the game in '96, they didn't know how to use the rich information available to them.

—*Evans Witt*
director of PoliticsNow

Political candidates may be bold and brassy behind a rostrum, firebrands in front of a crowd, but at heart they are not risk takers. They are inclined to go with what they know, to use again what has worked before, to trust the people and the policies that, in the past, have served them well. That is why they are as cautious as spring lambs around innovation, and it explains their hesitancy around new media.

The start-up media hold new promise, but also new perils and uncertainties, and office seekers are not quick to chance these risks. Today, voters see politics and the media as inseparable, but that view has taken generations to form. In the 1920s, at the birth of radio, and in the 1940s, at the emergence of television, the marriage of media and politics was not so certain.

Like the practice of medicine, political advertising holds to the advice First do no harm. Would putting a speech on the radio help a campaign? Yes, it might, but then again, it also might magnify a candidate's weaknesses, becoming more curse than blessing.

That's what happened in 1924 to Democratic presidential candidate John Davis, who was a stunning orator on stage but suffered from a "muffled and fogged" voice on radio.[1] Nor was he the only orator to bomb on the airwaves. Legendary public speaker William Jennings Bryan was frightful on radio, as was Warren Harding, the first American president to deliver a speech on the air and to blunder frightfully on live radio.[2] Evidently no one explained the difference between projecting the voice to a mob of 20,000 and speaking conversationally into a mike. They also may have missed the cautions necessary for live presentations.

On the other hand, radio was much kinder to Calvin Coolidge, who was the first to use radio extensively in his run for office. Later, Franklin Roosevelt, who played the instrument of radio like a Stradivarius, became known for the "fireside chats" that kept him in touch with the nation through the Great Depression and into World War II.

On the whole, the politics of radio was a win/lose proposition, offering some an extraordinary opportunity to reach voters, but an unhappy experience for others. Sometimes the media can do harm.

In 1948, as we noted earlier, Harry Truman and Thomas Dewey viewed television as a gimmick. They could have started the stampede to televised campaigns, but each had his own reasons for keeping the tube at arm's length, relying instead on conventional barnstorming. Truman saw television advertising as a crass promotion, better suited to selling cars than candidates. Dewey, who believed his rosy poll numbers, didn't see much point in rolling the dice on an untested medium.

In 1952, Adlai Stevenson, a celebrated orator, preferred the podium he knew to the camera he did not. The Democrat rejected advice to go on the air. Eisenhower, however, did not reject the advice. Franklin Roosevelt, Harry Truman, Robert Taft, Estes Kefauver, and other leading political figures used television for speeches and to extend the reach of congressional hearings,[3] but it took Dwight Eisenhower, one of the flattest political speakers of the age (although he was said to have an "interesting, mobile face" good for the cameras), to break into the medium that would later become inseparable from American politics. At the urging of his advertising agency, Ike used television with great success in the early primaries, and the old soldier, knowing a powerful weapon when he saw it, stayed with the medium through his victory in the general election. After Ike, presidential candidates recognized the do-or-die nature of network television. The medium was henceforth indispensable to American political campaigns.

And that brings us to 1996, the first year when the Internet, and more specifically the World Wide Web, became available for voter outreach in a major political campaign. True, various branches of the Internet were available earlier—for instance, E-mail[4] and text-based services such as Gopher—but for popular consumption, which is to say for political consumption, when we say Internet, we usually mean Web—the medium's graphical interface. Internet browsers in one form or another were available in 1992,[5] but the campaign of 1996 was the first in which enough voters and campaigns possessed a critical mass of equipment and software to make the Internet more than an academic tool or a novelty.

The earlier skepticism of political candidates toward a new medium was not evident in the 1996 campaigns. Office seekers couldn't get enough of the Internet. Andy Brack, Internet political analyst with Phil Noble & Associates, said that 85 percent of House and Senate candidates in the major parties had Web sites.[6] Many candidates in state and local races also put up pages to support their election bids.

So what accounts for the difference between acceptance of broadcasting and of the Internet? In every sense of the word, the Internet is here to stay, make no mistake about it; and when this medium takes a different course from earlier media, it's important to ask why. In addition to explaining how campaigns perceived the Internet, the answers may suggest how it fits alongside the other media, and perhaps how it will be used in the future.

Put to a number of campaign staffers, consultants, Web designers and others—people in the trenches during 1996—this question about why campaigns got on the Internet brings out an interesting view of the medium.

Before we examine the features that made the Web more approachable than early radio or television, however, we should acknowledge that the candidates and the campaigns today are different from those earlier in this century. By 1996, most political campaigns had become *media* campaigns. Candidates today earmark huge sums to buy media time, and they choreograph every move for media coverage. Their staffs include media-savvy operatives, and the candidates themselves have been well schooled in the ways of print and broadcast. Television has achieved near-religious significance; the evening newscast has become the candidates' vespers.

Theodore White, writing on the presidency, said, "American politics and television are so completely locked together that it is impossible to tell the story of the one without the other."[7] Eric Barnouw supports this view in the *Tube of Plenty*:

Politics had become sales pitches. Election campaigns belonged increasingly to the world of the television commercial. When candidates for major office went into the field to speak before crowds, it was often to obtain vivid moments of footage for 30-second and 60-second spots to be used in paid-for time—bought on the same basis as spots used for pain relievers, automobiles, cola drinks and ski equipment. The purchased slots had become the real arena of political conflict. Alone among major democracies, the United States had incorporated election campaigns into its merchandising procedures.[8]

Although television enjoys the spotlight for most national and statewide races, radio also serves these and smaller races at the local and regional levels. Radio is considerably less expensive than television, and it allows more audience targeting. Television draws most of the attention, but radio is still an active player in political advertising.

The media have transformed political candidates in two ways. First, candidates are mediawise; they no longer expect to meet all the voters face-to-face in rallies, at 4-H contests, or on front stoops, as candidates once did. True, some still work at "retail" campaigning, but these efforts are supplemented with advertisements, which are the real workhorses of political campaigns, and with news coverage. Many candidates "press the flesh" partly to present the media with a photo op. Baby-kissing is nothing new to politics, but with media looking on, the baby has become a more valuable prop.

Candidates today see political campaigns as media campaigns, but this was not always so. When radio and television first surfaced, candidates had to accept not only the new medium but also the logic of a media campaign. This time, that issue has been settled and the path to the Internet is clear. Candidates today are media-ready.

The second difference between candidates then and now is that office seekers today are prescreened media creatures. If you have a mortal fear of cameras and microphones, try insurance or carpentry. If you don't like reporters poking around in your unmentionables, stay out of the public square. Media skills are prerequisites for the job, and people not possessing the appearance, demeanor, and tolerance demanded by the media are soon eliminated.

What about consultants and others who can help the aspirant bob and weave through the media labyrinth? They don't exist. Consultants can polish a candidate who has a smooth surface, but they cannot coach rough-hewn, media-averse candidates to successful outcomes. Nor do they care to try.

Berkman and Kitch remind us that "Since fees are based on their record, consultants want candidates who have a chance to win. From the point of view of the consultant, it would be foolish to take on too many long shots."[9]

As we close out a century that has witnessed the birth of radio, television and the Internet, we see at the morning muster a band of political candidates armed for media campaigns. The rest wash out in boot camp.

Since our political environment is now a media environment and office seekers are seekers of media exposure, the Internet comes along at a much friendlier time for media in general. Still, environment alone cannot explain the rapid adoption of the Net. It caught on for reasons that are part of its very nature.

IT'S INEXPENSIVE

One of the most endearing features of the Internet for campaigns, and especially for campaign managers who guard the purse strings, is that it's inexpensive. Not just a bargain, and not just cost-competitive with other media, but damned inexpensive. You can add bells and whistles that run up the cost, you can hire Website development companies that charge a bit, you can add interactivity that eats up computer power and adds to the bottom line, but by running a simple, homemade site, a campaign could in 1996 get into this medium for pocket change.

Take the bare-bones campaign of Victor Morales, Democratic candidate for the Senate from Texas, running against Phil Gramm, who had some of the deepest pockets in politics. Gramm's philosophy was summed up well during his bid for the Republican presidential nomination when he said, "Money is a politician's best friend." Syndicated columnist Molly Ivins once remarked that even Gramm's friends don't like him, so maybe a dearth of real friends explains Gramm's affection for money. But, no matter how you figure it, Morales was at a disadvantage. Gramm entered the race with around $20 million, and Morales got into it with barely two nickels to rub together.[10] The dusty, white pickup truck he drove back and forth across the state was more than a symbol; it was Morales's transportation. This long-shot candidate ran a campaign on a shoestring and retreads.

He also had a Website that cost him $49.50 a month. Three volunteers designed the layout, wrote the code, answered E-mail and kept the site up to date.[11] And while it may have been done in a bargain basement, it didn't look it. The site had photos, facts and figures, speeches, news articles, downloadable brochures, even a link to a page about the Morales pickup truck—everything we've come to expect on a political site in 1996. Morales couldn't afford much media—a fact he often brought into his speeches—but with three volunteers and a few dollars each month, the candidate had a presence on the Web. (Not that he won. But he surely won the prize for the lowest cost per voter.)

The Web in 1996 was economical for the same two reasons that the other media were expensive: production costs and airtime. At least in 1996, when Websites were simple and formatted by hypertext markup language (html), the production costs remained low. New complexities are adding programmer time and costs, but during the election, html could be written by anyone. This meant that candidates were not obligated to bankroll high-priced talent. Grade school kids are writing their own code and setting up their own pages; bare-bones sites are not tough to assemble.

Setup was inexpensive, and so was maintenance. Some political sites in 1996 had an organic quality, changing daily and even several times a day. These campaigns added new speeches, fresh position papers, up-to-date articles and editorials. They kept the candidates' schedules current and posted the most recent reactions to unfolding issues. And, unlike costly radio and television spots, which cannot be updated easily or without some cost, site additions could append new information to the old, involving little more than a few minutes of time.

Many campaigns, however, did not keep their sites up to date. They assembled a page early in the race, then abandoned it. The impact of such neglect could not have been good on voters, who throughout the campaign were growing more accustomed to using the Web for breaking news. Deserted sites angered many in the press, as we discuss in Chapter 6.

Production simplicity and low costs make the Web the best populist medium since the tree stump, enabling hundreds of political candidates, hopelessly outgunned by Big Money, to even the odds, if only a little. The actual number of voters accessing this information in the 1996 campaign was small, but that will change. In the starkest terms, a candidate can produce for pennies a Web page accessible to audiences around the planet. There is nothing you can produce now, or ever could have produced, on radio or television at such a bargain. No wonder candidates quickly adopted the medium.

Site rental—compared with its closest cousin, airtime—is also a real bargain. A slick salesperson for the Web might tell you that for less than a dollar a day, you can have a site with a *potential* audience of millions, no billions, of people who can check it out any time of day, all day, every day. Compare that, he or she might say, with just one 30-second, prime-time network spot. It'll cost several hundred grand to buy a one-time audience of only a few million television viewers. Wow!

The catch is with audience potential. Yes, a broadcaster can guarantee a mass audience at so many dollars per thousand and then measure the reach. So far, no one can measure site hits with complete accuracy, although they're getting better at it. Still, despite the Internet's audience size—pretty small by network standards now, but getting bigger by the day—"airtime" expenses are trivial when stacked against conventional media costs.

Not all sites are $49.50 a month, but even the showy sites allowing visitor interaction aren't costly when compared with other campaign expenses. Moreover, site rental costs have little to do with audience size, so over the next few years, as the number of visitors grows, the cost per hit will become even lower.

No matter how you look at the expenses—production, maintenance, space rental—the Web is economical, and that was reason enough for many campaigns to take the leap. Adoption of a site meant few sacrifices.

A month's tab for the Web could tally less than the staff's monthly tab for donuts and coffee. Here is potential gain with little pain.

The low cost also meant that investment in a Website came with little risk. If a site didn't bring in the votes or do whatever else people claimed it would do, so what? The campaign would be out a few dollars. Little was ventured, and if little was gained, no loss. Of course, if the site *did* work, if it brought in votes and volunteers and contributions, then look at the payoff! In 1996, getting on the Web was like buying penny stock. If it took off and did great things, say hallelujah, sometimes you win. If it bombed, okay, you're out just a little, sometimes you lose.

IT'S A FAMILIAR FORMAT

The Internet is different from other media and very much the same. It differs in how you access it, what you do when you land on a site, and how you send information back to the source. These differences are extraordinary, although wrapped in a familiar package. Websites have text and pictures; so do newspapers and magazines. Audio on the Web is something like audio on the radio, and video on the Web is (or soon will be) like video on television. There was comfort in the familiarity of formats. For campaigns, a move to the Web was like returning to an old neighborhood. It wasn't exactly the same place, but it still had the feel of home.

But the capacity of the medium for feedback was new. At this point in its evolution, the interactive features have been little used. Visitors in 1996 could make cute posters and bumper stickers and type out friendly messages to the candidates. These activities were amusing, but the real story of interactivity lies ahead. Over the next few years, programmers will incorporate some remarkable feedback innovations into their Web pages and the full powers of interactivity will become more evident. 1996 was the first political campaign on the Web and the last to use it largely as a one-way medium. In that year, the Web displayed its conventional side—the text, sound, and pictures we have come to know—and that familiarity invited use.

IT'S FAMILIAR CONTENT

During the campaign, critics and Web users complained that most candidate sites were boring. They griped that the sites were formulaic, dispensing predictable content. Sites posted biographical sketches and the obligatory photos, sometimes with family and flag, always with the candidate grinning or staring longingly into the future. They carried quotable quotes and provided links to speeches, policy positions, and flattering news stories. At the end it was their custom to offer E-mail links to the candidate and to the Web design company or to the 18-year-old volunteer who assembled the site. Such cookie-cutter content dominated the political pages.[12]

A few of the more adventurous sites experimented with content, and they deserve credit for being brassy. Paul Wellstone, for instance, had a picture of his bus—no, he actually had an entire site for his bus, complete with a message from the bus-driving candidate, and an E-mail connection in case you had an urgent question ("What kind of gas mileage you getting with the bus, Paul?"). Victor Morales had a picture of his truck, so why shouldn't Wellstone have a site for his bus? It didn't stop at vehicles. Lamar Alexander made his shirt a prime attraction. Bob Dornan put his wife and grandchildren in the starring role.

When photos of buses, flannel shirts, and families mark the wild and crazy sites, you know that content was not far-reaching during the campaign. Curiously, although dull material may have disappointed many visitors, it actually contributed to the rapid adoption of the new medium. Risk-averse candidates were comfortable with the same old shoe. They didn't suddenly have to tell their darkest secrets or bare their backsides or offer anything with which they were not already familiar in a format with which they were not already comfortable.

In a manner of speaking, familiarity breeds content. A number of interviews with campaign managers, communications specialists, and Web designers made this clear. Jonathan Knisley, electronic communication chief for the Republican National Committee (RNC), said that he saw the Internet as an extension of *GOP TV*, a one-hour talk show focusing on campaign issues. The Web, he said, allowed the RNC to present the same information, but in a setting where users could examine details they might otherwise miss in the fast-moving television show. "I see the Internet as an extension of the other media," Knisley added. "It's really an extension of the 30-second sound bite, which doesn't handle issues very well. The Internet allows us to offer more depth for the topics presented in other places."[13]

Dick Bell, interactive media director for the Democratic National Committee (DNC), agreed with Knisley while stressing the need for comfort. "Campaigns are conservative, especially when they size up something new. Why? Because their game is all or nothing, so they go with what they know." Bell said the DNC used the Web to drive home the message of the day, reinforcing the other media with information that people could examine at their own pace.[14]

The notion of the Internet as an "extension of the other media" was echoed in a dozen other interviews. Clearly, campaigns fixed on features of the Web that made it part of the media family already accepted in American politicking. Even campaigns losing badly are unlikely to toss caution to the wind. They just double up on more of the same. The

Internet in 1996 was sold, in part, through its familiarity, not on a promise of extraordinary but little-recognized opportunities. And, with that, the Internet got its foot in the door.

IT'S CONVENIENT

It isn't easy to do television. You need writers, producers, camera operators, and people who, for no apparent reason, move wires around the studio. For television spots, you need someone to place the ads and buy the time, and someone else to make sure that you actually got what you paid for. And, if the candidates appear in the spots, they must prepare, report to a studio, and powder up before they sit in front of the camera. Television can be a lot more complicated than it looks to be on the screen.

Radio is less trouble, but it still requires that the campaign work with a station or recording studio, and that a group of professionals collaborate to assemble the spots, then pepper them into the broadcast schedules at the right times to reach the right audiences.

Candidates facing the prospects of buying time on early radio or television may have been deterred, for good reason, by the complexity of the process. It must have looked so much easier to walk behind a podium and give the same speech they had spouted a dozen times before.

The Internet posed no such barriers. In fact, campaigns were confronted by an army of young workers and volunteers who were eager to practice their skills and lengthen their resumes by working for candidates willing to let them write code for a functional site. Hundreds of kids signed on as developers of political sites. Some were friends of friends, or relatives, of the candidate. Many described in interviews how they started out as outsiders, but were quickly adopted into the campaign family. This became evident in their use of the plural. "*We* decided that *our* site should have something that makes *us* stand out, like a picture of *our* campaign headquarters." No third-party stuff here; these kids identified personally with the candidate.

The mostly young volunteers were the engines that drove the decision to get on the Web. Linda Muller, the Web designer for Pat Buchanan—but not a kid—created one of the classiest early political sites. She said that she presented the candidate with the idea at a restaurant one night. This was in April 1995, when the Web was little known. Muller said that Buchanan listened closely, and by the end of the meal agreed to let her run his site. The Buchanan page was a communication success—even if the candidate wasn't a success at the polls—because it conveniently provided a way to avoid the technical hassles of radio and television, and because the Internet was spring-loaded to work for minority candidates short of cash.

Of course, not all Website developers were volunteers. A cottage industry of professionals formed early around the medium and sold their services to political campaigns, as they had to businesses. But even these paid-for arrangements involved much less nuisance than the campaigns faced with radio and television. Once the campaigns and the pros worked out the initial design and strategy, the sites pretty much ran on autopilot. The campaigns periodically would send the developers new speeches, position papers, and updates of other site content, and the hired hands would take it from there.

So, whether the sites were home-grown or store-bought, the campaigns found that getting on the Web was a breeze. Eager volunteers made it easier to say "yes" than "no," and once these kids got going, they moved in with the campaign and stayed around to run the sites. No doubt, the "in-house" development of many sites helped candidates feel at ease with the medium.

Even the paid-for outfits offered a high comfort level. They provided one-stop shopping, and required little of the candidate. These companies, mostly mom and pops—or, more rightly, Jack and Jills—were start-ups that carved their niche into a new medium. They aimed to please, and interviews with campaign staffers and professional developers confirmed that the companies often exceeded contract provisions to provide the campaign with quality service.

IT'S CONTROLLABLE

Back to risk for a minute. As the DNC's Dick Bell said, political campaigns are risk-averse. They like to control every move, message, and event. That's why campaigns aren't comfortable with debates, television interviews, or press conferences, where candidates must yield some of their control. Front-runners sometimes have the luxury of rejecting these forums, and avoid the perils of an embarrassing question and the hazards of a misspoken answer. Candidates' loose lips sometimes sink electoral ships.

Recall Gerald Ford's disaster when, in a debate, the presidential candidate said to his great embarrassment that there were no Communist troops in Poland. As any sixth grader could have told you, in 1977 Eastern Europe was feeling the bitter winds of the cold war, and Poland was still thick with Communist troops. That blunder and his Chevy Chase pratfalls follow Ford to this day. Years later, vice presidential candidate Dan Quayle told a classful of school kids to spell potato with an "e" (thus, potatoe). To some observers, the candidate's slip was emblematic of larger inadequacies, and it even raised public discussion about his fitness for office. Candidates wince at the thought of similar mishaps.

By contrast, the Internet is about as risk-free as a medium gets, at least it was in 1996. It's your site, so you control the format and the content.

You set the agenda and discuss the things you find important. If you don't want to bring up the fact that you misled kids on the spelling of potato, you don't have to. Instead, you can brag about your proper spelling of most vegetables, or about your constituent services or your war record. You can even talk about your bus or your flannel shirt, if you think that will help your cause. It's your site.

Jeff Meyers, director of information systems for the Dole campaign, stressed the point. He said that Websites give candidates control of both agenda and content, and let them raise their strongest issues. They can offer a point-counterpoint discussion; they can talk about their own virtues or their opponent's sins. Meyers said that the ownership of political sites gives the candidate complete editorial control of what to discuss and how to discuss it, a handler's dream.[15]

On the Web, you also control time and space, both in short supply on traditional mass media. Campaign staffers frequently said in interviews that they used the expansiveness of the Web to flesh out the details often stripped away by other media. If you believe the polls, sound-bite journalism irritates voters, and if you believe the campaigns, it also irritates office seekers. (By this reasoning, you'd have to conclude that sound-bite journalism appeals only to sound-bite journalists.) The Web is a way for campaigns to get out all the news that *they* think is fit to print. The Web, therefore, gives campaigns a level of control they do not enjoy with traditional media.

For now, at least, most events on the Web are not real-time—or as television says, "live." Text dominated the Web in 1996, and most audio and video were taped. The conventions had live feeds, but these were rough and served mostly as technical experiments. Chat rooms were live, yes, but candidate exposure there was limited. For instance, Patrick Leahy ran town meetings on the Internet, and Lamar Alexander announced his candidacy live. But these were little more than novelties.

So, in 1996, candidates prepared the copy and answered the tough questions in advance. This, naturally, built a fire wall against risk because it allowed for prescreened responses. And, if candidates could not compile satisfactory answers, they could ignore the issues and set their own agendas. This static quality likely will change in the next few years as voters come to expect candidates to move from behind the fire wall and expose themselves to real-time interaction. But, for the first year out, candidates controlled the Websites; they had little to fear, and that eased their step into the new medium.

IT'S NONDISPLACING

Political campaigns, bound by the same natural laws as any other enterprise, confronted trade-offs in their allocation of staff, time, and money. The Internet, however, offered campaigns a rare opportunity to have it all.

For one, the Web's low cost allowed campaigns to set up a site without putting a dent in the media budget. A site cost from a few dollars to a few hundred dollars per month, so campaigns didn't have to steal from the bank account for radio or television time, brochures, or other traditional media. This sacrifice-free medium, therefore, did not require the green eyeshades to examine the trade-offs of the old media for the adoption of the new one. With the Web, there were no trade-offs. Good thing for the Web, too. It's doubtful that many campaign managers would have traded even a handful of television spots for a presence in cyberspace. Wonderful, if the sites did some good, and even if they didn't, nothing was lost because the candidates maintained their usual run of mass media.

Experimenting with broadcast ads years ago, candidates did not have such luxury. They paid what must have seemed like huge sums for production and time, and the money was siphoned from other activities. The Citizens for Eisenhower threw $2 million into a television blitz during the final weeks of the 1952 campaign. They had other options just as costly, but they chose television. With the Web, campaigns never faced such a trade-off.

Websites also didn't take much staff time, so there was little trade-off of human labor. Campaign managers shun speculative projects that soak up professional and volunteer time, and they would have been especially reluctant to invest much time in an unproven medium that reached only a fraction of the voters. Happily, previously prepared speeches, position papers, and biographies could be written, formatted, and recycled on a site in only a few hours. Design work and content meant the Website could be assembled quickly. Basic sites require much less time than is taken up by other media.

Finally, on radio and television, campaigns must cram messages into 30-second bundles, which compresses the selection and treatment of topics. In planning campaign spots, you must pick and chose among topics on your campaign agenda, advancing some, forgetting others. Then, when you write the spots, you must limit your arguments; there just isn't time to say all you would like to say about most public issues.

On the Web you can tell it all. No issues need to be displaced, no arguments dislodged to make room. Take all the space you want for each item. Include even minor issues of concern to only a handful of voters, then let the users decide what they'll read. The Website laid out a smorgasbord of issues and left it up to the user to decide how high to pile the plate.

A FEW OTHER REASONS

So far we've heard that campaigns have adopted the Internet for all the logical reasons you would expect to examine in a course on public communication. Costs, familiarity, convenience, and the rest are excellent reasons, but if you push campaign staffers a bit further, you'll discover they scrambled onto the Web in 1996 for another, perhaps less rational, reason: fear. A number of campaign officials said they feared the consequences of NOT getting on the Web during this inaugural year.[16]

Don't Be Left Behind

We fear being left behind, and this may have propelled some campaigns onto the Web. No one, of course, could know in early 1995 whether or not the Internet had any great potential for the upcoming campaigns. In fact, the odds were against it. Not all that many people were on-line.[17] CompuServe, Prodigy, and AOL were fighting over audience scraps so puny by television standards that electronic communication services looked like early Nielsen scores for cable TV. Hardly anyone understood what Al Gore meant by the "Information Superhighway," or cyberspace, although people freely tossed around the terms.

On the other hand, many campaigns asked, "What if this thing takes off, and picks up even a few percentage points for campaigns that use it, and we're not on board?" Some staffers involved in the 1996 campaigns described the decision to go on-line as insurance planning, just in case Websites held a little magic.

A few campaigns early on the Web laid down the challenge, and the race was on. Lamar Alexander was the first candidate to get on-line, so maybe he's responsible.[18] A fad or a trend, nobody wanted to be left behind, and certainly not for a few dollars and a few hours of time.

Don't Be a Luddite

Ned Ludd, a worker in Leicestershire, England, during the eighteenth century, opposed all new technologies and technological change, and thus lent the name "Luddite" to any movement that, over the years, has surfaced to challenge mechanical innovation.

The Internet, of course, was innovation and technology in its grandest form. The numbers of users continued to grow by hundreds of thousands per month, as the medium's adoption curve exceeded anything we have witnessed to date. Nevertheless, there are modern Luddites who swear against the Internet and all it stands for.

Being a Luddite in a society swept by innovation is not wise, especially not for political candidates who are promising to lead the country into the next century. Technology is business, technology is leadership, technology is forward-looking. Recall the Clinton–Dole battle of the bridges. Dole said he would establish a bridge with the past, and within hours, he was one-upped by Clinton, who promised to build a bridge to the future. The bridge metaphors became symbols that said as much as anything about the differences, real or imagined, between the presidential campaigns. The tone was set, the future was good, technology was good, and the Internet, as part of the future and an emblem of technology, was good. And it was in style.

It's an overstatement, of course, to say that candidates were actually afraid of the Luddite label, but it isn't a stretch to suggest that candidates enjoyed the occasion to tout their connection with new technology and their connectedness to a national movement. Campaigns often provided their Website addresses (URLs) in brochures, on the air, and in speeches. Bob Dole gave his URL on national television during the second presidential debate, and is now in the history books as the first candidate to do so.[19] He got his point across that Bob Dole was hip on the Web. Clinton somehow missed the chance to grab the honor, even though praise for his support of the Net is one kudo he deserves.

For some, the sites became a matter of pride and a demonstration of commitment to the future. Apart from any communication value the Web may have imparted to a campaign, it served as a symbol of progressive thinking. And, if nothing else, it warded off the charge that this seeker of public office was a Luddite!

Me, Too

A professional Website developer, working for several congressional campaigns, was asked what motivated most of his political clients to set up a site. He said simply, "Me, too."

"Me, too?"

"Right. Everybody else has one, I want one, too." You might see this as a variant of "don't be left behind," but it has a different spin. "Me, too" thinking is driven by friends and other candidates in the same party; "don't be left behind" thinking is motivated by the opposition, who just might get a leg up on you with some new device. "Me, too" is kin to the bandwagon effect said to drive so many decisions in this business, albeit for voters, not candidates. But here, candidates have approached professional programmers about sites because they want to climb on board the bus with everyone else.

The same may be said for polls, television spots, lawn signs, bumper stickers, and the rest, but this was the time for the Web. The political brothers and sisters have signed on, and besides, how can you get by at the club meetings if you can't talk about your own site when everyone else is talking about his or hers? Having a site that bears your name, boasts your virtues, tells your life story became irresistible for many candidates when it was apparent that others had them.

It was, therefore, important that a few brave souls—the early adopters, to use Rogers's term[20]—built their sites. They set the norm, and not only demonstrated the possibilities of this new medium but also showed that it was safe. Like kids who challenge each other to go first, once the first daredevil successfully crosses the stream or climbs the tree, the others feel obliged to follow. And so it was for some campaigns with Websites in the 1996 elections. The first few adopters lured the others into this new technology and the new communication fashion was under way.

A long list of reasons compelled the adoption of the Internet, and they explain why so many campaigns gave it a try. But to try to do what? Whether or not the Web was inexpensive and risk-free, there must be some expectation of even a modest return. What did campaigns hope to gain from its use? We turn to that issue now.

HOW DID CAMPAIGNS USE THE WEB?

It is unknown just how many of the 6,465 political races fought above the city level had sites, although, as noted earlier, Andy Brack estimated that 85 percent of the candidates for the House and Senate set up campaign pages.[21] The rate for candidates at all levels is, no doubt, somewhat lower. Candidates' sites ranged from dull, gray pages obviously assembled by someone thumbing through a just-bought *Web Sites for Dummies* book, to spectacular cyberfrescoes. The major party sites and the pages for Clinton and Dole were sensational visual displays filled with color and interactive options. Visitors could plow through detailed discussions and news stories, and they could skip lightly over dozens of topics tethered by hypertext and bit-mapped images.[22] No doubt, over the next few years, as the medium matures, these early sites will seem as primitive as silent movies, but for the first year on the Web, they were quite impressive.

Colorful, exciting, informative, interesting, interactive, okay—but this question stands out: What did they hope that a Website would accomplish?

This was a question put to dozens of campaign staffers involved with the Websites, people in the pits and people at the planning level. Some rattled off a rehearsed list of items that they had, no doubt, itemized many times in staff meetings. Others wondered why anyone would even *ask* such a question. They offered these reasons.

Avoid Press Interference—Get the Message Directly to the People

Nearly everyone agreed that a Website is custom-made to put the candidate and the voter nose-to-nose. Short of direct contact (which is uncommon these days), mass mailings (which are costly and seen by many voters as junk mail), and phone solicitations (even more irritating than junk mail), the Web was the only medium that allowed the campaign to speak directly with voters. In the politics of proximity, where candidates seek direct voter contacts, this is no small matter. One-on-one contact allows for message targeting, and it skirts the encumbrances imposed by the press. Much of what voters learn about candidates comes from the press, and every staffer knows what reporters want—sensation, scandal, something new or different.

Press reports insert the journalist between the candidate and the voter, with three effects. First, they filter the information from interviews or political events. What gets through the filter may not be what the candidate intended. After dancing around pointed questions for an hour, the candidate is never happy with a few column inches or 15 seconds on air. Candidates often wonder if they were in the same room with a reporter. That's the nature of the news business, of course, and experienced politicians understand that editing imposes filtering. What stays and what goes is out of the candidate's hands.

Second, reporters interpret. That's their job, and that's how news stories are assembled. Writers pack their own meaning around the words of the person interviewed, and in this way even the most meticulous reporter colors an interview. The context, explanations, even a description of the respondent's appearance can affect audience perceptions of candidates and their messages. The same interview, the same event can be interpreted differently by two reporters, sometimes leaving the audience with very different perceptions.

Old hands tell the story about a Moscow automobile show held during the cold war. Among the models on display were an American Ford and a Soviet Volga. According to reporters, the Ford beat the Volga in every category rated: mechanical, comfort, maintenance, everything. Accordingly, the American paper read: "Ford Beats the Soviet Volga." The Soviet paper wrote: "International Car Competition: USSR's Volga Takes Second Place. America's Ford Comes in Next to Last."

Apocryphal or not, it's this kind of slanting that politicians fear. Ford had no control over the Russian editor's interpretation of the car contest any more than American political candidates have control over how reporters interpret campaign interviews and events. It's the nature of journalism.

Third, news stories look for angles that may not square with the candidates' agendas. A reporter may seize upon one issue, chosen for novelty or controversy, raise it to the lead, and thereby give it coverage beyond its significance. From the other end, reporters may reduce or eliminate issues that candidates would give their eyeteeth to see in print or on the evening newscast. Again, that's the character of reporting.

During the 1996 election, AmeriSearch coordinated a national poll that dug deep for concerns of the electorate about issues facing the country.[23] Using open-ended techniques, the survey asked 1,500 people to talk about the issues and the concerns they might like to raise with Bill Clinton, Bob Dole, and Ross Perot. The results offered a collection of personal essays that conveyed the thoughts of average American voters. Unlike most political research at the time, this survey was not designed to rate the horse race—who was ahead, who was behind—but to unearth the deep-down thoughts of voters often missed through traditional polling methods. The survey reported nearly 1,000 pages of Americans talking to their presidential candidates. Boiled down, the results caught the eye of a network producer.

The principal investigator laid out the unique features to the producer, who set up a live interview on national television. The researcher duly explained how the poll differed in form and substance from the others, and how it elicited insights, not superficial nose counts.

Then the show went on the air. The split screens zoomed in on the anchorman in New York and on the apprehensive researcher in San Francisco. The first question, right off the top: "Tell us, professor, what's the horse race?"

The researcher thought, "Horse race? Horse race? Didn't they hear what I said? This wasn't a horse race poll, a winner/loser contest; it wasn't designed for that. It was designed to excavate deep thinking from voters. I thought you would ask me for an example of what voters said they would like to discuss with Bill Clinton or Bob Dole. I thought you would ask me how people's personal lives affect their concerns for public issues. Why are you asking me about the goddamned horse race?"

Fortunately, the horse race statistics were at hand. Nevertheless, the agenda of this interview was set around the horse race, not the raison d'être of the study. The researcher's agenda did not fit the news format or the producer's presuppositions about political polls.

Call it distortion if you wish, but that's the way it is when you work with reporters and the press, on live TV or for developed stories. You don't set the agenda, and even if you think the fix is in, even if you think you asserted your agenda so forcefully that no one could miss it, you're probably wrong. That irks political candidates to no end. Not many people who do interviews come away from a published story believing it offered the priorities they put forth. That being the way it is, many office seekers found the Websites a joy. Here they were the bosses, they set the agendas, and they could present them directly to the voters.

With traditional media, even when candidates do an end run around reporters and go directly to the voters with 30-second spots and quarter-page ads, they face problems. Forget for a minute the complaints about paid-for advertising that spots are negative and irrelevant. The fact is, there isn't an issue facing American political candidates today that can be examined intelligently in 30 seconds. But television ads are the way of the political world. It's a rare candidate (or one out of money) in a major race who doesn't succumb to the seduction of the 30-second commercial. Consultants push the spots, the media promote them, and the voters say they hate them. And, yes, the damnedest thing is, to one degree or another, they work.

Researchers Thomas Patterson and Robert McClure shook things up in the mid-1970s when they reported that political commercials were considerably more effective than the evening newscasts were in teaching voters about the issues.[24] What they communicate is another matter, but much of what gets across in a political campaign originates in the 30-second spots—simplistic, slanted, but effective.

Ironically, the campaign staffers interviewed for this book agreed that paid advertising limits the selection and treatment of important issues. In this respect they ally themselves with the voters who are repelled by the 30-second format.

During the 1996 election, the campaigns saw their Websites as a way around the press and as accessories to paid advertising. The TV spots flagged the issues and set the agenda; the Websites filled in the details. Most likely, this role will change in future campaigns, but in 1996 the fledgling Web flew lookout for television. Serving as their own writers, editors, and producers, campaigns used the sites to punch up the information presented in their wafer-thin spots.

For mainstream candidates with deep pockets, the Web may have afforded an opportunity to supplement press accounts and to fortify the ads on traditional media, but for candidates with limited resources, or out of favor with the mainstream press, the Web became more important because it put them directly in touch with the people and gave them a presence on the political landscape that they otherwise would not have had.

Look again at Pat Buchanan's experience. His Web designer, Linda Muller, said that during the primaries, the candidate was getting no press or bad press. "No one was covering Pat as they were covering other candidates. And worse, when they ran the occasional story, they distorted his views and made him look like a monster."

Muller said that she knew the Web didn't have nearly the reach of the established media and that a site would not give her candidate the national prominence enjoyed by the others, but it provided a presence and, moreover, it got out the word to the faithful. "On the Website, we could offer articles and other information that the Brigades could then disseminate further—for instance, to church groups, neighborhoods, and other grassroots places. This is an important tool to spread the word about Pat." Muller always referred to Buchanan's supporters as "the Brigades," those whose word-of-mouth communications fit neatly with the new culture of the Internet.

The effect was to fill a gap that had long existed in political campaigns. Without coverage by print and broadcast, peripheral candidates were orphans left with few options, none of them promising. Some tried political stunts and colorful novelties. Years ago, Fred Harris conducted his presidential campaign from a Winnebago, the result being little press, lots of flat tires, and even less national recognition. Victor Morales, you remember, ran his 1996 campaign from the back of a pickup truck. At first, he drew media attention, but it was not sustained. Novelty candidates seldom get top billing, and without press reinforcement, they fade quickly.

Into this gap raced the Internet with its growing public access and interest, with its promise of a reasonable alternative to traditional media, especially for those shunned by the mainstream press. It offers access to state and national audiences, and it comes at a cost campaigns can afford, with an independence they need to bypass the stone walls sometimes erected by the press.

Get the Word to Other Audiences

Disneyland is a city within a city. City One has all the glamour and glitz, the amusements, music, trinket booths, a dancing Mickey Mouse, and all the rest that for years have created the Disney fantasy world. It's the city on the surface, the conspicuous, the showpiece. Think of Disneyland and you think of City One.

City Two is Disney Underground. It's an extraordinary labyrinth of tunnels and underground railways, warehouses and maintenance rooms. It's inhabited by people you never see, uniformed workers who move like moles beneath the neon facade of City One. They dump the trash, repair the amusements, transport the boxes and barrels whose contents feed the restaurants and shops. Here are the invisible people inhabiting a hidden Neverland that is truly a magic kingdom of its own.

When political staffers answer questions about campaign uses of the Internet, most tell you first about City One. These are the Websites with four-color pictures, glitzy graphics, dancing, flashing logos, and the rest that draw in the crowds and hype the candidates. This is what voters see, and it's what most people have in mind when they talk about politics on the Internet.

Give them time, and the staffers will get around to their City Two. They'll tell you about the E-mail and less conspicuous sites that traffic in communications for other audiences. They'll describe underground channels that carry schedules, talking points, marching orders, and other items that maintain the daily operations of a campaign. Here is where the work is done, where campaigns coordinate daily activities and feed information to fieldworkers and, in some cases, to the press.

Like Disney's City Two, the Internet back channels in 1996 were remarkably busy and integral to the larger campaign operation. Start with E-mail. For most users during the campaign, this service was as dull as it gets, pure function, no razzle-dazzle, nothing pretty, yet it was the pipeline for campaign communication.[25] It is reasonably private, highly targeted, and allows receivers to read it when they're ready. E-mail can transmit charts and graphs, balance sheets, even photos and artwork that can be read with standard software. This is the pack mule of communication devices, and it can haul just about any digital file to any on-line computer. There is simply nothing like E-mail for speed and versatility. Campaigns relied on it for several key functions.

E-mail Within a Campaign

Campaigns used E-mail as a critical link between campaign headquarters and the staffers and volunteers in the field. The Dole and Clinton campaigns reported using E-mail to send daily updates or "newsletters" to all campaigns running on the party ticket. They also directed information to regions slated for a candidate's visit—their candidate or the opposition's candidates. They sent talking papers and speeches, and they discussed schedules and the candidate's intended message so the local campaigns could prepare supporters and the press. All of this was to ensure integration of local efforts with larger campaigns.

E-mail sent to the field also served to orchestrate national, state, and local elections and to give local candidates a sense of connectedness with other races. Dick Bell, interactive media director for the DNC, said the Internet, and particularly the E-mail messages, "flatten out the information pyramid." A perennial complaint of state and local races has been the lack of information from Washington and from other races at higher levels. Candidates running in smaller races have felt disenfranchised, and for years have sought better integration of their efforts with other campaigns.

Bell reports that E-mail, used at least as far back as the Carter campaign in 1976, has answered the call. In Carter's day not many campaigns were on-line, but the experiment showed promising results for campaign coordination. Bell's direct experiences with campaign use of E-mail reaches to 1986, when he was the research director at the Democratic Senatorial Campaign Committee. During the 1986 races, he said, "Every afternoon we would E-mail all Democratic candidates an update of the activities in Washington. This would bring them up to speed on party activities and provide information for responses to reporters working on the evening newscasts." Bell said this service was designed primarily for challengers, many of whom did not have their own links to Washington, but it quickly became so popular that many incumbents asked to be added to the mailing list. Over the years, as more campaigns adopted computer technology, the E-mail updates became increasingly popular. By 1996, they were a campaign staple and as much a part of the party coordination effort as the telephone, and as faxes and telex once had been.

E-mail also has formed a trunk line to voters, supporters, and contributors. Republican and Democratic officials pushed for voter E-mail contacts in 1996. They solicited the E-mail addresses through their own Websites and obtained them from other campaigns, from friends, usenet lists, and, although no one would go on record with this, from list brokers who sell addresses by the thousands. Most staffers agree that campaign use of direct mail and telephone appeals, which has soared in recent years, is likely to be displaced soon by E-mail.[26] It's easier, more efficient, and much less expensive, and now that people are logging on by the millions, it has become a practical alternative.[27]

What's in these messages? Lots of discussion that looks very personal, targeted material that singles out voters by personal characteristics. Information in E-mail messages was very much like direct mail, which had become the model for direct voter contacts. Recipients were usually pitched for a contribution, and of course, once they contributed, they were added to a different E-mail list that entitled them to yet more E-mail and even more personal treatment.

Some E-mail carried general campaign rhetoric to keep the voters pumped, but some was specific and action-oriented. Several major campaigns said that they would E-mail supporters who lived in areas where their candidate or the opposition candidate would be visiting. Supporters would be encouraged to attend speeches and rallies, to show the flag and be photographed by cameras feeding the evening news.

Campaigns kept close watch on the candidate's media schedule, and when a candidate or other official was scheduled for a call-in show, they would E-mail supporters with the time and offer information and ideas that could be used in the phone calls.

One source said that his staff sometimes sent over 10,000 messages for a single radio program. The objective, of course, was to set a candidate-friendly agenda and displace calls from supporters of the opposition—who, of course, were up to the same tricks.

No party monopolized this use of E-mail. Campaigns on both sides said they used the technique, and both said they customarily added a "multiplier" to punch up the potential number of callers. As with daisy-chaining, the campaigns urged supporters to call five or ten other boosters and encourage them to phone in with friendly questions.

There are no empirical data yet on the impact of these techniques, but in light of such information, it's hard to imagine that callers to political shows these days are anything but partisans with a bagful of preset agenda items. Not much room left on the phone lines for voters who are in the mundane middle. E-mail, in 1996, served as an often-used tool with which to manipulate the other media.

E-mail to the Press

The Internet's City Two provides for communication with the working press. Much of it, too, takes place out of public view, on the back channels and in the tunnels of electronic communication. Previously, campaigns transmitted critical information to the press through "power faxes"—the procedure of sending a single fax simultaneously to hundreds of media. This allowed campaigns to initiate communication and to respond instantly to charges by opponents.

E-mail makes the power faxes look like covered wagons. It's faster, more targeted (because it gets to the reporter you want—not the central mail room), and it's far less expensive and more flexible. Campaigns start with reporter lists that they use to distribute daily updates, and to fire off instant responses or preemptive messages.

Reporters on the road, or out and about researching stories, often write on laptop computers, which free them from the desk and from central faxes. E-mail, however, can be sent and received from any phone—even cellular phones that function on a bus or in a hotel room. With a key-stroke, campaigns can carpet-bomb reporters around the country with the information they once sent by other means.

As we discuss in Chapter 6, the Net has compressed time and space for all media. Breaking stories that once grabbed public attention through newspaper extras, then hourly newscasts, now reach the public through instant releases on cable TV and on the Internet. This pressure on the media, in turn, put pressures on campaigns to deliver information quickly.

The several hundred media sites available in 1996 often added information every few minutes throughout the day,[28] and a sleepy campaign not geared to the rapid delivery of information could quickly become overwhelmed. The large state and national races were expected to respond quickly in 1996, and by 2000 it will be true at the congressional and local levels as regional media increase their presence on the Web.

To supplement E-mail (rising to City One), many campaigns installed raw material on their Websites—speeches, position papers, questions and answers on popular issues—and while these were available to all takers, they were posted with the press in mind. Think of it as a convenient filing cabinet, usually up to date and stocked with much of the information published by a campaign. On-line, reporters could examine the latest installments and download the files for printing if they wanted hard copy. This saved the time of reporters and campaign staff alike.

John Bane, a doctoral student at the University of North Carolina at Chapel Hill, said his research showed that journalists used Website postings to provide more than the usual amount of unfiltered information in their stories. There were more speeches excerpted and more direct quotations from the candidate. He attributed this to the ease of access and the ready availability of this information.

The dissemination of information to the press, by E-mail or through Websites, is a gain for campaigns. On the other hand, the easier it is to send messages, the more messages are likely to be sent. This leads to overload, with too many campaigns chasing too few reporters for too little media time and space. The novelty wears off quickly, and gates will soon be erected by journalists against the mounting pile of campaign information.

How will this be resolved? One answer is "uplining," the interactive component of the Web. Reporters will configure candidate Web pages to receive only press releases about certain issues. They will be flagged by "urgent" messages that meet certain tests. Interactive computers will answer reporters' questions, possibly with stock responses at first but, over time, as the systems grow more sophisticated, with highly personalized responses. The computer will stand ready for interviews day and night, giving new meaning to nonstop campaigning. E-mail will continue, but it will merge with other Web functions that are reporter-friendly.

Gather Feedback and Interact with Voters

Visitor Feedback

In theory, E-mail from visitors should allow campaigns to better understand their audience. This feedback can benefit campaign strategies and improve the candidate's sense of the public mood. True, E-mailed information in 1996 came from a narrow slice of the electorate, and it could in no way be considered reflective of the general population. You would need to cull the jokesters from the pile and account for visitors with time enough to send several messages a day. And you would have to set up procedures to read the E-mail, categorize it, and report it to the campaign. Still, E-mail feedback could add another tile to the mosaic that, taken along with traditional information sources, could provide the campaign with a better sense of the views of constituents. Officeholders and office seekers, after all, like to tell how they listen to the people. Here's a way to do it.

But this was more promise than practice in 1996. It was surprising to learn how unimportant the *content* of E-mail was for the major campaigns. The messages were seen as a means of gathering E-mail addresses and signing up volunteers, both of immediate utility to the campaign. But as a conduit for constituent views—as an ear to the railroad track—E-mail was used poorly.

Roger Hurwitz, at MIT's Artificial Intelligence Laboratory, said that the campaigns were stuck in the broadcast model, which is the one-way flow of information. "They could have done so much with visitor feedback. They could have elicited opinions, measured views, defined the issues relevant to voters, but they didn't understand the medium. None of the campaigns had much of a grasp on how to handle the broad inflow of information."[29]

One senior campaign staffer, who asked not be identified, said that his site received between 80 and 100 messages a day. What did he do with them? Not much. Hurwitz was right. The staffer said the campaign extracted the addresses, but did no analysis of the contents and provided no summaries to campaign strategists. In other words, they licked off the icing and threw the cake away. This pattern emerged from Republicans and Democrats alike. Only staffers in smaller campaigns said they even read the few messages they received, and none reported that they regularly used information from these messages.

Such underuse of upline messages is a pity. Obviously, it robs the campaign of information that could help office seekers gain an insight into what voters want. Of course, campaigns had other sources for public views—polls and personal contacts—but would a periodic summary of E-mail messages have cost so much and been of so little value? This was an opportunity lost.

Worse, the site visitors were misled. They were invited to offer the candidate their views, and many did so in good faith, unaware of the fact that the campaigns simply scraped off their addresses and discarded their thoughts.

In one interview, this writer put the question directly to a campaign official: "How do you decide what information and features visitors want on your site?" He replied, "We sit around the table and decide."

"Do you run focus groups or conduct opinion polls or examine your incoming E-mail to find out what Web users want?"

"To tell the truth, we really don't have to. We've been running campaigns for a long time, and we know what the voters want."

In other words, one-way thinking for a two-way medium. When campaigns so blithely discarded those messages, they demonstrated their general disregard for the thinking of the people they were seeking to reach. In the final analysis, they didn't treat their visitors fairly, and they deprived themselves of information that could have improved the efficiency and effectiveness of their messages.

Interactivity

In the primaries, Bob Dole's page let you click on Guest Book, Volunteers, and Donations. Pat Buchanan invited you to Join the Buchanan Brigade, then gave you an enlistment form. Phil Gramm encouraged site visitors to contribute. Lamar Alexander urged visitors to click on his plaid shirt and send a check. Paul Wellstone said you could Get on Board his bus as a volunteer. Candidates in both major parties, for all levels of office, made uplining easy for visitors who wanted to commit time and money.

Website interactivity also was positioned as a novelty or "a lure," as one staffer put it. "Give people something to do on the site, keep it active and let them participate. This attracts visitors, and while they're playing with the interactive features, they may read the other items."

In an informal survey of journalists and political enthusiasts, Bob Dole's page was mentioned most often as the site with the best use of interactivity. Dole's home page challenged users to visit Dole Interactive, billing it as "the place to have fun and interact with the campaign." As far as political Websites went, it was a minor Treasure Island of amusements.

Ed Epstein, a reporter for the *San Francisco Chronicle*, raved about Dole's site at a Politics on Line conference, touting it as the best on the Web in 1996. He added that if Dole had run his campaign as he had run his Website, he would have won the race.[30]

One attraction, available even in the early days of the Dole campaign, was an interactive poster shop where visitors could configure images and slogans and enter the name of someone who might appreciate a poster declaring that he or she supported Bob Dole. The poster could be printed on any desktop printer. Visitors also could make up a personalized bumper sticker that proclaimed support for the Republican candidate.

Further, the site allowed visitors to download personalized screen savers and other graphics, all of which advertised Dole's candidacy. You could send electronic "postcards" from the Dole site. Select full-color "Dole for President" images, type in a personal greeting and the E-mail address of the recipient, and the program did the rest. When targets checked their E-mail, they found a message announcing that a postcard from you awaited them at a given Website address. The electronic post-card orchestrated personal endorsements and extended the candidate's message beyond the Website.

Toward the end of the campaign, Dole's site designers entered the future. It looked simple enough. Fill out a form that asked for informa-tion about you and your interests. Why? Because "Information on the following form will allow us to customize your personal Dole for Pres-ident Website."

It asked the visitors to provide their names, home addresses, phones, and E-mail addresses. Then it asked them to check off three issues from a list of 25 that were of particular interest. These included Balanced Bud-get, Immigration, Missile Defense, and Women's Issues. Next, visitors were asked to identify the coalitions they might be interested in joining (29 of them)—for instance, Women in Business, Rural Americans, Cath-olics, and High Tech/Information Technology. The site ended with a few options for graphics and formatting of the "personal Dole for President Website."

From that point on, when you logged on to the candidate's site, you were spared the generic page prepared for everyone else. Your tailor-cut page would serve up selected issue swatches most likely to interest you. That tactic may well be the future for Website activity: to each the in-formation he or she wants—no more, no less.

Savvy visitors knew that more was going on. While the campaign was constructing personalized Websites for visitors, it also was assembling a database and harvesting those valuable E-mail addresses. More than that, the campaign now could associate the E-mail addresses with indi-viduals by way of home address and phone and key topics of interest. Here was a treasure trove of data. Not only did it allow the campaign to assemble voter-specific Websites, it also gave the campaign a means of sorting people by issues in order to channel names and addresses to special interest groups friendly to the GOP. Visitors identified their greatest interests, which is tantamount to identifying their greatest vul-nerabilities. Indicate your interest in Greek-American issues and you be-come particularly susceptible to personal contacts by "Greeks for the GOP" or whatever organization forms around each visitor-sensitive is-sue.

Is this practice of data-gathering fair? From one viewpoint, yes. Visi-tors volunteered the information, they were not coerced. Instructions on the site said "Please Check Off the Coalitions You're Interested in Join-ing." One could argue that by checking off a box, the visitor has agreed to take the first step in joining coalitions that concern the selected issues. Not interested in joining? Fine, don't check the box.

On the other hand, it isn't entirely fair. For one, the site does not tell you that it might pass along your name and address to anyone else. It samples your interest, but doesn't explicitly state its possible use of your response. To make this clear, the site could have said, "We will, or at least we might, pass along your name and address to groups who share your concerns and interests."

Second, the site does not specify the names of the coalitions. It *says* coalitions, but only posts categories such as Doctors, Sportsmen, and Educators. This is especially troublesome because it asks people to identify concern for the focus of a coalition without reference to the political position of the coalition. Sure, you're interested in sportsmen's groups, because you love the outdoors and want to learn more about fly casting. But did you bargain for a slot on the NRA list? Your name and address easily could wind up there. To be entirely open, the campaign could have asked people to check boxes next to the names of specific groups, so they knew exactly what they were getting into.

Dole's site encouraged people to craft a personal page, and in the bargain picked up rich information with which to pinpoint messages and to direct personal contacts by GOP-friendly interest groups. The bone of contention here is not with such targeting but the failure to disclose the full use of this information. In 1996 this may have been just a lab test and operationally inconsequential, but in the years ahead, disclosure will become central to many valid concerns about Website targeting.

As interactivity expands along with the sophistication of equipment and software, information assembled from a wide variety of feedback mechanisms will be delivered personally and directly to Internet users, much the way a precinct worker in the 1940s may have offered a personalized message on your front porch. But then, you saw the face and heard the words from someone evidently trying to persuade. The virtual pitchmen will be less obvious, and their hidden agendas should be of concern to critics who fear the potential of this medium to manipulate the unsuspecting. Disclosure of all information uses will go a long way to offset these problems. In the meanwhile, it is caveat emptor.

NOTES

1. Charles Michelson, describing the radio speeches of Democratic presidential candidate John Davis, quoted in E. W. Chester, *Radio, Television and American Politics* (New York: Sheed and Ward, 1969), 18.

2. C. Press, and K. VerBurg, *American Politicians and Journalists* (Glenview, IL: Scott, Foresman, 1988); Chester, *Radio, Television and American Politics.*

3. Chester, *Radio, Television and American Politics.*

4. Jimmy Carter's campaign in 1976, is generally credited with being the first to make regular use of E-mail. His campaign used this computer communication to stay in touch with volunteers and fieldworkers and to arrange candidate visits around the country.

5. Phillip Hallam-Baker, who in 1992 was with the Artificial Intelligence Laboratory at MIT, said several browsers were available before the arrival of Mosaic, which is generally believed to be the first browser.

6. From telephone interview on Mar. 17, 1997.

7. T. H. White, *America in Search of Itself: The Making of the President, 1956–1980* (New York: Harper & Row, 1982), 165.

8. E. Barnouw, *Tube of Plenty: The Evolution of American Television*, 2nd ed. (New York: Oxford University Press, 1982), 483.

9. R. Berkman, and L. W. Kitch, *Politics in the Media Age* (New York: McGraw-Hill, 1986), 146.

10. S. H. Verhovek, "Phil Gramm's Offbeat Conservative Charm," *New York Times*, Dec. 27, 1995. Obtained from NYT Interactive Search Service, http://www.nytimes.com.

11. Morales's Web wizards were Tom Karches, Kara Bennett, and Mike Chorost.

12. British journalist Jonathan Prynn called most sites "little more than electronic notice boards." J. Prynn, "New Strand in the Tangled Web of American Politics," *The Times*, Nov. 6, 1996, feature Sec.

13. From an interview on May 3, 1996.

14. From an interview on May 10, 1996.

15. From an interview on Feb. 26, 1996.

16. A senior computer adviser to one of the campaigns said, "When we first got on a Web site, it was more out of fear than anything else. We said, 'Oh shoot, the other side's there, we can't let them steal the high ground.' " Reported in Prynn, "New Strand in the Tangled Web of American Politics."

17. Morgan Stanley reports that 9 million users had Internet/Web access in 1995. Reported in CyberAtlas (http://www.cyberatlas.com/market.html). Site observed Mar. 7, 1997.

18. E. Klineberg, and A. Perrin, "Symbolic Politics in the Information Age: The Presidential Campaign on the Web," paper on http://demog.berkeley.edu/~aperrin/infosociety.html. The authors note that Alexander's launch was not on the Web but on America On-line.

19. Dole's reference to his Website seemed to be forced and out of pace with the debate. Some have suggested that he may have given his URL as an antidote to his "bridge to the past" reference.

20. E. M. Rogers, and F. F. Shoemaker, *Communication of Innovations: A Cross-Cultural Approach*, 2d ed. (New York: Free Press, 1971).

21. With religious fervor, the Clinton administration in 1993, put the force of the White House behind an integrated computer communication system called the Information Superhighway. That term has since dropped from the national lexicon, but the concept of cyberspace remained and the business of the Internet flourished during Clinton's first term.

22. Hypertext—or hot text—is used to join one site to a related site. Bit maps provide images that are themselves "hot." Visitors click on areas within an image that link them to the next site.

23. AmeriSearch used the High Definition Research℠ technique, a survey procedure that allows respondents to set their own agendas. It uses computer-assisted coding procedures to analyze the data and computer search engines to

sort and deliver the data on the Internet. HDR was applied to the 1996 presidential campaign in a project called America's Voice.

24. T. E. Patterson, and R. D. McClure, *The Unseeing Eye: The Myth of Television Power in National Political News* (New York: G. P. Putnam's Sons, 1979).

25. During the election, most E-mail involved the basic text. Several programs surfacing just around election time, however, provided E-mail with a graphical component that added color, pictures, and even animation. For instance, General Magic, Hallmark Cards, Greet Street, and Prodigy offered programs that allowed users to send attachments along with their E-mailed messages. Receivers with Windows-based E-mail programs, such as Exchange and Eudora, could read the attachments as full-color messages. Eric Arnum, editor of *Electronic Mail & Message Systems*, said, "There is clearly a move in the industry to multimedia messaging. . . . With so many people using the net, the inclusion of a photo or map in your message makes it more interesting and improves your presentation tremendously" (quoted by Jon Swartz, "The Multimedia Is the Message," *San Francisco Chronicle*, Nov. 13, 1996, p. C4). No campaign staffer interviewed for this book reported using such programs in political communication during the 1996 elections.

26. For a discussion of direct contact campaigns, see G. Selnow, *High Tech Campaigns: Computer Technology in Political Communication* (Westport, CT: Praeger, 1994).

27. The use of programmed targeting in political communication is nothing new. Andy Glass, Washington bureau chief of Cox News, says that in the 1960s, when he was a member of a senator's staff, he would read constituents' letters and identify the key issues that should be addressed in a response. He then would select the appropriate computer cards that referenced each issue. The cards then would be run through a computer to generate a letter containing one paragraph for each of the key issues. Crude by today's standards, but the system offered a way of tailoring each letter to the concerns of individual constituents.

28. NewsTracker, for instance, reports searching 300 media sites for current news.

29. From an interview on Feb. 19, 1997.

30. Epstein's comments were made in a panel discussion titled "Virtual Media: Spinning On-line Political Coverage." The Politics on Line conference was held in South San Francisco on Dec. 12, 1996.

Chapter Four

The Rank and File: New Voices in Political Campaigns

In this and like communities, public sentiment is everything. With public sentiment nothing can fail, without it nothing can succeed. Consequently, he who molds public sentiment goes deeper than he who enacts statutes or pronounces decisions.

— *Abraham Lincoln*

In the early stages of the Vietnam war, the mainstream press bought into the Johnson administration's interpretation of the conflict as a "police action," and neither TV nor newspapers were willing or able to cover the groundswell of discordant views emerging from the nation's college campuses. Journalists covered the official views and explained official policies, so that during much of the war, the press was seen as an instrument of government by anti-war protesters. This perceived slanting of views by the establishment media galvanized groups opposing the war into the use of other information outlets—the most visible being the underground press.

Underground newspapers shared the counterculture look and tone. The rough-set type was sometimes barely legible, the typo-filled copy was opinionated and often ideological. The language, like the type, was rough, and the references to public figures were enough to make a sailor blush. The papers rarely published on schedule, and were distributed chiefly in coffee shops and dorm lobbies, at protest concerts and rallies, hardly ever at corner newsstands.

Few of these papers were funded through subscriptions and advertising; most survived on donations from sympathetic readers and small businesses, and on pocket change from people who published them. Pass-alongs were expected after a buyer had finished with a copy. Apart from *National Geographic*, they had to be the most reread publications in communication history.

As a rule, editions hit the streets when writers had the motivation to publish, and this often coincided with major military or political events such as the Tet offensive, the shootings at Kent State University, and especially the U.S. elections in 1968 and 1972. Underground papers typically reflected the views of people angry at the war, angry at the system that fed the war, and angry at the public officials who permitted it. Many also were angry at the denial of access to the conventional media.

Despite being crude, one-sided, and undocumented, the papers gave voice to the opinions of people outside the mainstream. The underground newspaper became a symbol of the counterculture and a reminder of the battle within a system where power is not equally shared and where those who wield the power control the flow of information.

Today, the Internet has picked up the action of the underground press, but with a difference. The Web puts all the publishers in the same place and gives the same "physical" access to undergrounders as it does to the *New York Times*. The vertically integrated Goliaths who control the nation's great papers and broadcast media, the telephone systems, and cable networks stand side by side on the Internet with the Davids who piece together sites of their own. On this medium, the size of an organization and the depth of its pockets do not tilt the scales nearly as much as they do in other media.

When someone today feels ignored by the major media or takes offense at their coverage, he or she is free to set up a site and tell his or her own story with only modest investment. This makes the underground press and the Internet cousins. With few financial barriers, with few limits on content, the Web offers the disenfranchised the same access once enjoyed by the undergrounders, plus a platform with unlimited possibilities.

On the other hand, some of the charms, if that's the word, of the underground papers are absent from the Internet. The rough appearance of the papers screamed "counterculture," which for some audiences signaled candor and trust. By contrast, Websites have a more consistent look; you can't tell this book by its cover. Not that this is necessarily a drawback for the public at large, since the renegade sites stand equitably beside the establishment sites in location, distribution, and status.

While the publishers of underground newspapers did not disdain mainstream audiences, they delighted in *le différence*, their independence from the conventional media being a matter of pride. The Internet does not bestow this distinction because all Websites use mainstream technology. Adoption of the conventional, always anathema to the counterculture, gives advocates the exposure they want but forces them to embrace a system that they often rail against.

During the 1996 election, successors to members of the counterculture, along with political campaigns, political parties, news organizations, churches, universities, businesses, and nonprofits took to the Web. For them, such access was a first in political communication. As recently as 1994, there was hardly a hint in the congressional campaigns that the Internet lay ahead, a situation easily seen in the fact that political campaigns used the same print and broadcast media they had been using for decades. It was only a few months before the new Congress took the oath of office in January 1995 that the first commercial browsers unlocked the doors to the new medium.[1] 1996, therefore, was truly a watershed year in political campaigning.

As the major candidates revved up their sites, the Internet was already displaying two traits that served the expanded roster of political players: (1) it was open to everyone, and (2) it consolidated all information sources into a single medium.

IT WAS OPEN TO EVERYONE

The Virtues

The twentieth-century record of the mass media is disheartening when it comes to the voices of the underfunded office seekers, small citizen organizations, and offbeat interest groups. As always, exposure in big media takes big money, so that the reach of a message depends on the size of a bankroll.

Challenging this relationship in communications, the Internet offers not only low cost but also high technology, the upshot being that you can be your own publisher, producer, writer, and director. This is truly a do-it-yourself mass medium at warehouse prices.

The numbers from the first campaign on the Web back up this egalitarian story. *USA Today* reports that more than 2,000 political sites were up and running during the election.[2] Although many of these sites were operated by the high rollers—established media, major campaigns and political parties—most were run by small organizations with no history of media use beyond in-house newsletters. They supported or opposed major or obscure candidates, ballot measures, legislation, world issues, and arcane philosophies. They dealt with tiny, local issues. A group south of San Francisco, for example, ran a politically charged site advocating the construction of tunnel![3] No issue was too small for the Web.

Thomas Jefferson, the "agrarian democrat" and advocate of the ordinary citizen, would have liked the 1996 campaign.[4] To be sure, he believed in the sunshine theory of government—let every policy be exposed to the people, enabling them to discuss and evaluate government activities and make informed electoral decisions. The Founding Fathers knew the value of public participation and the integral role of information in the democratic process. It is this character of openness and public activity wherein the Internet is superior to the established media, which have steadily developed their own bureaucracies and insular structures almost as inaccessible as the government itself. The Web gives all candidates, coalitions, and citizens the same public forum to make their voices heard, to become their own publishers and broadcasters, and to air their personal positions on public issues.

The Vices

The downside of this anarchic explosion is the problem of truth and accuracy. Amid this rampaging clutter, confusion reigns. The mass media, for all their faults of elitism and gatekeeping, at least come with a record and a reputation that cue the audience. As Charles Kuralt said in an interview, "If you read the *New York Times*, and if you read the *National Enquirer*, you make certain assumptions and know what you're getting. On the Internet, you can't be sure—at least, not always."[5] To trust a story or to regard it with a jaundiced eye depends on who tells it.

But the Web is rife with sites for which there is no "who." Although the spin-off news media sites use standard review practices, most of the hundreds of thousands of other sites lack editors to check the facts and parse the truth. The descriptions, statistics, and analyses may or may not have taproots in reality. Established reporters have, at least, some familiarity with the tricks and the tricksters of the trade, lessons learned in schools of journalism and on the street, and these skills help them cull many deceptions from the pages of mainstream media. Nothing like this is ensured on the sprawling Internet. For better or worse, a censorless medium that takes in all viewpoints imposes on users a great responsibility to weigh the information and to make their own judgments about its validity and usefulness. Perhaps the only protection for voters who turn to the Web for information is to be found in the very multiplicity of sites. Each voter must assemble his or her own mosaic from the many views expressed across a range of outlets on this new medium.

The process, applied to the Internet, may be more complex, but it is not new. Ideally, newspapers, radio, and television will seek to present an evenhanded view of every news story, an equal treatment of all newsmakers, a balance in the selection of stories and in the presentation of facts. In actual practice, however, no reporter, no publisher is without preconceptions that influence the choice of stories and their development. But most of the large news operations train their people to be as fair and accurate as human nature permits, and at the very least to be aware that each of us interprets events through very private lenses.

In the final analysis, though, no news report—in print, broadcast, and especially on the Internet—can provide perfect balance, and this is as it should be. The very notion of *absolute balance* is as frightening as *total lack of balance*. *Who* would hold the scales, and *what* scales would they hold to declare that balance has been achieved? Which of the critics is willing to legislate balance, for conventional media or for the Web?

America's premier essayist, E. B. White, responding to criticism that you can't learn *the* truth from a newspaper, said that he agreed, you cannot learn the truth. He said, "You can, however, buy at any news-stand a[n] . . . assortment of biased and unbiased facts and fancies and reports and opinions, and from them you . . . assemble something that is a reasonable facsimile of the truth . . . and that's the way we like it."[6]

E. B. White died in 1985, but were he alive, he might add the Web to the inventory of information sources that he saw contributing to our perceptions of the truth. Surely his "reasonable facsimile of the truth" would be realized more fully with the Internet's assortment of news stories, views and opinions, and all the biased and unbiased facts and fancies that never surface in the conventional press.

The Vastness and Variety

Barely two years after the public unveiling of the Web, more than a half-million sites had been installed. And we used to think 200-channel cable TV would overwhelm viewers! While the explosion testifies to the openness of the Web, it also jolts us to a recognition that a medium rich with so many choices presents Internet visitors with a daunting selection process. Won't many or even most sites go begging for an audience?

It comes down to mathematics, doesn't it—especially long division, when too few users are divided into too many sites? The 1996 campaigns offer an early example of what could become a familiar pattern for this medium. The larger sites of the national parties and major campaigns attracted their share of visitors. They had the best development teams, they were linked to many other sites, and they were most aggressively marketed in print and broadcast media. Their popularity should be no surprise. Web masters for these sites claim that just before the election, it was not unusual to receive hundreds of thousands of hits per day—a large number by Web standards.[7]

The smaller sites, though, tell a different story. If the "hit counters" are to be believed, the sites for many congressional and lower-level races did not have much traffic. Some sites, even late in the campaigns, reported only a few hundred hits. Why couldn't they assemble a more numerous audience?[8]

Many of the local-level races appear to have updated their sites only rarely, forgetting that stale information drives away business. In some districts too few voters had access to the Web, or more likely these tiny, lackluster sites could not compete with the bigger, flashier, better-promoted productions.

It's possible that smaller political sites were victims of a medium so full of options that the mathematics of division got the better of them, a condition that cautions everyone getting into the game. The truth is, it's a mistake to carry expectations of mass media-size audience into a targeted medium. Dividing audiences into a few dozen television channels is very different from dividing audiences into a million Websites.

Groups with unconventional viewpoints and modest purses, whose ideas struck the mainstream as novel or eccentric, found themselves in 1996 on the Internet cheek-by-jowl with the well-known and well-heeled. A look at the following list of diversified sites found among the thousands in a Web Crawler search on "U.S. politics" demonstrates the unprecedented expansion of political perspectives:

Ozone Action

Karl's Central Texas Handgun Reference

Space Activism Home Page

Contract with America Analysis

Workers of America

Cannabis Action Network

Group 133 Amnesty International Site

IWW—Hoosier Slim's Wobbly Page

Families Against Mandatory Minimums

Stop Prisoner Rape

Muddn' & Gun'n

HayMarket Martyrs

InfoQueer

Paul Teale/Karla Homolka Information Site

Get Government Off Our Back

Jay's Leftist and "Progressive" Internet Resources Directory

The Monday Lobby Group

Feminist Activist World Wide Web page

Sir Lou's Law Page

AdBusters

From Muddn' & Gun'n to InfoQueer, and from Space Activism to Feminist Activists, you get some idea of groups that read like the Yellow Pages of diversity. Like Noah's Ark, the Web seemed to have delegates from every quarter. They represented obscure organizations with something to say about their special passions in American politics. Where else but on the Web would you expect to see the political philosophies of the Cannabis Action Network? How could such a group afford television spots? How much coverage is the *New York Times* likely to provide them? They just don't make news that's fit to print. Most likely, neither does Muddn' & Gun'n or Hoosier Slim's Wobbly Page. The views held by these and thousands of other small groups without money enough to buy media or prominence enough to merit press coverage normally would never see the light of day. But there they were in 1996, for any voter interested in alternative political viewpoints.

Access, we add, is not the same as Web visits, but isn't that the issue? What matters is openness and a reasonable *chance* to reach the public, to be heard and to place an entry in the marketplace of ideas. Call it equity of access. From that point of view, the Web is an equal opportunity medium. What you do with it is up to you.

Of course, inequities remain, particularly in the formation of elaborate home pages plus the resources to promote a site, to act as one's own barker on the midway of information. The PeaceNet Group is unlikely to have adequate resources to develop a multimedia extravaganza like the one constructed by the Democratic or Republican National Committee. But PeaceNet has a presence, and it couldn't say that before 1996. Visitors can just as easily click on the PeaceNet page as they can the brand-name political party sites, and this gives small groups equity they could never enjoy on the conventional media. Near universal access makes the Internet a populist instrument and the most significant contribution to the democratic process since the Voting Rights Act of 1965.

Who else used the Web? The vastness and variety of participants in the political discussion exceeded all conventional standards. Visitors looking for alternative political ideas, groups, and philosophies in 1996 could turn to the National Political Index. On its Political Activist Groups list, it broke down nearly 600 sites into 21 categories.[9]

Agriculture

Campaign Reform

Censorship & the Media

Development & Sustainability

Ecology & the Environment

Economy

Education

Ethnicity & Race

Firearms

Health Care Reform

Human Rights

International

Labor Unions

Lesbian, Gay, Bisexual Issues

Miscellaneous

Nonviolent Action

Purely Political

Tax Reform

Trade

War & Peace

Women's Issues

If that lineup didn't connect with your interests, you could have clicked on to Adam Rifkin's Activism Links Page, which listed more than 450 sites grouped according to these categories:[10]

Activism Right Here, Right Now

Canonical Starting Points

Freedoms, Rights and Just Causes

International Organizations

Knowledge Can Be Dangerous

Law

Miscellany

News

Ordinary People

Readings

Technology

United States and Its Government

Project Vote Smart (PVS), one of the most information-packed sites on the Web, has been doling out political facts and figures since 1992. PVS, which began as an information-by-phone service, expanded to the Web in July 1995. The Corvallis, Oregon-based organization posted Links Where You Can Participate, an interesting collection of interactive sites that gave the visitor something to do.[11]

Vote Your Opinion on the Presidential Candidates

Vote Your Opinion on the Issues

Discuss Politics on the Web

Discuss Politics on News Groups

General Political Topics

Politics Related to Individuals

International Politics

Issues

Political Parties and Ideological Groups

Other Organizations

State and Regional Politics

These noncampaign sites went to the Web with an assortment of agendas including the advocacy of candidates, often from the fringe, and the promotion of political philosophies. Nonprofit organizations such as PVS and the California Voter Project churned out huge quantities of data. They polled the candidates and the voters, put up campaign finance data and focus group-like information in searchable form.

Much of the information found on political sites was not just adapted for the Web but created expressly for it. The Web's unique capacity to disseminate huge information files, for instance, led some organizations to create special databases suitable to the Web only. Because the Internet distributes data electronically and sorts it interactively, it is possible to offer information of the kind never before available to the general public.

A comparison of noncampaign with campaign sites, however, revealed a difference in the exploitation of the technology. The major campaigns could have afforded interesting interactive devices that pushed the science, but as we noted in Chapter 3, they chose not to, settling instead for a few amusements that turned flat through the campaign. They allowed visitors to make bumper stickers and posters, and some, like the Dole site, even let visitors configure their own pages. The real story of site creation with the finest tools is found in the development of sites by noncampaign organizations, sites such as PVS and Vox Pop. We turn to these in Chapter 5.

THE WEB CONSOLIDATED ALL THE INFORMATION SOURCES

Traditionally, political messages have been distributed through a blizzard of media from television to bumper stickers. While that continues, voters now can turn to one house for information from nearly every campaign, every organization with a point of view. This consolidation into an information flea market offers vendors and patrons of political information several advantages.

To begin, there is no privileged venue. For all its opulence, the MSNBC site provides no easier access (except fewer keystrokes) than a citizen's site wrapped in a plain brown bag. Thus, the counterculture viewpoint—once hard to find in some obscure underground paper—is as easy to examine as an editorial in the *Wall Street Journal*. The *Journal* editorial may be more heavily advertised, but with better search engines, even obscure sites can surface, and with links through other pages, they, too, can enjoy wider distribution.

Ease of access allows voters to compare information put out by different candidates and groups, and then to examine the arguments side by side. In the old days, in 1994, who could locate all the pamphlets, listen to all the speeches, ferret out all the positions of the candidates and of the groups and advocates staking a claim to the issues? Now, with the job made easier, a lot more voters may be inclined to sort through positions, at least of the sources most important to them.

Third-party candidates and peripheral groups traditionally have been consigned to the media ghettos—low-rent broadcast stations, thrift-shop publications—a state of affairs that not only limits their exposure but also comments on their candidacy. It would be hard to overestimate the advantage of the mainstreamer's 30-second TV spot over the fringer's handbill. Television is a first-class venue, the handbill is steerage. What does each say about the candidate who uses it? An ad in the *Los Angeles Times* is hardly on a par with midnight spots on a 1,000-watt AM station. Sometimes the medium *is* the message. But, because the Web houses all information vendors in one place, it evens up perceptions of the information sources. There are no penthouse addresses on the Internet, just one huge project with a million boxes.

The point about equity is demonstrated in a Web search of "presidential candidates." The results returned are arranged with the randomness of an alphabetized list: Sal Casamassima was listed alongside Bill Clinton, Bruce Daniels came up next to Bob Dole, and Pat Paulsen was mentioned just ahead of Ross Perot. The arbitrariness of alphabetical order puts the known next to the unknown, the prince next to the pauper. A search on "political parties" turned up site addresses for the Democrats and Republicans listed in their place with the Greens, the Libertarians, the Socialists, and the Veterans' Industrial Party.

This medium levels the playing field for mainstream and fringe candidates, major and peripheral parties, large and small organizations. Consolidation, in short, evens things a bit for players who, because of unequal resources and access, have never before shared the public stage.

HOW THE INTERNET MAY REVERSE THE EFFECTS OF
MONEY ON POLITICS

The 1996 campaign was marked by two occurrences that at first appear unrelated but in fact are entangled: (1) the record flood of money into the campaigns and (2) the arrival of the Web, where money matters little. Throughout this chapter, we have touted the openness of the Internet and made the point that the high participation and low costs go hand in hand. So, while this chapter deals with the broad populist participation in a new medium, the issue of campaign money is never far from sight.

To understand the significance of this point and to appreciate the Web's contribution to broader political participation, it is necessary to know about the influence of big money in the electoral process. In this section, we look briefly at money's influence on politics, and consider how the Internet may help heal this growing canker.

To begin, money has always played a role in politics, but never so much as when media management became the key to electoral survival. Earlier we extolled the Internet as the first exception to the rule of money-equals-public access. Crudely speaking, money buys votes—in Congress, in the White House. Some call it access, but it adds up to the power to put your concerns up front. That being true, how can we expect the beneficiaries of the system to change it?

The refrain is familiar. In today's TV environment, the visibility of political viewpoints depends on the size of campaign coffers. Money buys airtime and print space, phone banks and direct mail in such measure that these costs explain much of the frantic scramble for campaign contributions. Money bestows the power to persuade, the ability to assert an agenda, the threat to chase away would-be rivals in primaries and the general election. Most observers subscribe to this truism: Big money may not ensure success, but inadequate money ensures failure. Candidates without money cannot assert their views, or contribute substantively in the campaign give-and-take, or provide balance in the public dialogue over disputed issues.[12]

To make matters worse for poorly funded candidates, the amount of free media coverage often tracks the amount of paid media, so candidates with more money are twice blessed.[13] Moreover, less media exposure of poorly funded candidates translates into less funding and less exposure, and on it goes in a downward spiral.

A number of proposals have surfaced in recent years to deal with this daunting problem. For one, the Federal Communications Commission (FCC) could mandate free television time for qualified candidates.[14] Such a proposal has legal merit, given that taxpayers own the airwaves and grant the station operators the right to make private profits from a public resource.[15] Networks and station owners don't see it quite that way, and they have bitterly fought any such attempts to impose this requirement, even though they volunteered fragments of time for the major party candidates during the 1996 elections. The networks' gesture, however, does not provide adequate exposure, and it does not deal with the issue of unequal access.

Incumbent lawmakers who oversee the FCC are the primary beneficiaries of the current system, and with little gain for them personally, free network time is not an issue likely to appear soon on the congressional agenda. If networks finally yield more useful blocks of time, it will be the result of the pressures brought by outside interest groups and viewer coalitions, not of government initiatives.

The most often mentioned remedy to funding-related election inequities is to limit the amount of money a candidate can spend on a campaign. While some of the proposals bring together spending limits and free media time, all of the proposals, in effect, would flatten the media access differences among candidates who are not equally funded.

Concerns for political communication are not limited to the candidates. The parties have a huge voice in the political discussion, and with access to "soft money," for which there are no contribution limits, they continue to be particularly potent players. Soft money legally is earmarked for party-building activities, but the concept and the law are so loosely defined that practically any activity that doesn't support a specific candidate can qualify. When even the loose legal definitions get in the way, campaigns, in effect, play a shell game. They spend on items within the legal parameters, thus freeing money to be directed toward other items that might be questionable or patently illegal. Money, after all, is fungible, and soft money is especially so.[16]

The amounts of soft money contributed each year have been growing. The total for the 1992 election was $89 million. That figure jumped to $107 million in 1994, and in 1996 it was over $250 million.[17] In 1996, soft money accounted for 30 percent of all money raised by the parties.[18]

Voters may be struck by the unfair advantage that soft money buys in the public debate, but attempts to limit spending on such public expression have run aground on free speech guarantees of the First Amendment. In the summer of 1996, the U.S. Supreme Court ruled in *Colorado Republican Federal Campaign Committee et al.* v. *Federal Election Commission* that the FEC was limited in its control of the "Party Expenditure Provision." In other words, the FEC could not easily clamp down on party campaign spending. Moreover, the Court left a huge gap in the legal interpretation of what constitutes protected expenditures under the provision.[19] This added to the constitutional protections of spending in political campaigns expressed in a 1976 ruling in *Buckley* v. *Valeo*, where the Supreme Court said there could be no limits on the amount of personal funds candidates spend on their own campaigns.

These rulings cast doubt on any legislation that later may be seen to restrict political speech. With congressional foot-dragging on legislation restricting financial contributions, it doesn't seem likely that the full implications of the Court's decision will be pursued.[20] The novel idea that money is constitutionally protected speech has been characterized by some legal scholars as the worst decision since Dred Scott, but the Court seems unlikely to reverse itself.

So, what are we left with? Better-financed campaigns are better able to dispense their messages, and as long as conventional media and especially television are dominant information tools, that's unlikely to change. Individuals and interest groups, industries and unions with deep pockets can buy better public access, and that, ironically, is protected by a clause in the Bill of Rights engineered to ensure that everyone has a chance to be heard. As it is on Orwell's *Animal Farm*—where everyone is equal except a few who are more equal—in politics, everyone has an even chance to be heard, except those with more money, who have a better-than-even chance. Until now.

And here is where the Internet fits in. The funds required to run a television campaign are not required for the low-budget Web, and so the media-money-and-access cycle, up to now seemingly unbreakable, may be challenged. We have seen in the past few pages that thousands of voices never before audible in the political discussion have, for the first time in an American election, enjoyed a turn at the microphone. Media access, once limited by cost, has been opened. What has happened for peripheral players, some in offbeat groups with off-center philosophies, may also become common on a large scale for serious candidates who reject the system that places money and its ills at the center of electoral politics.

The Internet, in time, may stand nose-to-nose with the big and costly media, the difference between them being that the Net will not demand huge infusions of money, and that can break the lock. Campaigns will require less funding, and thus will be less dependent on and less beholden to moneyed interests. This, of course, is a dreamer's dream, but it is not unthinkable. Where political will has been weak, where legislation has failed and constitutional defenses have prevailed, where market forces have been powerless, the Web may succeed.

CONCLUSION

What happened on the Web was the explosion of diversity, the sudden entrance on the national political stage of a multifarious variety of caucec, claims, and aims. Today, the Internet throbs with a passion for ideologies so varied and dissimilar that it comes close to what the Founding Fathers envisioned when they "held these truths to be self-evident. . . ." One of the leading truths being the trust that out of the clashing current of ideas would come a more reasonable governance.

We began this chapter with an analogy comparing the underground press with the new political sites on the Net. That was, indeed, a prototype for the Web, since a homemade periodical was as inexpensive as the nearest mimeograph machine. But all analogies break down. In this case, the newspapers were not heterogeneous; they were homogeneous, certainly compared with the list of organizations mentioned here.

If underground editors had done a self-portrait, they would have posed as a family of look-alikes. Almost all were anti-establishment in the same tone, influenced by the same social philosophers with the same ideology, graduates of the same sorts of protest leagues. Further, they were convinced that they stood alone. For them, the *New York Times* and the *Washington Post* were as blind and colonialist as the *Wall Street Journal* or the *Chicago Tribune*. However outspoken, unpopular, poorly funded, outrageous, and courageous, most of the underground press was nonetheless run by people of the same stripe ideologically and politically. Editorial protesters were not known for their diversity.

The Web is very different. Thanks to the "democracy of access," any interest group from Planned Parenthood to the National Rifle Association comes aboard to an equitable site at the same affordable rate. And since no one has been barred and no one had been preferred, the groups, leagues, associations, clans, and tribes have jumped on the Web from every point of the social and political compass. That emergence of the Internet with its proliferation of warring ideologies was, of course, the organizational counterpart to the millions of souls who were splicing their PCs into the Web.

The economic conditions that invited in the wonderful variegated crowd of site builders during the campaign may also attenuate a huge problem building in the American political system. Money, the root of so many political evils but so necessary to get access to the American people, may become less of an affliction as campaigns join the multitudes on the Web. It's an outside chance, to be sure, but this low-cost medium may have implications for the political system beyond the transmission of campaign information.

The great distinction of the Web has been its friendliness to the innumerable races, creeds, and multihued interests that use it for their public communication. Here spread out among us in all its various shapes and colors is our modern Tower of Babel, a deliciously democratic confusion of tongues. In the midst of it all, we find in the wonderful new medium a grand collision within the diversity of opinions, conflicts, and prejudices that rock and roll across America.

NOTES

1. According to Robert Hobbes Zakon, Mosaic was released in 1993 and quickly proliferated "at a 341,634% annual growth rate of service traffic." The commercial and government applications, however, did not gear up until 1994.

2. M. T. Moore, "Begging Today, Clinton and Dole Clash on Internet," *USA Today*, July 10, 1996, p. 7A.

3. Save Our Coast and the Citizens' Alliance for the Tunnel Solution (SOC/CATS) set up a site to promote the construction of a tunnel rather than a bypass on Montara Mountain. This issue had drawn national attention since the early 1980s because it pitted a small, underfunded group of environmentalists against deep-pocketed, pro-development forces. The Website promoted the tunnel—the environmentalists' view. The tunnel position received overwhelming public support through a referendum on the November 1996 ballot. URL, http://www.tunnel.org.

4. Jefferson actively promoted citizen involvement and saw the press as an effective stand-in for the people in the chambers of government. When it came to a free press, Jefferson laid it on the line: "The basis of our government being the opinion of the people . . . were it left to me to decide whether we should have a government without newspapers or newspapers without a government, I should not hesitate a moment to prefer the latter" (Thomas Jefferson in a letter to Col. Edward Carrington, Jan. 16, 1787).

5. From an interview on with Charles Kuralt, writer and former CBS correspondent on Mar. 5, 1997.

6. E. B. White, *Essays of E. B. White*, (New York: Harper Colophon, 1977), p. 84.

7. From discussions with party officials on several occasions after the election.

8. Hit counters are software devices that keep track of the number of visitors "hitting" the site. Sites can host onboard counters, or install links with counters at other sites. The counters are known to be quirky, occasionally losing track and "resetting," or simply posting erroneous numbers that do not accurately reflect the number of hits. The author's observations, therefore, are subject to caution. Still, so many sites had only a few hundred hits, even in late October, that it is reasonable to suggest that many sites were not very popular among Web users. Verification of the numbers was difficult because site operators were not eager to confirm the number of hits, particularly low-count sites.

9. National Political Index. URL, http://www.politicalindex.com/sect10.htm. Information taken from the site on Nov. 14, 1996.

10. Adam Rifkin's Activism Links Page. URL, http://www.cs.caltech.edu~adam/LEAD/active_links.html. Information taken from the site on Nov. 5, 1996. Information on the site indicated that it was last changed on Aug. 25, 1996.

11. Project Vote Smart, Links Where You Can Participate. URL, http://www.vote-smart.org/other/participate.html.

12. The money contributed to political campaigns does not come without costs, and for taxpayers, payback can be painful. Many pols dispute this, but empirical analysis shows otherwise. Early in 1997, the Center for Responsive Politics (CRP),

a nonprofit think tank that researches the impact of money on government policy and actions, released the results of a study that demonstrates the relationship between campaign contributions and legislative votes. Take a vote on federal subsidies to the peanut industry, says Nancy Watzman, one of the researchers. In 1996 the House voted 212–209 to retain rich subsidies for agribusiness corporations. Those voting for subsidies received an average of $1,542 from the industry in 1995–1996. Those voting against subsidies received an average of only $152 apiece. That's ten times as much for members supporting industry subsidies. The same trend held true on timber salvage. Members voting in favor of the timber industry received $19,503 apiece. The same with votes on sugar supports (adding 50 cents to to the cost of a five-pound bag) and cable deregulation, passing on a 10 percent rise in home bills. That vote on cable featured a ratio of 7 to 1 in dollars destined for pro-cable members of Congress versus pro-consumers. (The CRP research reports many instances of correlations between money donated and legislative votes. Four are reported in the *San Francisco Chronicle*, Mar. 3, 1997, p. 8. The CRP's Website is filled with information about money in politics—http://www.crp.org/index.html.ssi.) The CRP conclusion: contributions and votes are linked. (While the correlation between contributions and votes is undeniable, the causal realtionship is in dispute. One explanation is that recipients of campaign contributions vote in accordance with contributors' wishes—the money buys the vote. An alternative explanation holds that contributors give to members who share their philosophies. They, naturally, wish to advance the candidacy of people friendly to their point of view, and this is reflected in their contributions. This explanation proposes no vote buying, no quid pro quo.)

13. M. Rosenberg, "The Power of Advocacy Advertising in Newspapers," *Editor & Publisher* (Feb. 11, 1995), 48.

14. The effectiveness of such an approach is not universally accepted. Marvin Kalb, a former CBS reporter and now director of the Joan Shorenstein Barone Center on the Press, Politics and Public Policy at Harvard, sees the free time only as an opportunity for candidates to do more of what they already are doing in their short clips on the evening news. "Nothing indicates that . . . stretching a sound bite from eight seconds to two minutes is going to change the essence of what the candidates are saying." Quoted in Edward Epstein, "Free TV Time Could Change the Face of Campaigning," *San Francisco Chronicle*, May 15, 1996, p. A4. In the same article, Kathleen Hall Jamieson of the Annenberg School of Communication at the University of Pennsylvania said that the format of the appearances must be controlled. She agrees with Kalb that an unstructured few minutes will lead to nothing more than a long campaign commercial. She argues for question-and-answer sessions or reporter-directed discussions to focus the candidates on the issues.

15. This position is laid out in G. Selnow, and R. Gilbert, *Society's Impact on Television: How the Viewing Public Shapes Television Programming* (Westport, CT: Praeger, 1993).

16. For information about money in politics, contact the Center for Responsive Politics, 13320 19th St., N.W., Washington, DC 20036 (202) 857–0044. Information for this discussion was taken from L. Makinson, *Follow the Money Handbook* (Washington, DC: Center for Responsive Politics, 1994).

17. D. E. Rosenbaum, "In Political Money Game, the Year of Big Loopholes," *New York Times*, Dec. 26, 1996, p. A1.

18. Taken from a reprinted *Newsday* article, "Republicans Widen Money Lead over Rivals, FEC Report Shows," *San Francisco Chronicle*, Mar. 27, 1997, p. A7.

19. Information from the Legal Information Institute and Project Hermes (http://supct.law.cornell.edu/supct/html/95–489.ZS.html) and a discussion with Lisa Rosenberg, director of the FEC Watch Project at the CRP.

20. Current limitations on campaign fund-raising have been summarized by the *New York Times*. Corporate contributions to candidates for president and Congress have been outlawed since 1907; contributions from labor unions have been prohibited since 1943. The 1974 law passed in response to Watergate limits individuals to total contributions of $25,000 a year to federal candidates and no more than $2,000 per candidate ($1,000 each for a primary and general election). The law allows individual donations of $20,000 to a political party and $5,000 to political action committees, which are formed usually by business, labor, or ideological groups to raise money and distribute it to candidates supporting their interests.

The 1974 law also provides for government grants to presidential candidates. Federal money matching that raised by the candidates is provided to them during the presidential primaries. A lump sum is given to the candidates in the general election. Candidates who accept the government grants agree not to exceed spending limits—a specific sum based on population for each state in the primaries and the lump sum ($62 million apiece in 1996) in the general election.

Chapter Five

Experiments on the Web:
Information Innovations

Who are to be the electors of the federal representatives? Not the
rich, more than the poor; not the learned, more than the ignorant;
not the haughty heirs of distinguished names, more than the humble
sons of obscure and unpropitious fortune. The electors are the great
body of the people of the United States.

— *James Madison*

INTRODUCTION

The donkey and the elephant were parties to a paradox in 1996. Both
used the Internet, if only marginally, to impact voters and both, in turn,
were impacted, if only a little, by voters using the Internet. The parties,
like the thousands of other site operators, large and small, during the
campaign experimented to learn something about format possibilities
and audience appetites for political information on this new medium.

Few observers would argue that the Internet was a smashing success
in the political campaign. There is no indication that it changed many
votes or boosted one candidate over another in photo-finish races. Some
site operators hoped to increase the salience of politics among American
voters, but there isn't much evidence of that happening either—that this
presidential election had the lowest voter turnout in three-quarters of a
century.

So, was this experiment at politics in cyberspace a failure? Far from it.
Even though the outcomes may have been less than convincing, the activities provided a valuable test of a new information source. Media
scholar Ben Bagdikian wrote: "To give citizens a choice in ideas and

information is to give them a choice in politics."[1] If nothing else, the experiment in 1996 was about choice, spreading before the voters a range of new options that expanded the choices in politics. This chapter examines some of the innovations that site developers hoped would bring voters new information and deliver conventional information in new ways.

POLLS AND SURVEYS

Polling has been part of politics for more than 60 years, and academic researchers have been gathering data from voters and candidates even longer than that. Until the Web came along, the public dissemination of poll results had fallen to research analysts and reporters. The analysts crunched the numbers and prepared the reports, the journalists synthesized the reports and published the results in news stories. The public got the results in a familiar package of narratives and tables.

This sports-crazed society likes poll results nearly as much as it likes box scores and batting averages, and accordingly, political survey stories have found an audience. Hardly a day goes by during an election without a story about the horse race or the political leanings of the public mind. The poll stories often are accompanied by reports describing surveys of public officials, candidates, campaign staffers, and others in the political limelight. Research is reductive, packaging in neat bundles the views of those who cast the votes and those who seek the votes; stories revealing the results have become staples of political coverage. All that will continue, but the Web can now deliver information directly to voters and sidestep the analysts.

Two categories of survey data surfaced on the Web in 1996: summary data and individual-level data. In addition, for the first time entire survey research data sets were made available for downloading by anyone interested in conducting an analysis. We look here at these three items.

Summary Data

Summary data are the results tables usually found in conventional news stories that report the findings of a poll. Sites offering such information provide the results of surveys in frequency distributions, or counts of responses for each answer, and crosstabulations—counts of responses for each answer broken down by group. A crosstab, for instance, would provide the separate breakdown of responses for men and women or for young, middle-aged, and older voters.

Organizations posted on their sites polling data obtained from the general population and from specific groups. For instance, the Gallup and Roper organizations offered data from their national voter opinion polls.

Table 1
Project Vote Smart (PVS) Results for Congressional Responses to the Balanced Budget Amendment Question

	Yes	No	Undecided	Didn't Answer
All respondents	56.8	30.9	7.6	4.7
All men	58.9	30.6	5.6	4.9
All women	46.1	32.2	17.8	3.9
All republicans	92.9	1.8	1.8	3.5
All democrats	34.8	50.7	7.2	7.2
All third parties	47.2	37.3	11.5	3.9
Republican incumbents	95.7	1.7	0.0	2.6
Democrat incumbents	38.2	54.4	0.0	7.4
Republican challengers	91.1	1.8	3.0	4.2
Democrat challengers	33.7	49.5	9.6	7.2
All incumbents	72.9	22.3	0.0	4.8
All challengers	53.0	32.9	9.3	4.7

Source: http://www.vote-smart.org.

Their sites offered tables of summary statistics and stories about the findings.

As for surveys of more defined populations, Project Vote Smart (PVS), for instance, provided results from a survey it conducted among candidates for public office, and it released its results at two levels: first, as summary data, similar to the results of opinion polls by Gallup and Roper; second, as we discuss next, as individual-level data.

The nonprofit PVS has run the National Political Awareness Test for the past few elections, and in the early days, provided the results over the phone and in brochures to voters and the press. In 1996, it installed the data on a site called The Virtual 105th Congress. PVS described the survey this way: "Project Vote Smart has interviewed 1,034 candidates running for Congress on the issues they are most likely to face if elected. The numbers in these charts represent what percentage of respondents in each break-out category selected that option on the National Political Awareness Test (NPAT)."[2] Table 1, taken from the PVS Website, shows the candidates' responses for the question "Do you support amending the U.S. Constitution to require an annual balanced federal budget?"

Although the Websites often provided summary data that were more complete than data published in magazines and newspapers, their layouts usually resembled the layouts found in conventional print media.

Individual-Level Data

As the name implies, this technique reports the answers of individual respondents in surveys conducted most often among political candidates. In these cases, voters generally are interested in answers provided by respondents they know or in whom they have a special interest— their own member of Congress, say, or the leadership.

In the PVS study, each candidate was identified with his/her responses, so visitors were able to search out the candidates that most interested them without having to plow through piles of unwanted details. The interactive Web presentation adds selectivity to these often large and unwieldy databases.

A number of nonprofits, such as Politics by the Numbers, Voter Information Services, Inc., and the League of Conservation Voters, reported individual responses to their surveys of the major candidates. In one of the most ambitious efforts, the Christian Coalition examined the voting records of incumbents on 15 key conservative issues.[3] Although not a standard pen-and-ink survey, it was a systematic gathering of individual-level behavioral information easily configured in standard database format. The study noted the member's agreement or disagreement with the Coalition's position, and scored each vote accordingly.[4]

The entire Christian Coalition database contained nearly 7,400 entries, too many to report in a newspaper or news magazine (forget broadcast), but a snap to report on the Web. Voters could run an easy search to find the positions of their members of Congress, and, as with PVS's information, they could search for any candidate in the country. The Web allows universal access to the entire database and thus dissolves regional limitations and frees voters to look beyond local campaigns.

Downloading an Entire Database

In addition to allowing visitors to browse individual data, some sites made it possible to download an entire data set. With these data installed on personal computers, users can examine a single record—say the response from one candidate, or summary statistics from all participants. While so much raw information may not concern most voters, it can be intensely interesting to journalists, interest groups, academics, and campaigns that have the capacity to conduct statistical analyses. With the complete data set, specialists can analyze raw data on their own and pull out information that has not been available until now.

Moreover, several databases can be merged into one large database for even more detailed analysis. For instance, with a little tinkering, the PVS database and the Christian Coalition database could be merged to determine how incumbents agreeing or disagreeing with the Christian Coalition answered the National Political Awareness Test. This would help Congress watchers track voting patterns and develop more accurate predictive models for the likely passage of certain legislation.

The capacity of the Web to transfer large data sets will likely spawn innovative research over the next few years. One experiment, run in 1996, was called America's Voice. It placed on the Web a large survey database designed for journalists, academics, and interest groups. Anyone could access the information, but the 12-megabyte file was a disk hog, and deciphering it required knowledge of statistical analysis procedures. These limitations made it less useful for average voters. Easier-access versions are planned for future presidential campaigns.[5]

This research reported telephone interviews of 1,500 randomly selected respondents who gave spontaneous answers to a few very simple questions: "What advice would you give Bill Clinton or Bob Dole if you could sit down over coffee with him and talk freely? Given the chance, what question would you ask each candidate?" The result was freewheeling conversations, from a national sample of voters who discussed the questions *they* would like to ask, and the advice *they* would like to offer the major presidential candidates. More than 1,000 pages of data were coded and prepared in Microsoft Access files.

From these files, users with some knowledge of Access could examine statistical summaries, review key phrases from the conversations, and read the entire interview of each respondent. They also could sort the interviews by respondent demographics and category of response. The mountain of material could not have been made available without the Internet.[6]

In the next few years, data from interviews, polls, and research of all kinds will make their way to the Web in searchable form for interactive use. This public availability of source information will have several implications for the news media and especially for journalists who report what the numbers mean.

For one, the media won't have the final word. Reports and stories, based on interpretations by journalists and researchers, will be dissected as others with access to the source data analyze the results for themselves. As it is today, most newspaper and broadcast stories that cover polls report what the numbers "mean," but meanings are subjective. With Internet primacy, the interpretations will be open to cross-examination. This is salutary because poll stories often present open-and-shut cases, whereas in reality the numbers they use so impressively can be interpreted to yield different conclusions. Reporters and pollsters will have to anticipate that people will second-guess their stories as they examine the results from different perspectives.

The second implication is closely related. The availability of raw data means that average voters can get in the act. Uninterpreted data from many sources can help voters size up a candidate on key issues, and they also can effect the agenda on which they make electoral decisions. As McCombs and Shaw reported in the early 1970s, traditionally the press, and to a smaller degree the campaigns, have had a big hand in setting the voters' agenda by telling people what's important.[7] Both are likely to continue their influence, but their strength will ebb with the availability of narrow interest sites and primary research data. The process of personal agenda-setting will increase with the availability of raw data and the sophistication of search engines.

How will this happen? Today, voters who read a news story based on the PVS data are exposed to an agenda set by the reporter, whose agenda, in turn, may have been set by a PVS press release. This has a homogenization effect: all audiences are exposed to the same lineup of issues. But, with direct access to the raw database, voters can examine only the issues in which they have a particular interest and ignore the rest.

Let's say some people examine the candidate's views on the balanced budget, but skip a dozen other issues that form a complete picture of the candidate and a total view of policy matters that will concern the officeholder. Won't the news stories and other information provide that balance? Perhaps, but the profile of news exposure may change in the next few years as voters are drawn away from the spectrum of issues now presented in the mainstream press and toward the narrow bandwidth of personal concerns as they chase down special interests on the Web.

The availability of raw data stands along with other targeting features of the Web to realign the public agenda. Voters pursuing only the issues that hold personal appeal tend to come away with a restricted view of the big picture and of the topics that affect other people. This may lead to diminished empathy with other voters, an erosion of the sense of community, and a failure to see the ties between issues in public policy. We look at this critical issue more closely in Chapter 8.

The third implication of raw data on the Web is that journalists will have more information from which to assemble a story. With the America's Voice data, for instance, reporters writing about character issues of the presidential candidates could weave into the story a thread from the voters' perspective. They could report which character traits concerned voters most and why they were a concern. They could integrate statistics about voter thinking, using quotations that exemplify the views expressed. They also could break down responses by voter demographics to show commonalities or divisions within the population. A writer on the *Charlotte Observer* could evaluate voter views from North Carolina and compare them with the views of California and New York voters. Such custom analysis can add a new dimension to political reporting, and it will become more common with the increase of Web-delivered data.[8] But simultaneously, this burden of riches will require reporters to develop new skills with which to extract the information. Perhaps reporters will learn to rely less on expert interpretations and more on their own reckoning of source data.

RELEASE OF CAMPAIGN CONTRIBUTION DATA

A few forward-looking cities in 1996 experimented with the electronic filing of campaign contribution reports. It was only a start, but it demonstrated one of the most promising applications of Web technology in the release of political information. The wisdom of electronic filing is seen most clearly in light of the huge increase in the flow of money into American politics.

The 1996 campaigns for president and Congress took in and spent more than $2 billion.[9] Not only was this a record-breaking sum, but it was nearly twice the amount spent in any other election.[10]

Although Republicans outspent the Democrats, both parties took in record amounts, and both major candidates became embroiled in campaign finance scandals.[11] The parties ran effective damage control that convinced the public that the scandals were minor, and by Election Day, voters came away thinking that these incidents were just a few more examples of politicians being politicians.

For many critics, the amount of money, where it comes from, where it goes, and what it actually buys are the real scandal in American politics. Two years before the 1996 election, Bill Clinton and Newt Gingrich shook hands on a pact to reform campaign finance laws, and the Congress even examined legislation to bring it about. But by election time, the leaders forgot their vows, and a Senate filibuster stopped the legislation cold.[12] So many ills in this democracy are seen as a direct results of dollars chasing influence and favorable legislation, that it is stunning to see the perennial defeat of campaign finance reform legislation.

As the Internet becomes more popular, maybe something can be done. One simple but elegant idea, noted above, is the electronic filing and reporting of campaign finance data. In short, electronic filing puts on a Website all the campaign financial data now reported on paper, and makes it easily searchable and downloadable in standard database format. The wisdom of electronic filing is based on something Arthur Hays Sulzberger once said about public information. In a discussion of the newspaper business he said, "We tell the public which way the cat is jumping and the public will take care of the cat." Tell the public where the money is coming from and where it's going, and maybe the public will take care of campaign finance offenses.

How does electronic filing work? Instead of submitting financial information on standard, paper forms as they do now, candidates prepare the data on a computer file that then can be installed on a central Website. Within hours of the filing deadlines, the registrar or other agency posts the data on-line, enabling visitors to run on-line searches. In addition, they can download the results of a search, or the entire set of records, for further analysis on personal computers.

The bugs are already worked out and electronic filing is ready to go, but, to hear some tell it, the process is too difficult and needs more testing. That's not so. Electronic reports pose no greater burden. Inexpensive, tested software is in the box, ready to ship with the morning mail.

Electronic files allow campaign watch groups and voters to analyze information with an ease and sophistication not possible with the current paper-based data. Analysts could spend days with paper forms and never discover information that they could find in just minutes of electronic research. They can scan all receipts and disbursements and examine who has been giving how much to whom. They can even compare the records of contributors and lobbyists against those of the candidates—a cross-check procedure that otherwise would take months of painstaking work.

To sense the value of this process, look at how people now have to examine campaign finance data. In 1991, before electronic filing was mandated in San Francisco, this writer wandered into the records section of City Hall to meet an investigative reporter who was examining financial records for an article on campaign funding practices. An employee of the registrar's office opened a double-locked door to a caged-in room where banks of file cabinets lined the walls. On a worn pine table in the middle of the room, the reporter leaned into a small canyon of documents and painstakingly copied columns of numbers on a yellow legal pad. He had been working for nearly five hours but still had only a fragment of the information he needed. With such plodding work, it's no wonder that in-depth, investigative pieces about campaign finances haven't been as common as you might expect, given the importance of the subject.

Since 1992, San Francisco has been one of a handful of cities to require electronic filing. With the data on-line, the reporter with a laptop can find the statistics in less than a minute. He can do the job from his living room, his Honda, or the corner bar. The easy access to campaign finance data might not produce stories as exciting as sex scandals, but it could make them as common, to the great benefit of the commonweal. The public visibility of these records would be the first step to finance reform.

To sum up, electronic data on the Web are not merely a convenience. They do more than save a trip to Washington or City Hall, although that alone is reason enough to implement the plan more broadly than the few cities now mandating it, and the few states now considering it. It puts the raw campaign finance data in the public's hands as soon as it is submitted, well before Election Day.

The other advantage goes to the analysts and number crunchers. Easy sorts and searches on the Website allow quick, more accurate, and more sophisticated analysis of downloaded data, making this approach a lot friendlier than the old paper system. It's the difference between horse-and-buggy transportation and a rocket to the moon. Not only is the rocket faster than the horse, but it can go places the horse cannot.

The forward-looking jurisdictions that already mandate electronic filing demonstrate conclusively that the process works. In the absence of campaign reform, and in the face of a whittled-down Federal Election Commission, whose funding the Congress has cynically cut in the past several years, the Web can go a long way toward letting voters know which way the fat cats are jumping. This offers the best hope for voters to keep tabs on the people who contribute big money and on the politicians who spend it.[13]

EXPLOITING INTERACTIVITY

We have discussed feedback and interactivity elsewhere, but this unique feature is so inherently a part of the Internet that without it, the medium would be no more than a poster board. Descriptions of interactivity are therefore marbled throughout many discussions, as in this section, where we look at how upline information, more than any other feature, stands to alter the flow of political infomation. Here, we focus on how Web sites in 1996 experimented with interactivity as they sought to bring the voter more fully into the give-and-take of a political discussion.

Ten years of experience with video games and interactive learning programs has taught communicators the value of involving an audience. Active communication holds the users' attention, it engages them intellectually, and it is more gratifying emotionally. From the outset, the major campaigns saw the value of interactivity, and integrated it aggressively into their sites. Jeff Meyers, director of information systems for the Dole campaign, and Dick Bell, interactive media director for the Democratic National Committee, reported early in 1996 that interactivity would be central to their sites, leading them to discover activities that held visitors' interests and kept them on the site.

Quite often, interactivity on a Website was used to bait visitors. Interactive sites used games, posters, and other devices to get people on the site, thereby exposing them to other information. Sometimes it was a political message, sometimes an advertisement. Consider the following examples.

Poll and Quiz Sites

U.S. News baited visitors with a political quiz. "Here's your opportunity to find the candidate who thinks like you do. U.S. News Online has compiled candidates' positions on 10 campaign issues. Answer these questions and meet your dream candidate—the results may surprise you."

Questions covered current events such as the balanced budget amendment and U.S. involvement in Bosnia. Visitors weak on the issues could click on hypertext for background information. Several seconds after visitors submitted their answers, the site came back with the name of the "dream" candidate.

CNN and *Time's* AllPolitics page offered a Candidate Rate-O-Matic. (That had to be the most retro title on the Web.) It functioned like the *U.S. News* site. Visitors were told to "Gauge your personal opinions by answering the questions below, and the Rate-O-Matic will come up with the perfect . . . okay, okay . . . the best match for you." Answer 23 questions, then click on Find My President.[14] Rate-O-Matic then responded with the name of the candidate whose views you agreed with most often.

Congressional Quarterly prepared a political poll. The site asked visitors to identify their House or Senate member, and then to agree or disagree with ten key issues. Here, too, visitors who were confused by a given issue could click for additional information. Responses were instantly compared with the actual votes of the senator or representative.

The *U.S. News*, AllPolitics, *Congressional Quarterly*, and other sites that matched up voter and candidate were favorite games. But it isn't hard to imagine a day when similar sites attempt the more serious business of guiding voters toward real electoral decisions. They may list a more complete array of issues and weight their importance to each voter. They may offer tutorials, commentaries, and opinion pieces that suggest how the voter should lean on any issue. Then, they could match a voter's concerns with a candidate's record, whether for president, member of Congress, mayor, or votes on ballot measures. Once a match was made—in heaven or in hell—the sites could print out a checklist for convenient reference in the voting booth.

Is this far-fetched? Bear in mind that we use tests for all manner of decisions, practical or trivial. Look at the SATs, GREs, MCATs, LCATs, psychological tests, and job placement measures. Multiple-choice tests tell students the disciplines for which they are best suited, tests tell employers which applicants to hire and which to turn away. Why wouldn't a test-conditioned public, which doesn't care much about politics in the first place, find it convenient to identify electoral choices by answering a handful of questions and letting the computer pick the candidate? There's a lot here to lose sleep over, but it's unlikely we'll get through another election without someone coming up with a fuller and more serious version of the Rate-O-Matic.

The San Jose Mercury News's Wonk Corner posted five new questions every week ("Take the test and see if you're qualified to be running a think tank, or need to go back to civics class."). *The Boston Globe* produced a one-page trivia test with tongue in cheek (E.g., "In Berlin, which president unintentionally said 'I am a jelly doughnut' when he meant to say, 'I am a Berliner?' "). The S.H.O.E. Poll (Strategic Harassment of Electorate) asked you to "bare your sole and stand up and be counted." Then it proposed to match nine recent presidential candidates with their running mates. This site, whose only apparent purpose was to produce bad footwear puns, promised to send the results to the candidates and the media "so they remain instep with America."

Several features were common to the many poll and quiz sites—good or bad. For one, each actively involved visitors. They had to fill in a blank, check a square, or click on hypertext. Most sites also identified issues—however trivial—and thereby had the effect of setting an agenda, underlining what people think is important in a campaign. Paraphrasing Bernard Cohen, the list of questions may not tell voters what to think so much as it tells them what to think about.[15] The result: shape the voter's options simply by raising certain issues and ignoring others.

Many sites provided links to additional information. Such tutoring is a bane for survey research because it influences respondents, but if visitor education is the objective, it isn't a bad idea. Together with the questions, the tutorials form an interactive one-two punch. The questions flag knowledge gaps, and the tutorials provide short courses. How many people turned to this information is unknown, but information focused on key issues may be a benefit to a notoriously ill-informed electorate.

Fun-and-Games Sites

If you thought the polls and quizzes were fun, batten down the hatches for the political games. These sites pushed interactivity to the limit, and they usually succeeded in creating pages as exciting as a midterm exam. They often relied on the tried-and-true Q&A format, which by the end of the campaign was wearing pretty thin. But some sites were educational, and many offered an interesting, if not wild and crazy, pastime heavy on data and light on entertainment.

A large number of these sites dealt with the federal budget, a natural for political games. The Third Millennium organization, for instance, put up a Balance the Budget Game that challenged visitors to estimate the proportion of the $1.5 trillion federal budget spent in nine categories.[16] Players keyed in their estimates, submitted the answers, and received a score and a comparison of their answers with actual government statistics.

The Center for Community Economic Research (CCER) at UC-Berkeley offered The National Budget Simulation, where visitors could make budget decisions to balance federal spreadsheets in a year: "This simple simulation should give you a better feel of the trade-offs which citizens and policy makers will need to make to balance the budget." Along with the game, the CCER provided basic budget information and links to related sites. Other universities offered similar games, some on site, some requiring the visitor to download software to a personal computer. At the very least, this drill forces citizens to face the hard truth of such trade-offs as whether to increase the defense budget at the inevitable expense of, say, the welfare budget.

Developers eager to push the technology experimented with a range of games, most of which had an educational bent. Here are a few:

- *iguide* asked visitors to match the candidates with their sound bites.

- *Carmelnet* had visitors write news stories by filling in the blanks of a puzzle.

- *Pathfinder* posted a budget-based game that involved not only interaction on the Website but also research, on-line chats, virtual voting, and other activities that culminated just before the election. "At the end of the game the final results will be presented to Congress and the nation at a press conference in Washington, D.C. Your voice will be heard in the corridors of power."[17]

- *Trillium Software* developed a downloadable shareware program that let visitors make their "own projection of the outcome of the election for the entire USA and every state. You tell it who the candidates are, how well the economy is doing, whether the parties are united or divided, and it forecasts the November election."[18]

- *The Landmark Project* developed an ambitious educational site designed to meet five goals:
1. Promote exploration and examination of information related to the issues of the 1996 presidential campaigns using digital information tools (word processing, spreadsheets, databases, and Internet navigation). 2. Develop digital information processing skills. 3. Using databases, spreadsheets, word processing, and electronic information retrieval as tools to assist in making decisions. 4. Promote an awareness of how digital information is used in political campaigns. 5. Promote an awareness of how digital information can be used by voters.

An impressive integration of skills went into the Landmark Project, and once accessed, it required much more from thoughtful visitors than a few mouse clicks.[19]

Whatever the range of game sites, from the silly to the serious, they all had audience interactivity in common. Not since radio listeners played with crystal sets in the 1920s has there been as much public curiosity about a new media feature, namely, the upline information suddenly available on the Internet.

This was fed, in part, when the spotlight focused on formats, not content; this was often the case. The game sites marked success by how many people played their games and how much data the sites collected. As for the lessons visitors took away or the number of souls converted by the po:'tical catechism, they either didn't care or were too busy to find out. The technicians were still at work in 1996; it wasn't yet time to talk about effects.

The problem with these sites—if indeed it was a problem (except for a spoiled and pampered population whose expectations have been honed on high-speed video games)—was that they ran in "batch," not interactively. The difference? In batch mode you assemble the entire program, then submit it all at once. In the interactive mode, the computer reacts to each response as soon as the visitor enters it. Batch mode is like a personal letter where you say everything you want to say, mail it, then wait for the recipient to send back a response. The interactive mode is like a conversation where each comment is met with a reply.

No question about it, the batch mode is the weak link in all the interactive sites; the game sites just highlight the weakness. In time, with faster transmission speeds and faster computers at both ends, the interactive mode will become more common and Website interactions will be a lot more interesting. Even in batch, though, many of the political sites were engaging, if only for their novelty.[20]

THE WEB PROVIDED A FORUM FOR NEWS AND INFORMATION

1996 was the time to pile on information, news, commentary, reports from major politcal events, any tidbit, no matter how small or inconsequential. With few space or cost limitations, developers loaded up the sites, often without much thought about the purpose or effects of their messages. The philosophy was simple: dump the information on the Web because someone, somewhere might want it. And if they don't, so what?

The outcome was a blended heap of stories, observations, critiques, and analyses that individually may have enlightened, but collectively had the effect of being buried under 200 pounds of turkey feathers. Even the best search engines failed to resolve the tangled pile, according to some observers. Too much information had become as troublesome as too little.

The on-line databases, polls, games, and other interactive ventures often grabbed the spotlight, but the information sites dominated the political corner of the Web. They became the workhorses of media, interest groups, and campaigns.

To mention only a fraction of the sites in this category: the networks —NBC, CBS and ABC; newspapers—the *Washington Post, New York Times, Boston Globe, Los Angeles Times, Denver Post*; the mainstream and fringe political parties and related committees; political news sites— PoliticsNow, PoliticsUSA, Project Vote Smart; organizations—there were hundreds, from the National Rifle Association to Greenpeace. (See Chapter 4 for lists of organizational categories.)

The assortment of news and information sites was like a cyberversion of the main newsstand at Grand Central Station, which at one time boasted more current events information per square foot than any place on the planet. Every inch of countertop and wall space in that stand was covered by a newspaper or magazine. Only a tiny island of breath mints and cheap cigars was spared. On the Web in 1996, the newspapers and magazines, reports, personal observations, and other news and information sites covering politics would have filled not just the Grand Central newsstand but Grand Central itself.

The sites maintained by conventional media, information firms, government, nonprofits, special interests, and individuals offered hard news and commentary, wacky reports and silly critiques. It was a blend of the conventional and the unorthodox, but it wasn't always easy to tell which was which. Web users report getting sucked into believing an article, only to have it strike them midway through that the writer was a crackpot or the site was a spoof. The Dole Pineapple site got more than a few people.

The news and informaton sites ran continually through the campaign, but many of them became especially busy on three occasions: during the conventions, at the debates, and on Election Night. That's no surprise. On the same occasions, the conventional media go into a frenzy, so the industry is spring-loaded and the public is well conditioned to expect media dog-and-pony shows. On the Web, that's what they got.

Conventions

The San Diego and Chicago conventions were the first in many years where the nominees were a foregone conclusion. Political conventions used to be worth the price of admission. Not since the violent 1968 Democratic National Convention in Chicago has there been a truly spontaneous convention, but 1996 was a drowsy stage play, the blandest in recent political history.

Scripts-prevent-slips mentality in both camps led to drum-tight direction of every event. Participants in both conventions marched through their paces like troops on a drill field, every speech was timed to the minute, every Sousa tune synchronized to the tapping of a schoolmarm's baton. Spontaneity was a four-letter word. But, even with real excitement wrung from the conventions, many Websites, like the major national media, played up the events as through they were the greatest shows on earth.

Weeks in advance, the major sites—CBS, *USA Today*, PoliticsNow, AllPolitics, and the rest—staged convention setup pieces. The focus of some Web pages was not the activities of the conventions but the format of the sites—they didn't promote the convention so much as they promoted the means by which they would cover the convention. This was, after all, the first time that the media could invite voter participation, and they took advantage of the opportunity.

CBS hyped its real audio and video feeds, tempting visitors to take the site to the convention floor, where they could experience the excitement firsthand, moment by moment. Pity the poor soul who didn't realize how painful it would be to watch the CBS camera locked on the podium, transmitting a nerve-racking few images per second. MSNBC promised spine-tingling coverage and invited visitors to the convention chat rooms. Other sites prepared visitors with speaker bios, schedules, and the ubiquitous cyberpolls. Get ready, get set for the big conventions that—barring Mrs. O'Leary's cow kicking over another lantern to create some excitement in Chicago—didn't have a chance of offering much of real interest to American audiences.

It didn't take the public long to get wise to the conventions' painful blandness, and many ducked out. Website operators reported hundreds of thousands of convention hits, pretty encouraging until you realize that the on-line audience was some 40 million strong. Convention site visitors most likely were political enthusiasts and technology buffs curious about the first convention covered in cyberspace. Being part of history, no matter how dull the event, has its own attraction.

The major media and political party sites posted an impressive amount of information in the schedules and speech texts, platform positions, commentaries, news releases, and facts about the convention, the conventioneers, the convention halls, the convention souvenirs, the convention bus schedules. It was a virtual convention trivia fest.

Many of the speeches, schedules, and other data were posted on sites run by both the political parties and the media, and this sometimes blurred distinctions among the site operators. The DNC even ran ads for Sun Microsystems, AT&T, CNN, and other commercial companies, and assumed a decidedly commercial look.

The CBS convention site had links to 18 video clips of conventions going back to 1948. They included footage of Harry Truman, John Kennedy, and Ronald Reagan accepting their party's nomination. They showed Chicago police wrestling Mike Wallace to the convention floor, and for real excitement, they stocked clips of the police shoving around Dan Rather. CBS also included an extraordinary clip of Congresswoman Barbara Jordan's 1976 convention speech, perhaps one of the most spell-binding political speeches to be delivered in decades.

Soon after the Democratic National Convention, it became evident that the voters would not develop an interest in this campaign, with or without the Web. Public lethargy in American politics is nothing new, but the apathy in 1996 reached new proportions for a modern presidential election.[21]

As a point of explanation, the America's Voice poll found two possible reasons. First, people were generally satisfied with the course of the country. We weren't at war, our cities were relatively calm, no issue towered in the public mind, and most important, the economy was humming along. Unemployment and inflation were down, and the stock market was up. Corporate layoffs aroused some concern, and many people worked two jobs to make one salary; nevertheless, public confidence was strong and, consequently, interest in the political elections was weak. Angry, fearful, driven people closely follow elections and go to the polls, but these were not the emotions of the electorate in 1996. The poll also found that people looked to small, local, and personal issues, and they were not much stimulated by larger national concerns. Voters played this election close to home.

Debates

The candidates learned important lessons from the bitter political fights plaguing Washington from the Gingrich revolution of 1994 to the counterrevolution of 1996. The spark came from the government shut-downs around Christmas 1995. Voters were angered by the sights of politicians carrying on like school yard bullies, shouting at each other and refusing to compromise. As Maine Republican Senator Olympia Snowe remarked, "All they see is kids bickering in the sandbox."[22] So for the learned candidates, name-calling and public confrontations were out; decorum and the show of cooperation were in. The risk of public indifference was greatest for Bob Dole, who needed a charged-up public. Nonetheless, he, along with Bill Clinton and the veeps, took the vow of civility. Very few voters complained that the candidates were not well behaved.[23]

Making nice is what people say they want, but when candidates make nice, voters go to sleep.[24] Campaign 1996 thus evolved into a wearisome and villainless skit. Voters, whose sense of excitement had been culti-vated by theatrical blockbusters and envelope-pushing TV dramas, were not much interested in the overcivil, overscripted campaigns.

Undaunted by the voters' indifference to the conventions and the ongoing campaign, Websites billed the presidential debates like a Hollywood extravaganza. They approached the three debates (two presidential and one vice presidential) with the same passion that they approached the conventions, promising great coverage, excitement, and involvement. To be sure, a few sites offered real audio, and most hyped interactive amusements—chat rooms, questions for the candidates, ratings of the performances—hoping something would grab an audience and hold it in place. Some sites measured voters' interest in key issues through on-line surveys and hinted that these responses would somehow figure into moderator Jim Lehrer's questions to the candidates. There is no evidence that visitor-derived information ever got to Lehrer or, if it did, that he used it.

Digital Equipment Corporation adapted a Madison Avenue survey technique used to measure audience reactions to TV spots. Digital set up an on-line version that took the audience pulse at 10-second intervals throughout the debate. Preselected visitors were asked to click "approve" or "disapprove" to gauge which of the candidates' answers hit pay dirt. Thirty minutes after the debates, Digital posted audience reaction to each answer.

The instant tabulation of Website feedback holds promise as a useful assessment tool for political themes, TV ads, speeches, and other items now tested in focus groups. Digital's sampling technique needs work, but its successful test of the technology demonstrates an extraordinary application for the medium in venues like the debates.

Like conventional media, many of the media on the Web examined debate styles and strategies, handicapped the outcomes, and sized up the odds that Dole and Kemp would take off the gloves. Sites often used boxing analogies to promote debate coverage, as though billing verbal fisticuffs might stimulate voter interest. It didn't work. Websites didn't draw much of an audience, but neither did other media. Television ratings for the debates were dismal, in fact the lowest ever for the presidential and vice presidential contests. But, as they say in Hollywood, "only" ain't so bad if it runs into 70 million. Web audiences, however, ran only into the thousands.

Election Night

Then, in the final breath of the 1996 election, something remarkable happened in cyberspace: on Election Night, Web traffic was so heavy that gridlock beset some of the major sites. Such a wonderful mess! PoliticsNow, MSNBC, AllPolitics, and a handful of others turned away users, and for visitors who could get in, moving through many sites was plodding at best. MSNBC saw its hit rate increase fivefold; to handle the extra load, it increased its computer servers by 50 percent—and still it could not meet demand.[25] Such success! PoliticsNow had a shutdown between the East and West Coasts, a problem that, in part, may have been due to the heavy traffic. What a night and what an ending for Web coverage of a campaign that earlier was so disappointing!

Only the largest, most promoted sites faced this bittersweet problem,[26] but their experiences on Election Night were testament to the popularity of the medium and a foreshadowing of the demand for information. What drew the crowd was the immediate posting of returns.

The sites heaped on huge piles of data and let the visitors sort through them. For the first time in 40 years, people could avoid television's run-down of races that didn't interest them as they searched for the results they wanted. These sites displayed the Web's strongest features: its capacity for large quantities of data and its usefulness in allowing people to flag for themselves the things that most interested them. Information-targeting is this medium's greatest asset, and the story on Election Night offers the strongest example yet of its success.

Visitors did not look for commentary and analysis as much as they looked for fast returns. Indeed, they may have been tuned to television news for discussion while they tuned to the Web for specific facts, but it was the raw facts—the data—that drew them in.

Not to throw a wet blanket on the Election Night experience, but we should note that the total Web audience did not increase much on Election Night. Analysts believe that the usual Web audience simply left its customary Websites in search of the few political sites posting election returns. The traffic problems therefore simply may have been a matter of shifting habits among the committed that resulted in congestion around a handful of special sites.

Such an explanation, however, should not undermine the lessons learned on Election Night. Give people what they want, and they will come. They wanted specific information quickly, and they were willing to stand in line for it.

CONCLUSION

Sleepy Campaign 1996 was not the most rigorous test of the new medium. The number of people on-line was not large by media standards, computers had not yet reached appliance status in most households, and the skewed demographics of people on-line clouded inferences about how this medium would play with a broader audience. Moreover, voters avoided campaign coverage on conventional media and on the Web as in the end they would avoid the election booths. Nobody knew if people would flock to the Web for political information, but hopes hung on the conventions and the debates; the results were disappointing.

Nonetheless, so early on, there is evidence that this medium has the

capacity to alter the flow of political information. It will provide voters with infusions of raw, uninterpreted information, allowing them to uncover their own agendas and to provide their own insights into the meaning of surveys and other data that customarily filter first through the analysts and reporters.

The Web also will establish a more equal footing for voters in the political dialogue, giving these traditionally passive recipients a voice in forums where they have too long been silent. 1996 was a clumsy test, yes, but it was filled with promise that the flow of information in American politics has been forever changed.

NOTES

1. B. H. Bagdikian, *The Media Monopoly*, 3rd ed. (Boston: Beacon Press, 1990), 223.

2. From the Project Vote Smart Web site, http://www.vote-smart.org/congress/virtual/balancedbudget.html.

3. Fifteen items posted in the Christian Coalition Scorecard, http://www.cc.org/voter/scorecard/tx.html. (1) Partial-Birth Abortions; (2) Putting Parents Back in Charge of Education; (3) Family Tax Relief; (4) Foreign Aid for Abortion; (5) Balanced Budget Amendment; (6) Defense of Marriage; (7) Taxpayer-funded Abortion Referrals; (8) Parental Consent; (9) Term Limits on Congress/Citizen Legislature; (10) Taxpayer-funded Divorce; (11) Taxpayer Funding for Pornography; (12) Overhaul Welfare to Strengthen the Family; (13) Tax Limitation Amendment; (14) Anti-crime Legislation; (15) No Welfare for Lobbyists.

4. In the Texas delegation, for example, Dick Armey, who agreed with the Christian Coalition all the time, received a 100, and Sheila Jackson-Lee, who never agreed with the group, racked up a 0.

5. America's Voice was provided by MSNBC. The research was conducted by the Public Policy Research Laboratory at Texas A&M University. The author was codirector along with Dr. James Dyer.

6. In the next generation of this project, a specially designed search engine will allow site visitors to examine the databases directly on the Website. They will sort by demographics, search for key words, examine the responses of people who addressed selected issues.

7. M. McCombs, and D. Shaw, "The Agenda-setting Functions of Mass Media," *Public Opinion* 36 (Summer 1972); 176–187.

8. We must note that while the Web distribution of data is groundbreaking, the concept of a computer-literate journalist is nothing new. Since the late 1980s, computer-assisted reporting—a concept much broader than statistical analysis—has been gathering interest in newsrooms and journalism schools, and with the Web, it has become even more critical. Wesley Pippert, dean of the Washington Reporting Program at the University of Missouri, says that an elective course in computer-assisted reporting has become the hottest journalism course on campus. He says this generation of young journalists must be computer-savvy, not just in Web searches but in all computer applications used by the campaigns and industries they cover (from an interview on Dec. 7, 1996).

9. D. E. Rosenbaum, "In Political Money Game, the Year of Big Loopholes," *New York Times*, Dec. 26, 1996, p. A1.

10. The *San Francisco Chronicle*, Jan. 1, 1997, reported that congressional campaign spending in 1996 reached $626.4 million in the general election. That's a 6.3 percent increase over the 1994 races, which until then set the spending record. Note that this is only spending by the candidates' campaigns, and does not include the parties and other organizations.

11. Dole's finance vice chairman, Simon Fireman, was found guilty of money-laundering and fined $6 million. Clinton fund-raiser John Huang created an Election Eve scandal involving Indonesian contributors. The incident brought Democrats unwelcome excitement in an otherwise uneventful campaign.

12. An Associated Press story reported the final financial data of the 1996 campaign calculated by the Center for Responsive Politics. It said that the parties raised $263.5 million—mostly in unregulated "soft money"—in the two years prior to the election. This total was almost three times the amount raised for the 1991–1992 campaign ($89 million) and 2.5 times the amount raised for the 1993–1994 campaign ($106.4). According to the report, in 1996, the Republicans raised $141.2 million and the Democrats $122.3 million. " 'Soft Money' Donations Almost 3 Times '92 Total," *San Francisco Chronicle*, Feb. 17, 1997, p. A7.

13. In 1996, the Federal Election Commission issued electronic filing guidelines, and although it could have imposed mandatory reporting, it established a voluntary system instead. Voluntary compliance is meaningless. Candidates are unlikely to submit their records for on-line scrutiny if their opponents aren't required to do the same; and if everyone doesn't submit records, no one will do it. The FEC's voluntary approach lets the lowest common denominator set the standards—and that will bring down the system.

14. The CNN/*Time* Candidate Rate-O-Matic II questions: (1) Do you support a woman's right to choose [to have an abortion]? (2) Do you support a balanced budget amendment to the U.S. Constitution? (3) To reduce the budget deficit, should the federal government eliminate the U.S. Department of Energy? (4) Should there be a single income tax rate? (5) Do you support deployment of an anti-missile defense system? (6) Do you think U.S. troops should be in Bosnia as peacekeepers? (7) Would you support a ban on political action committee contributions to federal candidates? (8) Do you support development of national educational standards and goals? (9) Do you favor eliminating the U.S. Department of Education? (10) Do you support the principle of amending the U.S. Constitution to allow voluntary prayer and/or a moment of silence in public schools? (11) Should the government maintain affirmative action efforts in hiring and contracting? (12) Should the government maintain preferences for minority students applying for college admission? (13) Do you support capital punishment for federal crimes involving murder? (14) Should there be more restrictions on purchase and possession of firearms? (15) Do you favor restrictions to further limit the number of legal immigrants entering the United States? (16) Do you support a universal federal health-care program to guarantee coverage to all Americans, regardless of income? (17) Do you favor providing homeless people with apartment vouchers they can use to supplement the cost of an apartment? (18) Do you favor creation of federal enterprise zones in communities with high unemployment rates? (19) Do you favor a constitutional amendment limiting the

number of terms that U.S. senators and representatives may serve? (20) Do you favor increasing the funding for national job-training programs? (21) Do you favor limiting the time that people who are able to work may receive welfare benefits? (22) Should the government deny welfare benefits to unwed mothers who continue to have children? (23) Do you favor an increase in the minimum wage? The response array for all questions is Yes, No, Undecided.

15. B. Cohen, *The Press and Foreign Policy* (Princeton: Princeton University Press, 1963).

16. The Third Millennium site URL: http://www.thirdmil.org/debt/debt.cgi. The nine budget categories are Domestic Spending (Education, Environmental, etc.); Social Security; Welfare (AFDC, Food Stamps, etc.); Interest on the National Debt; National Defense; Medicaid; Medicare; International Affairs; Other Entitlements (unemployment insurance, veteran's benefits, etc.).

17. From Reinventing America II, posted on URL: http://pathfinder.com/@HhHilAcASHP6am6/reinventing/.

18. From Projecting the 1996 Presidential Election, posted on URL: http://ourworld.compuserve.com:80/homepages/trillium/.

19. The Landmark Project. http://wwww.landmark-project.com/PowerVote.html.

20. Most experts agree that, in the very near future the speed of information upline and downline will increase dramatically. Early in 1997, U.S. Robotics Corporation, the largest manufacturer of modems, announced a 56K modem that increased by 60 percent the speed of the fastest modems (33.6K) available at the end of 1996. With compression technology and fiber optics, the delivery speeds will increase manyfold.

21. Voter turnout in 1996 was the lowest in 76 years.

22. S. V. Roberts, "The GOP: Civility vs. Civil War," *U.S. News & World Report* (June 24, 1996), 10.

23. Results from the America's Voice poll showed little public dissatisfaction with the deportment of the candidates.

24. The same paradox holds for negative ads: voters say they hate attack spots, yet these ads benefit candidates who use them.

25. H. Wolinsky, "Internet Users Clog Political Web Sites," *Chicago Sun-Times*, Nov. 7, 1996, p. 8.

26. Matrix Information and Directory Services (MIDS), an Internet usage tracking service, reported that the Internet had only a slight increase in traffic on Election Night. Congestion occurred around only a few sites that offered instant returns and analysis. Some critics, including Bob Metcalf, a columnist for *Info World* magazine, have argued that increased usage of the Web will, in time, crash the system. Metcalf told the *Washington Post*, however, that "Election night was 'yet another opportunity for the Net to go down, and it didn't. . . . That would tend to refute my hypothesis.' " Taken from David S. Hilzenrath, "Mixed Returns on the Net; Election Night Surfers Saw the Web's Weakness, Power," *Washington Post*, Nov. 10, 1996, p. A1.

Part Three

The Press, Politics, and the People

The belief that an informed citizenry is the foundation of a successful democracy and an antidote to tyranny is central to American constitutional protections. It guided the Founding Fathers in 1789 when they drafted the Bill of Rights, and it pointed the way for the Supreme Court in 1976 when it reaffirmed the rights of political speech in *Buckley v. Valeo*. It's no coincidence that all practicing democracies ennoble a free press, nor is it by chance that a despot's first act is to muzzle the news media.[1] Information is the lifeblood of a free society; it is a toxin to totalitarianism.

Michael Gartner, president of NBC News, said, "The great thing about democracy is we're free to take in all this information and make up our own minds about what is truth."[2] Gartner is at least half right. It's true, we are free to take in all this information, and if the arrival of the Web means anything at all, it's that Americans have more information available about more subjects from more sources than we could have imagined a few years ago. It is an irony that the information abundance itself causes trouble for the rest of Gartner's statement—making up our minds about the truth.

In theory, there can never be too much information, too many data, too much commentary and analysis about issues and events. But even in the Information Age, an overabundance doesn't translate into rational judgments. F. E. Smith, first Earl of Birkenhead, told about a judge who said, "I have read your case, Mr. Smith, and I am no wiser now than I was when I started." Smith replied, "Possibly not . . . but far better informed."

While the avalanche of political information on the Web is impressive and potentially beneficial to the electorate, the real question is not how well *informed* voters will become, but how *wise* they will become as a result of all this information, and how that wisdom will be expressed in the public dialogue and in the polling booths.

We have many problems with our electoral system, but an information shortage hasn't been one of them—even *before* the Web came along. Through most of this century, we have had available in print and broadcast media and campaign literature a generous supply of data on which to make informed electoral decisions. The Internet just piled on more. This new inventory of information has yet to evidence a measurable increase in good public sense for electoral politics.

For one thing, there has been no increase in public involvement. The turnout in 1996 was the lowest for any presidential election since the 1924 race, when no one owned a television and the illiteracy rate was much higher than it is today.[3] Thus, we must suspect that an information bounty does not have much to do with the electorate's political involvement.

Worse, it might have a negative effect. The late Claude Pepper, a 33-year veteran of the House and Senate, might have been on to something when he said, "A dollar ain't much if you have one." Maybe information ain't much if you have it. Paraphrasing JFK, when information is so abundant and obtained so easily, maybe we esteem it too lightly. One thing for certain, information may be necessary, but it is hardly enough to motivate nonvoters. You have to question the civic virtue of an electorate that doesn't vote.

Thomas Jefferson, the most celebrated early defender of a free press and a chief proponent of the First Amendment, knew that the right to *publish* information was not enough. He felt that putting the information on the street was only half of it; getting people to use it was the other half. Historian James Pollard described Jefferson's philosophy thus. "A free press must be circulated among the mass of the people sufficiently educated to profit from this information and opinion."[4] Jefferson was concerned that the people use the information intelligently and profit from it by making wise political judgments.

Ken Burns, in his documentary on Jefferson, interviewed a stable of historians who pictured this remarkably accomplished president as a child of the Enlightenment, that radical change in elite thinking about the masses. Jefferson embraced their utopian hopes in the perfectibility of man. Just give the people the truth freely, and wisdom will follow. Neither Washington nor Hamilton was quite that sanguine.

For true believers, however, the Web is an extraordinary repository of knowledge that archives more political information than the sum of the nation's newspapers, magazines, and broadcast media. We celebrate its abundance, but maybe we're missing the downside, or at least the limitations of knowledge. What about political wisdom? What will the Internet do for that? The critical issue absent from Gartner's statement, and from much of the talk about the information profusion on the Web, has to do with the power of information to cultivate wisdom, and if that's too ambitious, at least to enlighten political decisions. That's the issue that won't go away, because information is not necessarily truth. Ultimately, we have to reckon with what impact this cornucopia of information, and the interactivity between visitor and computer, visitor and visitor, and the one-stop shopping for political ideas, will have on the individual judgments of voters and on the collective wisdom of the people.

It's been said many times that political campaigns are communication campaigns,[5] and that the study of American politics is a study of the information flow between the electorate and the elected. To understand that flow, we have to understand how information makes its way to the population and how people use it in forming electoral decisions.

Until this century, the lion's share of political information came out of a newspaper, and then traveled through the population by word of mouth. The newspapers, like the people who convey information over backyard fences, became known for their reliability. The value placed on much of what you heard was determined by where you heard it, and the weight you put on a report or a rumor depended on the credibility of the source. As the old saw goes, "If you can't trust the messenger, you can't trust the message." Further, if you don't know the source, you keep your guard up. The veiled "they"—as in "They said the horse is a sure winner"—inspires more suspicion than it does confidence.

Through the rest of this century, radio and television stations joined the media mix and, over time, forged reputations that shaped the perception of the information they delivered. The credibility of entire networks was linked to the trust people placed in the anchors for the evening newscasts. That's why networks choose their anchors as carefully as the cardinals choose a pope. Walter Cronkite was more than a news reader, he was the CBS icon whose light shone over all that network's programming. The reputations of the media remain a powerful influence on the public perception of the information they deliver.

Journalists contributing to Chapters 6 and 7 expressed concern about the credibility of information sources on the Web and about the capacity of audiences to distinguish among the tens of thousands of contributors. The names of unknown writers and site developers offer few clues about their credibility. More perplexing are the many anonymous sites that sometimes are no more enlightening than graffiti on a highway overpass. Then, as the well-researched, documented news stories stand alongside the opinion-filled essays, there is a risk that audiences will blur the distinctions and give both the same weight. The journalists see this as some threat to their profession, and a growing risk to the electorate as the abundance of often undifferentiated information becomes more widely available.

The mainstream media benefit the public agenda in ways that the Web may not. For one, traditional media acknowledge several sides to most issues. They may not cover all sides equally or fairly, but most at least, let the audience know, that other opinions stand in opposition to the one presented. This reminds people of our pluralistic population and that the country is not of one mind on any issue.

Next, the mainstream press also covers an assortment of issues. You'll find a variety of stories from Washington, state capitals, and towns among items on culture, the arts, sports, and other events that form the matrix of American public life. This blend reminds audiences of a shared public agenda and that no single issue is all-consuming.

Some journalists expressed concerns that voters chasing down topics of personal interest on the Web will be exposed to a restricted array of issues and to a limited range of viewpoints on those issues. It's easy to see how this could happen. The Internet is a highly targeted medium that allows users to pursue their interests and bunker themselves into sites with parochial concerns. "Push" technology, which hand-delivers information on only the topics you select, caters to that inclination and stands to limit even further a Web user's exposure to a healthy blend of issues and a "show me" attitude toward opinions.

Moreover, many sites offer decidedly partisan views and ideologically narrow perspectives that collectively mislead users into believing the views are prevalent. Visitors who load up on right-wing sites and dwell in right-wing chat rooms, for instance, may come away believing that these views circumscribe the political norm. This clusters users around a narrow point of view and estranges them from people who don't share that philosophy. This concern was on the minds of some journalists and political commentators.

Part III looks at the effects of the Internet on American journalism and on the national community, and while the chapter titles suggest a clean break between the press and the people, it is impossible to tease them apart. Nearly all the information available in a political campaign and all the issues surfacing in daily discussions about government and politics originate in the media. Therefore, like a pebble thrown in a pond, any change in the media ripples throughout the population. This has been true of radio and television, although for them, it took some years for the effects to become dominant. The Internet, as we have already seen, became an overnight attraction and a surprisingly promising force in the dissemination of political information.

We examine how the Internet has influenced the way journalists gather information for political stories. As we have seen, unlike any other medium, this one is well stocked with raw data and original information from campaigns, government, and interest groups. The Web is more efficient than previous delivery systems, moreover, because it provides data that could not be had at any cost in previous campaigns. We'll examine what this means to journalists and then to the audiences of political stories.

Obviously, the availability of information must be distinguished from its application. Raw data, analyzed information, and pure opinion are dumped into this medium. For some, a knee-jerk reaction is to praise any system that delivers such knowledge so generously. If inadequate information is bad for a democratic government, then surely an outpouring of information must be good. Not necessarily, if people confuse fact with fiction, and if they pigeonhole themselves into isolated groups whose information may be deep but not very wide. At the end, the matter comes down to wisdom and the expression of sound electoral judgment. How does the Web affect that?

NOTES

1. *Los Angeles Time* reporter Tracy Wilkinson wrote about the importance of the news media to Serbian President Slobodon Milosevic: "For the opposition, control of City Hall means access to electronic media that is run and censored by Milosevic or his allies. That access is considered crucial to the opposition's ability to run in future elections, build a party base and crack Milosevic's grip on power.

" 'By losing TV and radio, Milosevic would lose part of his media dictatorship,' said Vidosav Stevanovic, a writer who has been designated head of the television station by the new opposition government. 'The moment he loses media, he loses power. His regime is based only on media and police.' " Wilkinson, "Yugoslav Police, Opposition Clash over Media Control," *Los Angeles Times*, Jan. 24, 1997, p. A1.

2. *Brown Alumni Monthly* (May 1991).

3. The illiteracy rate in 1920 was 6.0 percent, and in 1930 was 4.3 percent, compared with the 1996 rate, which is around 1 percent. The early statistics are reported in *The Statistical History of the United States* (New York: Basic Books, 1976), 382.

4. J. Pollard, *The Presidents and the Press* (New York: Macmillan, 1947), 53.

5. The integral role of information in politics has been presented in many writings, and particularly well in K. H. Jamieson, *Dirty Politics: Deception, Distraction, and Democracy* (New York: Oxford University Press, 1992); and R. Berkman, and L. W. Kitch, *Politics in the Media Age* (New York: McGraw-Hill, 1986).

Chapter Six

The Use and Impact of the Internet on Journalism: The Reporters' View

I have yet to see a piece of writing, political or non-political, that doesn't have a slant. All writing slants the way a writer leans, and no man is born perpendicular, although many men are born upright. The beauty of the American free press is that the slants and twists, and the distortions come from so many directions, and the special interests are so numerous, the reader must sift and sort and check and countercheck in order to find out what the score is.

— *E. B. White*

POLS, PRESS, AND THE PEOPLE: A CHANGING RELATIONSHIP

In May 1777, six months before the Continental Congress agreed to the Articles of Confederation, and 12 years before George Washington took the oath of office, the press was already causing trouble. While Washington was knee-deep in British soldiers, the patriot press was hard at work publishing information "of an injurious nature" tampering with the general's battlefield ventures. Except for a few letters of complaint, Washington didn't do much about press intrusions, but it's clear that he didn't much like what the press was up to.[1] For the rest of his professional life, Washington would be dogged by the press, as would each of the 41 presidents to follow.[2]

Throughout our history, antagonism between the president and the press has been consistent, although the relationship between the two has been through many changes. Early in the republic, the press was visibly partisan, sometimes serving conspicuously as a house organ for the administration, sometimes steadfastly opposed to anything the president did or said. Later, due largely to the economics of ownership and to the force of personality, powerful publishers and editors asserted a new control at the White House in a era of "personal journalism." Forceful editors such as Horace Greeley, James Gordon Bennett, and William Cullen Bryant talked with presidents as equals, and at times—in writing and in person, as well as on the news page—told them what they ought to do.[3]

The current relationship between the president and the press began to form with Theodore Roosevelt. Here was a personality custom-made for the job of injecting life into a dormant relationship that had developed between the president and the press just after the Civil War. Roosevelt's grandstanding and force of personality helped establish a new, lively, and surprisingly productive relationship. In his administration, the working press corps had greater access to the White House, and specifically to the president, through press conferences, previously a little used forum.

The presidential press conference floated all boats. It elevated the prestige of the White House press corps, it provided the president with a direct link to the country, and it gave voters access to the thinking of the president on key national issues, delivered in a forum that had an air of spontaneity. The energetic, congenial, headline-making Roosevelt forged the die for a relationship that brought the press more fully into the activities of the executive. This, in turn, stimulated public interest in government more broadly, reaching to the other branches and to the activities of the federal bureaucracy.

Whatever the nature of the relationship between presidents and press and, for that matter, between the press and all other government entities, there remains one constant: the media play a central communication role, a bridging role between political leaders and the voters.

As the country grew and the population became more dispersed across the continent, political figures became increasingly dependent on the media for any meaningful contact with the electorate. Stump speeches and other face-to-face forums were staged to draw in the press more than to convince the spectators. Without the press, voices in Washington could not have been heard beyond the Potomac, and so for most of our history, the press has been an unofficial member of the American political system and, like it or not, the intermediary between the government and the people.

The integral role of the media has been maintained by the size of its technology and the cost of its operation. Up to now, the mass dissemination of information has required a centralized medium that gathers the news and distributes it to large audiences. News organizations, like funnels, take in data, process it, and through big printing presses and powerful transmitters send out the digested information in the papers and the newscasts. This machinery has guaranteed publishers and broadcasters their key roles. You simply cannot move information to the masses without the large hardware, an obvious fact that has kept public officials tethered to the press. Moreover, this huge investment in technology has made it difficult for new publishers to get in the game.

With newspaper consolidations and broadcast buyouts, fewer news operations are feeding more of the public. News media of even modest heft thus remain in the hands of moneyed interests, ensuring that access to a public forum depends largely on access to adequate funding.[4]

There are hundreds of small-town newspapers serving communities, some with as few as several thousand subscribers, but they flourish on a strict diet of local happenings with scarcely a nod toward national or even state news.

At the other end of the scale is the condition that drove dissenters to publish underground papers during the Vietnam war. Whether or not the alternative press had any consequence for national policy, it effectively symbolized the failure of the established media to represent unconventional views. If there is no ready cash nor friends in high media places, some information just doesn't make it into the public arena.

None of this holds for the Internet. Its information machinery operates less like a funnel and more like a sieve. Information does not channel through a central processing plant, and it does not have to pass muster with the editors, writers, and producers who prepare it for mass distribution. On the Internet, information sources can bypass the filters of news and distribute directly to the people or, more accurately, distribute for the people to access themselves.[5]

Without high-tech presses or transmitters, and the support staff needed to operate them, the Internet does not incur the expenses of conventional media ownership. As we have seen, for pocket change, anyone with an idea, even someone without a clue, can set up an information site. The lower threshold for entry opens the medium to anyone interested in taking on the assignment.

What do the decentralized distribution system and universal access of the Web mean to the traditional media structure?

Without a doubt, the media will have to endure new competition. During the 1996 campaigns, this was inconsequential, but over time, alternative news operations will form on the Web, some of them arising from a handful of like-minded people with something to say. They will collect information and disseminate news, they will offer more opinion and commentary, they will shade the information with an organizational bias, and they will concentrate the topics on focused interests. In other words, they may be more newsletter than newspapers, and their audiences will be more targeted than mass.

Competition will also come from nonjournalistic operations. Recall that Linda Muller, Pat Buchanan's Web designer, said the press was not adequately covering her candidate during the Republican primaries, and this neglect pushed his campaign onto the Web. Supporters and curiosity seekers did not have to wait patiently for a story about Buchanan in the mainstream press; they could turn directly to his site for news every day. Muller said many visitors hit the site daily, along with their perusal through the morning papers and their viewing of the *Today Show*.

Like any good editor, Muller kept the stories fresh because she understood audience expectations and, unlike so many other political activists during the campaign, she figured out that the value of the Web was its capacity to deliver new information quickly.

Sites like Buchanan's will evolve in the next few years as candidates and political figures exploit their direct access to voters. The established press may not have met its equal, but it soon will meet a horde of pushy competitors in the information marketplace.

What about the media bridge between pol and people? Will that TV/ newspaper/radio/magazine bridge collapse? Maybe not, but the decentralized Web *will* allow the political leaders and the voters to communicate directly—while avoiding the big media funnel—and as a result, the old relationships will change.

This does not mean that the system has finally achieved the Founding Fathers' long-sought ideal in which people and political leaders engage in constant, personal dialogue. No doubt, the direct, unfiltered communication can benefit both sides, but there are hidden dangers in a process where pols and voters can meet out of public view.[6]

Aside from the likely changes between political leaders and voters, the relationship between political leaders and the press stands to change as well. Now, there is a convenient course around the big media, although it didn't amount to a breakthrough in the 1996 campaign. But, as the Internet matures, alternatives to the conventional press—and this includes the Websites of conventional media—will offer beefier information in exciting formats that the public will notice. The simple fact is, as alternative information sources grow, the centralized media will lose their status as the only game in town.

The same thing happened before the Web came along, when cable television, with its 40 channels, cut deeply into network lineups of news and entertainment. Just as cable didn't kill the networks but chipped away at their supremacy and altered their style, so the Web won't kill the conventional media, although it will further reduce their dominance and alter their style. It's safe to say that newspapers and networks will not go belly-up, nor will jobs in journalism go the way of the blacksmith. Historically, America has never lost a medium; we have only altered the existing media to accommodate a new one. But when the Internet muscles in, it will challenge the mainstream press politically, and one of its impacts will be to diminish the latter's central importance to the voters and political leaders. When that happens, campaigns will change the course that has altered many times since George Washington's first run-ins with the patriot press.

THE JOURNALISTS SIZEUP THE WEB AS AN
INFORMATION SOURCE[7]

Reporters, who are the suppliers of so much information during a political campaign, are also among the most aggressive consumers of information. Their daily mining of facts and opinion about the candidates and campaigns, public policy and voter reactions gives them a distinct position from which to size up the usefulness of a developing source of news and information.

This section considers how a handful of nationally ranked journalists and media watchers evaluate the Internet for its information content. This is not a random sample, to be sure, and the discussion does to attempt to provide a sweeping examination of how reporters used the Web in 1996. It does, however, look at how a handful of respected news specialists from a range of media and news organizations view the value of the Internet in their work.

To begin, they failed to agree on the usefulness of the Web for political research. Some, like Barbara Saffir, a research assistant for David Broder at the *Washington Post*, found the Web a convenient resource for campaign and election-related information and opinion. Along with other advocates, she said that she built the Web into daily research routines, using verified information directly or as a lead to other sources.

Others weren't so convinced. Elaina Hadler, director of National Public Radio's *Talk of the Nation* program, a national call-in show, took a more cautious view, declaring that the overwhelming volume of unsorted and unfiltered information was often more trouble than it was worth. She said it was tough to track down useful information, and then to verify its accuracy. She described how Web research slows when it hits sites that are abandoned, under construction, or loaded with bulky graphics.

Researchers also stumbled over irrelevant and unusable information that clutters Web searches. Anyone who has used this medium knows the chaff is out of proportion to the wheat. Hadler said she found that frequently the investment of time did not justify the paltry amount of information that resulted. The Web in 1996, she said, was more of a promise than a practical information resource. She was not alone.

If there was a consensus among the group, it was that the Web yielded lots of information, but that landing something useful took too much

time and effort. The culprit was the search engines—the programs designed to sift the Web for sites that may address one's interests.

Most of the reporters said they ran into trouble because the search
engines failed to discriminate adequately among the jumble of sites. They
often got a chaotic mass of addresses, forcing the investigator to go
through the list site by site, a process that could take hours or days.

That's not good enough for a profession that lives and dies by the
clock. The reporters interviewed agreed that until programmers im-
proved the search engines, the Web would remain a second-string research tool for reporters. Nevertheless, for a resource so new, the
reporters found several uses, most avoiding the use of search engines.

To Learn the Candidate's Position on Current Issues

The journalist's use of a candidate's site depended largely on how
much substantive information it held. "Sound-bite sites" and sites that
looked like a high school yearbook were understandably of little value.
Not only was such content frivolous, but for some reporters it tarnished
perceptions of the Web as a serious campaigning tool. Kathy Bushkin,
vice president for news at *U.S. News & World Report*, said that campaigns
could serve reporters better by posting hard position statements, policy
descriptions, and concrete discussions of the candidate's views by key
issues.

Ed Epstein, a political reporter for the *San Francisco Chronicle* who also
writes about the Web for *PC Magazine*, said he used Website information
from candidates running in other parts of the country where he otherwise would have few contacts and little access. For local races, he said,
reporters usually develop personal contacts in campaigns, and this ensures regular discussions and press releases, position papers, and other
campaign material. Moreover, local campaigns are quick to respond to
a reporter's questions, so Websites for local races don't add much that
is not already accessible to a reporter.

Before the Web, Epstein noted, he would spend a good deal of telephone time running down sources in out-of-state campaigns, and even
then it was tough to assemble a reasonable view of more than a handful
of races. This time, the Web made that easy, he said. In an hour a reporter
could check out several candidates' positions and assemble a consensus
story that examined trends across the country.

Epstein complained that many sites were hopelessly out of date; some
never changed a word throughout the campaign. That's like candidates
developing a stock speech in February and not changing a word of it
through November. A reporter who returned periodically for updates
on evolving issues would come away empty-handed and disappointed.
The freeze-dried sites also reflected poorly on the campaign, suggesting

that at best, the staff was lazy, if not clueless about operating the new medium. On balance, Epstein felt that the Web was helpful early in the season, but over time, as fewer campaigns freshened their sites, it became less and less useful in tracking candidates' positions on key issues. Why waste the time?[8]

Kathy Bushkin, at *U.S. News*, said that she found many uses for political research on the Web, but that going to the candidate's sites was not one of them. "They didn't seem to know what to do with the medium," she said. "We're on the cusp of something new and everyone, the campaigns staffers and the reporters, are figuring out how to work it into routines they've developed over the years." It was a toy for the campaigns, it didn't cost much, and many candidates went along with it because it was the "in" thing to do. Her complaint echoed Epstein's: many campaign staffs lacked enthusiasm for it and displayed little knowledge of its potential.

The *Washington Post*'s, Barbara Saffir agreed that many of the candidates' sites over time became museums, but when that happened, she said she turned to other sites that monitored the candidates. "Lots of other groups were looking at the candidates and the campaigns, and when the campaign sites ran dry, I could turn elsewhere, at least for some of the information, such as transcripts and position statements." Saffir, probably the most avid Web supporter of the journalists interviewed, said that she often could find media or interest group sites that had something to say about the candidates' positions on current issues. She said this should be a warning to the campaigns: if you don't provide your own information, someone will do it for you, and you may not like the spin they give it. When the candidates figure out how valuable a well-maintained site can be to reporters, she said, they'll keep it stocked with usable and updated information.

Several journalists said that they used the Web to explore the policies and issue positions of third-party candidates. Public—and press—recognition of these typically underreported, underpublicized campaigns is, of course, a dream of the smaller parties. The Green, Libertarian, United We Stand America, and Natural Law parties have suffocated in the traditional media environment that favors the major candidates.

No doubt, some journalists looked in on the sites of smaller parties and less-covered candidates. Common sense suggests that minority candidates would be shrewd to elevate their visibility by crafting reporter-friendly updates on their Websites.

Elaina Hadler of National Public Radio deplored the shoddy appearance of some third-party sites. She said that the Web pages offer many voters and journalists their first exposure to a third-party campaign, and first impressions are critical. Hadler expressed disappointment in the writing, spelling, and grammatical errors, disorder, and sloppy layout of some sites. No matter how she tried to evaluate some candidates' information, she said, she couldn't get around the second-rate presentations. "A handful of them were a mess. They were hard to read, they had no order, and they were filled with writing problems. How could someone visiting these sites come away with a positive impression of the candidate? I went in hoping to learn about the campaign and found myself coming away distracted by the appearance."

Given the simplicity of this technology, it's hard to understand why campaigns tolerate such shoddiness. It takes little more than apprentice-level formatting skill with html code and a spell checker to put out a simple, clean site. The underground newspapers used inferior equipment, so they had a good excuse for their rough look, but the Web delivers easy-to-read pages so naturally that a programmer has to work at creating a crude appearance. Conceivably, the authors consider their political ideas more important than the layout and the writing, but the reality is that those ideas can be tarnished by a poor presentation.

To Get Leads for Follow-up Contacts

Philip Davis is a political reporter for National Public Radio. His deadlines are as tight as any in the news business, and his need for good and fast information has all but put the Web off-limits as a routine research tool. Davis repeated the usual drawbacks: inadequate search engines, piles of hopeless sites with nothing to offer investigative reporters, and undocumented information that takes too much time to verify.

Davis did say, however, that Websites maintained by many campaigns, parties, interest groups, and other political organizations provided names and phone numbers for quick entry points to many sources. "The phone is still the fastest and easiest way for me to get direct answers, and I've found that contacts posted on the Websites can be a great help."

Ed Epstein confirmed the value of contact leads on the Web. After examining the site to determine a given position, he would phone the organization and ask the spokesperson for comment and clarification. The contact information hastens the process of tracking down someone authorized to speak for the organization.

Barbara Saffir said, "Think of it as a big indexing system." Sites with something interesting to say often provided leads for follow-up discussions, a custom-made feature for reporters. "You have a position statement, then a live person who can verify that the organization is responsible for the claim. You also can flesh out the information and adapt it better to the direction of your own story."

To Get Information About Ballot Initiatives and Political Organizations

California's law on ballot initiatives makes it a challenging setting for grassroots political activity. In 1996, for instance, the state ballot contained 15 measures concerning such wide-ranging issues as legalizing the medical use of marijuana, clamping down on campaign financing, and eliminating affirmative action programs. True to its reputation, most of the state's measures were controversial, and some attracted national attention because they had human interest value and a potential impact on other states.

Hot and heavy issues also draw the attention of interest groups. For instance, dozens of organizations found a stake in the marijuana measure. This referendum, roughly similar to one in Arizona, called for the legalization of marijuana use by patients for whom it is prescribed by a physician.[9] The American Medical Association, along with other professional medical groups, got in the game, and the National Organization for the Reform of Marijuana Laws (NORML), of course, took a front-row seat. Sometimes it was difficult to tell which group took which position on this matter. Traditional states' rights groups, which usually want the federal government to keep its hands off state laws, argued this measure violated federal law. Liberal groups, which typically invite federal intervention, said this was a state matter.

Sorting it all out—what the law said, what it implied, who stood for it and against it—was a lot easier with the Web. In San Francisco, Ed Epstein said the Web paid off for its coverage of the state's propositions. To start with, the official site set up by the secretary of state produced an on-line voter handbook. It provided wording of each ballot measure, discussed the pros and cons, and reviewed the measure's implications.

Then, Epstein said, a reporter could run a search to discover which groups spoke out on the issue and what position each was advocating. An hour-long Web search, even with balky search engines, could flag the key players and deliver the names of people to contact. Reporters could then complete their research on the phone. "The Web's remarkable, given all the propositions we have around here. It gives you a new way to find the players on these sprawling issues."

Journalists also reported using the Web to track down interest group perspectives on issues like the budget, foreign affairs, and environmental concerns. Kathy Bushkin (U.S. News) said that while the Web was still too new to capture the serious attention of most candidates, the interest groups, with a passion for their treasured issues, were a different story. Their goals were different from the candidates' goals, and they exhibited more flexibility in how they communicated. They saw the Web as a way to reach broader audiences beyond direct mail and small meetings. "They saw this as a more serious medium, and they used it better than most of the candidates. Their sites usually had more information and were up to date."

The interest groups work without the sword of Damocles hanging over the candidates, so they are freer to experiment with new approaches. "Why do you think the NRA [National Rifle Association] site got 30,000 hits a day?" asked Tanya Metaksa, chief lobbyist for the NRA. She said she specialized in posting innovative and relevant information that voters and reporters found useful. Unlike so many others, she constantly updated the site and tied it closely to events unfolding during the campaign.

On-line Data

Journalists sometimes used the Web in 1996 as a portable library. They would "bookmark" a collection of information-dense sites and hit the road with their laptops, which provided a useful take-along archive.

"In the old days, the 'boys in the bus' had to lug around huge boxes of files when they followed candidates on the road," said Wes Pippert, a 30-year UPI veteran and now dean of the Washington Reporting Program at the University of Missouri. "We would use these files for background information, to put the daily events into context, and to confirm the candidates' earlier statements and policies about something they may bring up in a speech somewhere. Of course, they could spring anything on you, so you traveled with all the files you could carry, but what we could carry is a drop in the bucket compared to what you can pull off the Internet today."

Modem-equipped laptop computers give journalists on the road instant access to government records, transcripts, schedules, and a huge collection of periodicals, newspapers, polls, and newscasts. Sites run by the parties, candidates, interest groups, universities, and the government offer rich background data.

Consider the stark contrast between this largesse and the information scarcity in the 1940s. In 1948, Herman Cohen was the announcing supervisor for radio station WSUI at the University of Iowa, later he became a communications professor and president of the Speech Communication Association. He was interested in Harry Truman's whistle-stop campaigning and, curious about the local broadcasts of the president's rear platform speeches, he sought out the train schedules.

Cohen found no local sources for such information, so he wrote a letter to the White House, describing his interests and requesting the list of stops. Several days later he received a personal letter from Charles G. Ross, secretary to the president, along with a typed copy of the 19-page schedule, complete with handwritten, marginal notes about the broad-casts. Ross wrote, "My secretary has gone through the schedules of the President's trips . . . and has marked the places at which the President spoke."[10] Someone in the White House had spent hours on the assign-ment.

The personal letter, annotations, and typed schedule suggest that such information at the time was a novelty. Apparently, few journalists thought to ask for such data, because obtaining it was just too much of a nuisance. Several decades later, information about Clinton's whistle-stop tour to Chicago was posted on the Web and available instantly to all takers. Unless one infers that the Internet is merely a tool for making lazy reporters look good, this is progress.

Some particularly useful Web research tools have sprung up. Electric Library, for instance, provides access to more than 150 full-text news-papers, 800 periodicals, news wires, classic books, maps, and more.[11] The service carries a nominal charge, but it is updated daily, and its onboard search engines use the effective Boolean system, which uses standard query procedures. Anyone can also search the online archives of the *New York Times*, the *Washington Post*, the *Los Angeles Times*, the *San Francisco Chronicle*, and many other papers.

For the "boys in the bus," a thorough search of past news stories may have included the *Reader's Guide to Periodical Literature*, the *New York Times Index*, and the morgues of large newspapers. In more recent times these tomes have been replaced by NEXIS, a proprietary on-line news and information research service with access to all major publications and broadcast news programs, government publications, and other sources. NEXIS has become indispensable in newsrooms, allowing com-prehensive searches that simply could not be accomplished by the old methods. The problem for many bare-bones news organizations, how-ever, is that NEXIS, which charges by the hour, is prohibitively expen-sive. Could the Web provide an inexpensive alternative?

When reporters were asked if the Web could replace or supplement NEXIS as a key research tool, the answers were mixed. Elaina Hadler (National Public Radio) said that she has used the Web for research where she might otherwise have used NEXIS, and she's been pleased with the results. "It's cut down on our NEXIS use dramatically and it's saved us a lot of money. Of course, you have to pick and choose your sites, but I've come up with a handful that are reliable and supplement my use of NEXIS. Does it replace NEXIS? No, but it cuts way back on the use of it."

Philip Davis, another NPR journalist, is less sanguine. For much of his background research, he still relies heavily on NEXIS. "It just doesn't do the same job. I find that I can't get through it fast enough, so I still use NEXIS primarily for rapid background research." Davis added that he used the Web often in his research for campaign coverage, but that it only supplemented his use of NEXIS.

Hadler and Davis may look at the Web differently because their jobs at NPR differ. Hadler runs a daily talk show, which requires the use of information research tools to assemble backgrounders for the program host. Much of her work can be done well in advance of the programs. Davis, on the other hand, prepares stories only hours or even minutes before airing, and in so doing, the Web taxes him twice. First, without adequate search engines, the research can consume valuable time and in the end yield little. Then, the special need to verify Web information takes up yet more time. Whether or not Electric Library or a similar service, with superior search engines and documented sources, can replace NEXIS depends on how well it lives up to its marketing claims. The jury is still out.

The *Post*'s Barbara Saffir offers a middle ground on the use of the Web and NEXIS. Not constrained by a tight research budget, she uses the Web as an extension of NEXIS. "Sure, I use NEXIS, but there are things on the Web that are not on NEXIS, so I don't see the two as competitive. The Internet is an extension of NEXIS, adding yet more information to my research."

The Convention

The convention sites of the parties and the media featured a lot of sound and fury, but amid it all, they had only a few items that interested the journalists interviewed. Barbara Saffir used them to track the schedule of events and to download the transcripts of platform speeches. She could have obtained this information via fax or regular mail, but the Websites were faster because she didn't have to go through the hassle of making arrangements with party officials.

Saffir and other reporters for top national journals were not dependent upon the Web because the parties are not likely to neglect the premier press organizations. On the other hand, campaign staffers are not apt to jump through hoops for the *Asheville Citizen-Times* or the *Mapleton, Saler & Siuslaw Oregonian*, or a thousand other mom-and-pops around the country. So, for the thousands of small print and broadcast media, the Web postings of raw convention information were more than a convenience. For the first time, every publisher and broadcaster had access to the same convention information at the same time. That's what the DNC interactive media director, Dick Bell, meant when he said the Internet evens things out.

Furthermore, the burden of information access has shifted from the supplier of information to the user of information. In the past it had been the obligation of the political parties to distribute the text of speeches, schedules, platform statements, and the other convention information to news media and organizations. The process was expensive and time-consuming, and it was bound to offend those missing from the mailing list.

Now, the parties' obligations end at the monitor. They post everything and wash their hands of the matter. It saves them money and staff time, and it broadens their exposure to a potentially huge audience, fulfilling the prime directive of any convention.

Election Night Coverage

On Election Night, most journalists, like average voters, watch television for the returns from key voting districts statistically chosen for their demographic symmetry. Like the voters, most journalists first learn about the outcomes of an election from television. For everyone but a handful of network and affiliate insiders and some of the major newspaper chains, it's a game of watch and wait—watch all the returns and wait for the one you're interested in.

Andrew Glass, Washington bureau chief of the Cox News Service, said, "Election Night coverage on the Internet demonstrated that voters and journalists were no longer tethered to television. Print journalists, even the 'moms-and-pops' had the same access to data at the same time as the TV reporters—the Hal Brunos and Bill Schneiders. They could access the results themselves, and they didn't have to wait until the announcer got around to the races that interested them."

For journalists, the data flow on Election Night can make a real difference in getting out the news. Reporters can keep a close eye on key races or referenda and, seeing which way the wind is blowing, arrange interviews and write up results in time for the morning paper. Local radio stations, without network feeds, can access real-time data and broadcast it throughout the evening.

Philip Davis and the National Public Radio news staff kept abreast of the nationwide trends through the exit poll results delivered on the Web: "The editors still used other resources extensively in their coverage, but the Web provided another source of information and helped track the quick pace of the returns." Davis recalled that he was in NPR's London bureau on Election Night (his early Wednesday morning) and monitored the results from there. Based on his own experience, he surmised that the election outcomes not only reached U.S. audiences very quickly, but also sped to audiences around the world. For most journalists, on Election Night, the Internet provided a novel resource that stands to improve local, regional, and even international coverage of voting results.

Interaction: E-mail, Chat Rooms, Town Meetings

E-mail

By 1996, E-mail had become for many professionals a routine method of interpersonal communication. The *San Francisco Chronicle* cites industry sources who claim that more than 3 million Americans use E-mail daily.[12] E-mail has been around since the early 1970s, and it has been in widespread use since the 1980s, when many students gained access through campus computers. Graduates brought the habit with them to the job, and used it in their work long before the Web became a reality. For many professionals, E-mail is becoming as unremarkable as the telephone, and so common that one reporter said, "I haven't even considered that part of the Internet."

The reporters used E-mail to communicate with colleagues, with the office, and occasionally with campaign staffers. Several reporters responded through E-mail to this author's request for an interview, and offered follow-up information through E-mail after the initial discussions. It's a natural medium for people who are on the road and have irregular schedules. It permits easy responses, it archives the incoming and outgoing messages, and it simplifies the distribution of correspondence to third parties—through "cc's" and forwarding. Reporters can attach documents and, with new graphic facilities, they can send photos, voice files, and formatted program files.[13] The E-mail that once was thought of as a simple conveyance of messages has become the U-Haul of cyberspace. In addition to all of these things, E-mail is inexpensive, and that puts it within reach of all takers, even the small players in the news business.

Some larger campaigns used list servers, which are like bulk E-mail. Staffers develop recipient lists and, with a keystroke, send press releases, speech texts, and other campaign information to targeted groups. Several journalists said they agreed to be on these list servers, but few found useful information. Andrew Glass said that he received a lot of information through the list servers, but it never amounted to much in his reporting. Barbara Safir, who delighted in most of the information she found on the Web, did not find great interest in the list server information.

Part of the problem is that list server information is aimed at groups, not specific individuals, and that puts it in the junk-mail category. People have come to recognize E-mail as a vehicle for interpersonal exchanges, and list servers violate that expectation. Over time, the information flood can be overwhelming, so that many recipients delete it like so many unopened letters with bulk-sort postmarks.

Elaina Hadler at NPR's *Talk of the Nation* said that many in her audience communicate with the show through E-mail. Staff members monitor the incoming messages and flag interesting questions and comments for use on the air. "I even found many of these to be more intelligent than the call-ins," she said. "People hear about our topic from the promos and call even before the show gets under way. Their comments are often nonspecific or loaded with other agendas. The E-mailers, though, tend to be responsive and reflect more thoughtfully the flow of Ray's [show host Ray Suarez] conversation."

Chat Rooms

Another of the Internet's interactive forums is chat rooms, where visitors hold electronic discussions about designated topics. Chat rooms originally were set up by proprietary on-line services. America Online and CompuServe have been the main players for several years, but more recently, chat rooms have been opening on free Internet sites, some of the most active ones being maintained by Yahoo.[14]

"Dissing," the hot give-and-take once associated with chat rooms, diminished through 1996, according to veteran moderators. It depends on the subject matter, of course, but the old hands say that wider audiences joining the Web have reduced the concentration of "flame throwers," so chat rooms today aren't always the brawls they once were.

During the election season, the Web was packed with chat rooms about politics, but these well-trafficked sites were little used by the journalists. The freewheeling discussions may have offered insight into voter thinking on the elections, sort of like sitting in on coffee klatches around the country, but monitoring these took time, a commodity always in short supply for the press during an election. Moreover, this would have been a bad sample of public opinion. Chat room visitors do not represent a valid cross section of American voters, so discussions on-line could never be extrapolated freely to the wider population.

Not only that, but the candor of participants is problematical. It is not uncommon for people to play devil's advocate or to assume a provocative stance just to stimulate a lively debate. Such tactics keep chat rooms active, but they are not helpful for political observers trying to make sense of the public views toward the election. In short, chat rooms make for an entertaining pastime, but they are an awful place for journalists in search of mainstream views, which is why reporters were wise to walk a wide circle around them.

Town Meetings

The interactive capacities of the Web also could have been applied to more formal sessions, such as virtual town meetings, press conferences, and other public forums. In fact, late in 1995, before most campaigns got under way, some experts claimed that the Web would provide the great cyberspace meeting hall, but that just didn't happen. Lamar Alexander launched his primary campaign by announcing his candidacy on the Web, but after that, he tuned to the conventional media for coverage of most of his public activities.[15] Patrick Leahy held a few town meetings on-line, but these never amounted to much more than early demonstrations of the Web's potential as a two-way medium. They capitalized on the novelty of the medium, but they didn't follow through to make these public forums a more functional component of the campaign.

Kathy Bushkin said, "The great cyberspace debates never really got off the ground, even though the electronic frontier guys promised this was to be the year." She added that as the Web becomes more populated over the next few years, the candidates will find the incentive—the critical audience mass—they need to allocate their scarce campaigning time.

On-line interaction is an interesting idea and not a bad way for candidates to hear firsthand what's on the voters' minds. The second presidential debate in 1996, where people in the handpicked audience posed questions to the candidates, came across as a wooden, overorganized affair. At one point, moderator Jim Lehrer had to all but plead for a question about foreign affairs. It's not likely that an on-line session would need such prompting: indeed, the challenge might be to quiet down the fans.

Ed Epstein was disappointed that the town hall concept fizzled, and he thinks that candidates can initiate much more interaction in future campaigns. Real on-line debates with voter involvement can give the press a chance to observe candidates in a forum where they don't exercise complete control. A principal complaint among many journalists and voters has been the lack of spontaneity by the candidates, who dispense prepackaged answers in settings for which they have been well prepared. On-line audiences are unlikely to tolerate plug-in answers or to let them slip by without appropriate comment. Epstein sees a scenario in which candidates will be unable to avoid on-line debates, town halls, and press conferences as more voters gain Internet access.

THINGS WEBSITES COULD DO BETTER

The Web's first entry into a political election gave developers and users a chance to learn how the medium can be most effective. The process is evolutionary, but successes and failures sometimes become clear from the start, as they did for the other media.[16]

When it comes to advice, you get what you pay for. Nevertheless, after this first campaign on the Web, site developers might profit from the journalists' free suggestions for improvement of their pages. It appeared that many campaign site designers saw voters as their only customers, and ignored reporters, who were positioned to carry the message beyond the site. As we noted, sites offered color and pizzazz, the kind of hype seen in campaign brochures, but they often were short on hard information that gave reporters a fix on the campaign and the candidates' policies. That was an opportunity lost. Serving reporters makes good sense.

So, what do the reporters want? First, they would like more hard information. They suggested items like the texts of speeches, schedules, position papers on issues of both local interest and national prominence. Quick and detailed responses to challenges from the opposition, special interests, and the press would help reporters track a candidate's thinking. The key is to be responsive and fast.

All campaigns might take a page from the Clinton playbook, which says to never let the sun set on a charge. The traditional fast-response tools have been phones and faxes, but the Web can be swifter yet. In time, reporters will turn first to the candidates' sites for an early response, then, if necessary, follow up with a phone call. A Web response is instantaneous and universally accessible. This is particularly important to journalists reporting for Website media—indeed, for any reporter whose beat requires quick news delivery.

In the best of all worlds, the candidates' Websites would post campaign finance information. That isn't likely to happen, however, unless, like nuclear disarmament, all candidates agree to do it; and history suggests that voluntary release of financial data is a pipe dream. Still, hoping against hope, some journalists said the Website posting of campaign finance data would be useful and save them a lot of time. More likely, in time, the Federal Election Commission and other government agencies will post the financial data for all candidates.

Several journalists suggested that campaigns keep their press sites simple. The texts of speeches, policy papers, and the rest don't benefit from pictures, graphics, blinking text, and animated icons. Uncluttered, text-only sites are easier to read, and they download and print more quickly. Understandably, Web site *designers* were drawn to the rich graphic features, and some used them liberally during this first year of Web campaigning. There is nothing wrong in pushing the medium to its fullest potential to impress voters, but a professional audience wants data quickly and the bulky bunting gets in the way. Elaina Hadler summed up the thoughts of several observers: "Make it fast."

Another suggestion. Campaigns that post information for the press will need to index it well and make the sites easy to navigate. Some journalists tell of campaigns that dumped information into their sites like garbage into landfill sites. Visitors had to move inch by inch down a site, hoping to stumble onto a usable item. Other sites had cumbersome indexing systems that, in an effort to be cute, became useless, and some sites didn't deliver what the hypertext promised.

Other reporters were irked by a related issue: the hypertexts to no-where. Click on these and be told "Not Found: The requested object does not exist," or "Site Under Construction." Not only do these responses frustrate, but they waste time, which for reporters is unendurable.

In sum: streamline the indexing system to save time. Deliver what the hypertext promises. Double-check links to related sites, and test them periodically, because sites start and fold like cheap diners. The point of better indexing and accurate links is to save visitors time and demon-strate a developer's concern for detail and accuracy.

Keep sites current. One of the big complains was out-of-date sites. Ed Epstein said that it looked like some campaigns set up a site, then walked away from it. A Website is not a billboard. A billboard may sit for years on the side of the road, and some even become landmarks. But the Web has another mission. It allows content change by the minute, often beat-ing live radio and television with a breaking story. Sites built on the billboard model violate audience expectations, discourage repeat visits, and denigrate the candidate whose name is on the masthead. An aban-doned site isn't likely to convince anyone that the office seeker is on top of his game. Candidates can be forgiven for missing the point in 1996, but that period of grace is coming to an end.

The press catches on quickly when there is a reasonable expectation that a candidate's site holds current information. Journalists are likely to check frequently updated sites as regularly as reporters on the crime beat check the police blotter.

Finally, several observers said that they would like to see more inter-action on the candidates' sites. A few national campaigns made a point of the candidates' connecting with voters on-line in chat rooms and town meetings. These are likely the kinds of events that will become more common in upcoming elections as candidates discover how to use a two-way medium to advance their message. Voters may expect more "face-to-face" time, and reporters, eavesdropping on the exchange, may be reading their expressions for a clue about the chemistry developing be-tween the pols and the people.

Journalism and the Web

The histories of the traditional media haven't told us much about what to expect during these early days of the Internet. As we have discussed elsewhere, the centralized model is limited in forecasting the evolution of a decentralized medium. Two hundred years with newspapers and over 70 years with broadcast have taught us little about a medium that has few barriers to entry, one free of editorial oversight and lacking standards for accuracy and taste. Furthermore, the traditional media have shed no light on what we can expect when information choices number in the hundreds of thousands. How will people find the truth among these sources? How will they arrive at balance in their understanding of a story? How will they respond to the working press when they and reporters share the same access to national events, databases, and other primary sources? There are no precedents and few clues arising from the traditional media.

Nevertheless, these are intriguing and relevant questions because the Internet *will* change the flow of news and information into the public arena, and it *will* have an impact on the traditional media and on the relationship between journalists and American audiences.

In the next few pages, we will explore several issues, related to journalism and public information, that are likely to surface as the Web integrates more fully into the national—even global—information structures. We begin with a look at how journalism itself may change.

Wes Pippert, veteran reporter and director of the Washington Reporting Program at the University of Missouri, believes that for increasing portions of the population, the Web will become a staple of political communication. "The campaign in 1996 was the last to be covered in the traditional way. It's a watershed in political reporting. Already you could see changes that I attribute directly to the Internet." Pippert said that stories about day-to-day activities of the candidate, once fixtures on the front page, were buried deeper in the papers in 1996. Front-page stories focused on analysis and critiques, the reason being that increasing numbers of voters could track the candidates on CNN and on the Web hour by hour. They could see the campaign events in real time on TV and read the speeches and follow the latest policy updates by looking at Websites maintained by the candidate, interest groups, and the media. This "as it happens" availability of information dampens the spontaneity of newspaper coverage and changes the role of newspapers in the priority of news sources. The broadcast media continue to change. The Internet will change the changers, television and radio.

And it will change other practices in the news profession as well. According to Pippert, the boys in the bus, whom we looked at earlier, that pack of journalists who followed the candidates from stop to stop, already have become less important to campaign coverage due to the ascendancy of cable television. Now, he suggests, they will become even less needed because the Internet will do much of the job for them. How?

Traditionally, reporters took to the road to record the events and examine the candidates' speeches. They looked at the meaning and the consistency of statements made in different places and at different times, and they reported their perceptions in daily feeds. Much of that will be picked up by the Internet. A small handful of journalists can cover the events, post the speeches and position papers, give an account of the events. The candidates' own sites will add to the information stockpile.

In seconds all this data can be on the Web, and in the near future, not only the text but the audio and video as well. Every reporter in the country will be able to read, hear, and see the event; do his or her own research; and examine the meaning of the day's events. The boys in the bus will be trading in their tickets for a laptop.

Reporting techniques already have changed in subtle ways. The pace of news is quickening, and the telling of it is tightening.

Philip Davis at NPR said that the Web has imposed new time pressures on journalists working in all the other media and especially in broadcasting. "Web news media can update the sites every few minutes: How can you beat that? In time, radio and television reporters will have to assume that audiences are already familiar with news developments and the breaking stories." Reporters will put a stopwatch on hot stories and keep a close eye on key Websites.

As for the tightening of a news story, Randy Reddick, director of PCSNET, suggests in an article that traditional story structures don't hold on the Web, and that the most effective news reporting requires two kinds of writing. First is the core piece, short and to the point, giving readers the gist of the event but not burdening them with detail. The early evidence is that they just won't read lengthy stories.

Second are background pieces linked to the core story. These are more complete and detail-rich, and they usually are less time-sensitive, in that they offer historical analysis that does not change by the second. Reddick calls these "archive pieces" and says they can be stored indefinitely and linked to many core stories.

Describing an interesting outcome of the two-step method, he writes: "Such a story, written in several distinct modules with an eye to an interactive environment, leads to a situation in which the audience takes part in creating the story it reads. Six people reading the same 'core' story could create for themselves six different story packages as they follow different combinations of links."[17]

Reddick's approach works for audiences and is a blessing for harassed reporters. Writing to deadline, reporters can quickly develop the core piece to rush out the hard facts. This delivers the essential details fast and gives readers what they want. Then, relieved of pressing time demands, reporters can work on archive pieces or, in many instances, simply link to, or modify, existing archive pieces that serve the purpose. The two-step approach, already used on many Web news sites, gets out the essential facts quickly while embedding the report in useful context.

Speeding up the delivery of a story and writing in a new format are only some of the changes facing journalists. Pippert predicts that the journalist's job will change from chronicling events to analyzing them, from fixing on the "who, what, where, and when" to the "why and what-does-it-mean?" Voters, who can track the campaign events themselves, will turn to the journalists for interpretation, perspective, and context, and this will require a reapportionment of skills needed for the job. According to Pippert, the Web will impose on reporters the obligation to stay current on a wider range of contemporary issues and political developments, and to gain a deeper sense of history. These are the building blocks of news analysis that reporters will need to stockpile for the new journalism.

The journalist's role has changed through time, and the concept of the journalist-observer-historian is nothing new. The transition from reporter of events to interpreter and analyst of news began before midcentury, when the telephone and other electronic communication tools became widely available. The Washington correspondent assumed the role of news commentator and interpreter when the disclosure of events was instantly transmitted to newsrooms everywhere by the wire services.[18] Papers needed correspondents who could analyze on the hoof, and that, according to journalism historian James Pollard, was a major change in the newspaper profession. With pressures from the Internet, the analyst's job will continue its evolution.

To prepare for this, reporters will need to broaden skills identified over a decade ago by former CBS newsman Charles Kuralt. He declared that good journalists must be good collectors of wide-ranging facts that they can use in analyzing and explaining events. In a 1986 speech honoring the late sports writer Red Smith, Kuralt said:

I am sure that felicitous writing comes only from felicitous musing on the contents of a kind of jumbled file cabinet or wastebasket of the mind. It's all right with me if Red Smith's mind was cluttered with facts about the Kentucky Derby, which it was; or if the reporter's mind is cluttered with facts about corruption in Chicago, as Mike Royko's mind is; or the political philosophy of William Howard Taft, as George Will's mind seems to be.[19]

In his examination of journalism in the mid-1980s, Kuralt recognized a weakness that, if anything, is growing more acute with the Web's context-scarce posting of facts:

If American journalism has one great weakness, it is that we lack a sense of history. I advocate a journalism of context. . . . It would require writers with exquisitely cluttered minds, and editors able to relate today's wire service bulletin to events of the past. It would immeasurably improve our newscasts and newspapers . . . and it would serve the country.[20]

Relating wire service bulletins to events of the past is child's play, given what Pippert describes as the journalist's approaching job. The Web will produce bulletins by the minute and disjoined stories by the warehouseful, and American audiences will turn to professional journalists for the context and meaning. This new demand will overhaul the profession, shift the focus of journalism curricula, and reshape the thinking of professionals who cover the news.

Cox Washington bureau chief, Andrew Glass, added that the universal distribution of information on the Internet also will overhaul the relationship between the news professionals and their audiences. Everyone with a computer has access to all the information—the sites, databases, information archives—and therefore, "Journalists become end users and end users become journalists."

That's an interesting way of putting the shifting roles and the newly forming relationships between journalists and their audiences. With access to the raw information, average users can do much of the job that traditionally fell to professional journalists. When journalists and voters drink from the same pools of information, it alters the traditional hierarchy. Until now, information delivery has always been at least a two-step process, with journalists at the top serving as the gatekeepers and the interpreters of news, and everyone else as recipients of the information that results. Most items that voters came by during elections first passed through the gatekeeping press. The journalists set the agendas by passing along some information and blocking out other information; but the readers and viewers caught only the items that passed though the filter.

The Internet will change traditional relationships by cutting a course around the press, giving users and voters the raw information with which to draw their own conclusions. (We noted an example of this earlier when we looked at the Web availability of survey databases.) As a result, as gatekeeping lessens, interpretation functions of the press will change as well. For instance, peripheral players, which in the past had almost no coverage in the mainstream media, will have direct access to voters, as will the advocates of third-string philosophies, theories, and ideas that often were overlooked in conventional coverage. Voters may explore and interpret these views for themselves and make judgments that the press earlier made for them—if it covered these items at all. In Glass's term, voters will become their own journalists.

How many end users—average consumers of news—actually will care enough to track down all the information is another matter. As to balance, there has been little evidence that voters themselves are all that meticulous about forming their judgments. People may start out looking at both sides of an issue, but once they lean toward a decision, they usually seek information that confirms their view, avoiding the rest. Not many socialists opt for Pat Buchanan's page, and few militia members are likely to spend time on the Greens' site. Usage patterns among Internet audiences are still forming, but as end users become their own journalists, doing the interpretation for themselves, they are not likely to assemble the balance they generally get from the professional corps.

This returns us to the relationship between reporters and their audience. As users cobble together their own ragtag collections of sources, they will increasingly need the fusion skills of journalists for analysis and context. This will not only keep journalists in the loop, but it also will impose on them heavy obligations to serve as arbiters, judges, historians, and teachers. The credibility of journalists will depend not only on their analyses but also on their abilities to divine the truth, an increasingly difficult task in this anarchic medium.

The Web and Problems of Source Verification

The time pressures noted earlier by Philip Davis, and the free-for-all spirit on the Web, impose new demands for source verification on reporters. Much of the information is undocumented, put up for no other reason than that someone has a wild idea and $25 rent money for a Website. The sites often look as authentic as the *New York Times*, but appearances on this medium can be painfully deceiving. Look at the conspiracy sites that sprang up in 1996, claiming that TWA flight 800 was destroyed by U.S. Navy missiles. They were so convincing that even veteran newsman Pierre Salinger was duped into believing their validity when he carried their charges to the mainstream press and put his professional reputation on the line. The sites were wrong and Salinger was wrong—and *he* had the time and the competence to check the facts.

What happens when competitive pressures driving reporters to stay on the crest of a story permit little time to authenticate the information, whether it comes from conventional or Website sources? There is a growing concern that reporters will be lured into shortcuts that can impair the reputation of the profession and lead to tragic consequences. The push for speed already may be testing reporters' resolve to corroborate the facts. Quoting Ronald Reagan, who was speaking in another context, Philip Davis said that journalists must not yield to the time pressures, they must "trust, but verify."

Charles Kuralt tells about his research for a piece he was writing about Galileo. He couldn't lay his hands on a reference book he had on the subject, so he took to the Web. "I found all sorts of interesting things on the Web. I was reading one piece about Galileo's dispute with the Catholic Church, and I thought that it was a bit different from what I had remembered. It put the Church in a little better light than I recall. I discovered at the end of the site that the article was written by someone from the Vatican."[21]

Kuralt tells the story as a reminder that the interpretation and presentation of facts on these sites can color a reader's interpretation. As it turns out, Kuralt knew something about his subject, so he recognized the slant provided by the Vatican source, but an uninformed visitor could easily be misled. Couldn't it happen in any medium? Of course, but everything is tossed together on the Internet, the divine next to the demonic, doubtless a recipe for confusion.

" 'Trust but verify' is an occupational imperative for journalists who would venture into this shady environment," said Gordon Sabine, retired professor of journalism and former dean of the College of Communication Arts and Sciences at Michigan State University. "This entire profession is founded on the expectation of truth. Details matter, accuracy matters, getting the facts checked and double-checked matters. Why? For the simple reason that what journalists say resonates throughout the population. Their stories are carried to thousands or millions of readers and viewers, and what's more, they can be picked up by other reporters whose stories may resound yet further."[22]

That's not all. With systems such as NEXIS, Electric Library, and Excite's NewsTracker now in place, where anyone, anywhere can lay hands on a news story, these reports are no longer confined by geography or time. Electronic storage of news accounts ensures that these stories last across the years. True enough, journalists do write the "rough drafts of history."

Widely disseminated inaccurate information, therefore, not only tampers with the telling of contemporary stories, but runs the risk of contaminating historical views many years in the future. There was a time when only the papers of record held such significance, but now hundreds of papers and broadcasts enjoy that distinction. All the more reason for the sacred responsibility of accuracy and source verification.

Marvin Kalb, former CBS newsman and now director of the Joan Shorenstein Center at Harvard, raises an issue that has plagued journalists for years. He calls it the "tyranny of the file": Assume that you're a reporter working on a story, and you wish to include as part of your research a review of other news stories relevant to your issue. For such information you would turn to the "file," which is the collection of clippings—maintained generally by a newspaper or newsroom librarian—that has to do with the event you are covering.

The tyranny of the file occurs when a reporter uses data from a tainted file. The inaccurate information from that file is then embodied in the next story, which, in turn, can become part of subsequent stories. Reporters working on related issues also might use the bad information, and before long, the effects of the error can be compounded exponentially.

It all occurs because reporters have come to trust the information that made it to print. As Kalb put it, "You will not have checked the accuracy of the file because you assumed that if the information was in the file, and in the library, that it was worth using. Besides, it was published, so you can cite the source. This is the 'tyranny of the file,' and it stems from the journalists' willingness to accept the validity of information."

Innocently, such reporters assume that the story, or facts, or statistics, or editorial comments have been vetted by writers and editors whose names were on the story or the masthead. When the truth surfaces, those led down the garden path may at least point to their guides. But what happens in a medium where little or nothing is known about the source? Eyeing the Internet, Kalb said:

On this new medium the problem compounds into a journalistic nightmare. Journalists can turn to the Internet, where there is so much information. But it is often undigested and unsourced, and even if it is sourced, what is the validity of that source? If you use it, you then give it legitimacy through your own stamp, and spread the error not only to a limited group, but to tens of millions of people around the world who then are fed bad information, bad insights, bad perspectives. The tyranny of the file is compounded in the nightmare of the Internet.

Kalb voices the suspicions you often hear from veteran journalists who take seriously their professional role as a fire wall separating the public from unreliable information. The Internet is new and untested, and while that alone is enough to raise suspicions about its use in a newsroom, its free-for-all, no-holds-barred design calls for yellow flags. Kalb agreed that many sites are rock solid and carry information every bit as accurate and as valid as clips on the evening news or articles in the morning paper. Many sites, in fact, derive from broadcast clips and newspaper articles. Nevertheless, traps await the unsuspecting.

For instance, the Web carried a number of bogus sites during the election. They looked legitimate, with all the proper signs, including believable URL addresses and convincing text that smacked of material originating from campaigns or other legitimate sources. Sometimes the real and the counterfeit differed by only a URL extension (e.g., .com .edu .org) or even a dash. Consider that "www.dolekemp96.org" was the Republican candidate's site, and "www.dole-kemp.org" was a spoof. You would be forgiven if you confused the two—except if you're a reporter. In 1996 most of these were playful parodies. Kalb fears, however, that the good-natured deceptions could take a malevolent turn, and not only dupe voters but involve unknowing reporters in the ruse. "And another thing, if you tell me the software can help, that the search engines designed to sort it all out will help, I'd have to say that I don't find any comfort in that. I don't know the person who put together the software, and I don't know his agenda, and that's what concerns me."

What's to stop search engine developers from embodying prejudices in the algorithms of their programs? Turned loose to scavenge the Web, these tools could stack the deck in favor of sites that espouse handpicked philosophies or candidates. They could deliver the bogus sites or the commercial sites that paid up, and they could do other mischief that could be tough to detect.

Several sources have told the story about the president of one major Web search engine company who pulled the addresses of organizations that did not agree with his position on the personal liability of trial lawyers. The company denied doing so. Proving the charge is difficult, but the prospect is haunting.

The bogus sites could pollute the pool of public information if their pranks were carried by the mainstream press. Imagine disaffected campaign staffers sabotaging a site by putting words in the candidate's mouth. How about hackers? They have cracked the codes of the FBI and CIA, so why should we believe they'll respect information on a campaign or a media site? As long as these possibilities exist, the unwary reporter is vulnerable to a new and more dangerous tyranny of the file, and the medium can have awful consequences if its errors are carried to the public through the mainstream press.

That danger was on the minds of most journalists interviewed. Everyone who acknowledged using the Web in a story said he or she verified the Web information by phone or though another media source, such as newspaper files or NEXIS. Nonetheless, it was evident that while this caution may have been the rule, there were significant exceptions.

For instance, some reporters quoted speeches and cited policy positions directly from Web postings. They reported results taken off the Web on Election Night and quoted poll results posted on research sites. All of these items were taken from well-known and legitimate sites, and there haven't been any real horror stories to come out of it, but the unchecked information still raises questions about the long-term policies toward the practice.

As we noted, lying at the heart of this issue is the pressure of time. In the late 1960s James Reston said, "A newspaper column, like a fish, should be consumed when fresh, otherwise it is not only indigestible but unspeakable."[23] The standards for freshness have changed considerably since Reston wrote that. As we have noted, one of the Web's great virtues is its capacity to get information out quickly. This *potential* for quick delivery has created the *expectation* for quick delivery, and it has put new pressure on reporters to hit the stands fast. Reporters writing for Websites feel the pressure, as do reporters in conventional media, who are up against the changing standard of information freshness. The clock now runs faster for everyone in the business.

As a research resource, however, the Web is vexed by the pressing need to verify every detail in its vast information stores. It takes time to cross-check the contents of a speech, or to corroborate a policy statement, and traveling down this road can take hours—a lifetime in a medium that runs by the second hand. How do reporters authenticate returns flying across the computer monitor on Election Night? Do they wait for confirmation from the networks? That's silly. For the first time, reporters for small papers and broadcast stations have the same information access as the big media. Why would they give it up and return to the lethargic old system?

The temptation to run at the head of the pack will test the reporters' good sense to verify the data. It isn't clear just when a citation is enough or when a source must be contacted directly or when a second source is necessary.

Verification, we quickly add, has never been as clear as Journalism 101 would have it. When is one source adequate, and when does a reporter need two or three? What about anonymous sources? They place huge responsibility on the journalist. "According to a highly-placed administration source, who spoke on the basis of anonymity. . . ." That lead has, in the past few decades, contributed to public cynicism toward the press. On the other hand, some of the most important stories of the century would never have made it to public light were it not for sources who would talk only in the shadows.

For years, newsrooms have followed documentation procedures, but none is airtight or assures error-free verification. We already have seen that newspaper clippings may err; trusting them can compound original blunders, yet every day thousands of reporters "trust the file." Spokespersons sometimes misstate candidates' positions, pollsters sometimes publish incorrect statistics, printed speech texts sometimes deviate significantly from delivered speeches; and these mistakes make it into print and onto the air. No medium reports error-free news, and the Web is not the first to sin, even if its temptations are new.

End Users Tackle Verification

Andrew Glass's "end users who become journalists" are not likely to revere the importance of documentation, and even if they do, they may be too limited or too unconcerned to conduct their own checks. Besides, where do average users turn to verify facts in this medium? One site looks like another, and there are no apparent distinctions among the credible, the noncredible, and the incredible displays of information. The trappings of presentation on this medium are so beguiling, even Pierre Salinger, a news veteran of 50 years, could be seduced into buying a fake bill of goods. What hope is there for the novice?

Several of the Internet's characteristics in combination create the problems. Start with the aforementioned failure to distinguish between sites. At least during the election, there appears to have been a widespread misunderstanding about differences among the categories and sources of Web sites. Many users didn't differentiate among the candidate, party, media, and government sites. Take, for example, Adelaide Elm's story about the Project Vote Smart (PVS) visitors who thought all links on her site led to PVS productions. The destination site may have said "Welcome to the DNC Home Page," but that didn't matter. If visitors got there from the PVS site, they figured it must be a PVS creation.

As we noted earlier, many users don't understand the concept of a link, and their confusion is compounded when they jump frenetically from site to site, watching the screens change but not understanding that their browser is whipsawing around the planet. Channel surfing on television only half-prepared Web audiences. It got them used to the scavenging process, but it did not prepare them for the vast range of options that they would confront. It will take people time to recognize that when they change sites, they also are changing authors, and that while some sources report verified facts, others express opinions and still others create pure fiction. "Look alike" is not "trust alike." It's asking a lot of visitors to make these credibility calls on the fly.

Another factor contributing to the misunderstanding of Website information springs from the authority of the medium itself. It's a condition that has long existed among television audiences. Media researchers have found that viewers naively believe that television purges and filters information so that only the truth emerges. Early on, before the networks vetted their standards and practices divisions, where advertising claims were subjected to empirical tests, there may have been some basis for such a trust. But even the editorial censors could not guarantee truth.[24] No matter, people believed the information because they believed the medium.

The Web may have the same effect. Like television, it is becoming mainstream and a big industry. The mighty ones on the Web, such as NBC, Microsoft, CBS, and Gannett, are traded on the New York Stock Exchange and are household names. Web information is referenced in public discussions and political speeches. You can read about the Web in newspapers and magazines, see stories about it on the evening news, listen to public officials tout its virtues. You even can hear presidential candidates give their Web site addresses in national debates.[25] Why shouldn't people believe what they see and hear on this medium? Its impressive résumé is filled with convincing references.

Moreover, today's audiences have been groomed during an era of centralized news and information. They are accustomed to reading major papers and attending to conventional broadcast media with the confidence that builds when information is vetted. For good reason, audiences give credence to the mainstream media. For all the charges of sensationalism and even hucksterism leveled at reporters and media bosses, information from the mainstream press has been reasonably sound and the facts arguably straight. American consumers of news have assumed accuracy from the press the way they assume potability of the water supply. People say they're annoyed by reporters, but trust in the final product is high and proven exceptions to the rule are rare.

Moreover, our long history of media conditioning has not instilled in us the natural skepticism found in other cultures, where the press answers to other masters. Nor have we been alerted that the information born of this new medium is different from the information found elsewhere. Except for a handful of stories about sexual predators on the Internet, the medium has drawn good ink, most of it fixing on the abundance of information, the ease of access, the virtues of interactivity.

It isn't in the interest of any major player to raise red flags. Service providers, such as AOL and CompuServe, will avoid it; they, least of all, want to frighten off the audience. The major news media sites won't do it. They have little to gain if, so early in the life of this medium, they arouse suspicions about the validity of information; an anxious public might sink all ships. So the industry and the major press have tiptoed around the danger that this freewheeling medium will artfully package false information.

Consequently, large portions of the audience are unaware of the differences between the Web and responsible media. They have learned to draw a distinction between the *New York Times* and the *National Enquirer*, but not between one Website and another. The sites themselves often conceal their sponsors. Few users give much mind to the thought that once on-line, they have engaged a decentralized medium. More than ever, verification is now the user's responsibility, and a misunderstanding of the critical differences can be risky to the benighted individual, and ultimately to the population of benighted users.

The prospects concern Marvin Kalb, who said that access to accurate information is central to individual voting decisions and to the outcomes of public elections. He referred to something Arthur Hays Sulzberger once said about the centrality of information: "A man's judgment cannot be better than the information on which he has based it."[26] Significant changes in the sources and composition of information that make up our knowledge pool can change public judgments, Kalb argued.[27]

Kalb worries about the captivity of information users when they shift from conventional media to the Internet.

We are all prisoners of the information we have, therefore, prisoners to the sources of that information. If we read something in the *New York Times*, we believe it is probably accurate and reflects many points of view, and probably provides a good summary of complicated problems. If we go on the Internet, however, we compose our own answers to difficult problems. We become prisoners to the answers that the Internet provides.

Users must contend with more than the validity of information sources. As Kalb points out, they also must assemble the facts into meaningful answers. The magnitude of the job is overwhelming and difficult for people not trained for it. This is why Kalb argues for a broad exposure to the news: "It is crucially important that in addition to the Internet, there continue to be newspapers, TV, books, and many other sources of information to serve as counterweights to essentially unfiltered sources of information—and unknown sources of information."

CONCLUSION

The press is already under the gun. Some research suggests that public confidence in the news media is at an all-time low, reporters rating only a little better than politicians.[28] Much of this is a "shoot the messenger" reaction and not due to sins that the press itself has committed. Responsible journalists are unfairly tarred by TV reporters, for example, who shove a mike in the face of the grieving parent and ask, "How does it feel to lose your child?" The public doesn't always understand the distinctions among legitimate news operations, talk shows, sensational programs, docudramas, and the rest, so when one crosses the line, all are tarred by the same brush.

Not that the press isn't sometimes its own worst enemy, giving due cause for public cynicism. Aggressive network news teams sometimes draw fire, as ABC did when its reporters concealed their identities in pursuit of a story at the Food Lion grocery chain. The network drew a $5.5 million fine (afterward appealed) and a finger-wagging from the jury. Public reaction against ABC and undercover journalism was not unanimous.

Much less defensible was the paparazzi persecution of Richard Jewell after the Olympic bombing in Atlanta. Police and FBI leaks contributed to the feeding frenzy, but news stories often came up short on the tentative nature of the investigations; with a wink and a nod, they let on that the culprit was in hand. The relentless hounding of Jewell, who later was declared blameless, created a spectacle that is slow to fade from the public memory.

The press cannot afford a deepening public mistrust, but more important, the public cannot afford to lose trust in the press, especially not now. American news media have always been at the center of public debate over national policy and political decision-making. The press sets up the public dialogue, then fosters it by tracking public reaction. Playwright Arthur Miller once said, "A good newspaper, I suppose, is a nation talking to itself." The country needs to talk to itself, especially in the era of the Internet, when media will scatter people in many directions, and it needs to trust that the media, although occasionally stumbling, are reliably reporting the news, faithfully auditing public reaction, then feeding it back again. Nonprofit institutes like Poynter, which subject papers to relentless evaluations, declare that reporters have never been better and mainstream papers have never been more responsible. That evaluation may be accurate, it must now become widely accepted.

As for the Internet, it will not reduce the role of the press; it will likely increase it. Nor will it relieve the press of the need to maintain its standards. If anything, it will increase the need. In an uncensored, open-access medium where everyone *can* have a say, everyone *will* have a say in one way or another. What people say will be opinionated and partisan, it will play fast and loose with the facts, and it will largely be undocumented. Much of the Web already is information by mob rule, and that isn't likely to change as this decentralized medium becomes more populated.

Wes Pippert's observation that the Internet will push journalists further into the analyst's role was right. Audiences will have direct access to campaign events and to an expanding range of political information and points of view. They will hear firsthand from the candidates, their supporters and detractors, interests groups and unallied critics. Eventually, voters will look for someone to sort it all out, to analyze the claims, statistics, and promises, and to explain what they mean. There will be a need for someone to help voters separate the wheat from the chaff, and that job will fall to the reporter-analyst, whose role will take on increasing importance with the growing inventory of Web-based information.

Analysts who operate in this environment will feel the need to be accurate and evenhanded. After all, they will serve as the arbiters and the referees, the neutral voices that offer the trusted perspectives. It is critical, therefore, that journalists operating on and with the Web, even in the face of time pressures, maintain the long-held need to document and verify information to preserve their role as trusted observers and analysts of public information.

NOTES

1. James E. Pollard offers an excellent and detailed account of these issues in *The Presidents and the Press* (New York: Macmillan, 1947).

2. It's surprising to see Jefferson on this list, since he is one of history's staunchest defenders of a free press. But he, like the others, often suffered from harsh press accounts of his public and private life; yet such treatment did not distract him from his strong support for a constitutionally protected right to publish.

3. Pollard, *The Presidents and the Press.*

4. For an excellent treatment of big business control of American media, see B. II. Bagdikian, *The Media Monopoly*, 3rd ed. (Boston: Beacon Press, 1990).

5. Direct and unfettered access is good for the free flow of information, but it troubles some journalists because it skirts the editorial responsibility, the purging and branding functions provided by the established press. *USA Today* may feature capsule reportage, but you know what you're getting. The *National Enquirer* may be scandalous, but you know what pushes those editors. With Websites, however, you can't be sure. Those that bill themselves as news sources, even name brands like MSNBC and the *Los Angeles Times*, are still on probation. They need more time to prove their reliability as a constant, trustworthy source. But information found on the partisan, special interest, and individual sites deserve a close review to see if there is probable cause for suspicion.

6. See a discussion of problems with direct mail and personal campaign phone calls in G. Selnow, *High Tech Campaigns: Computer Technology in Political Communication* (Westport, CT: Praeger, 1994).

7. The following news professionals participated in the discussions reported throughout this chapter: Herman Cohen, former professor of communication at Pennsylvania State University, face-to-face discussions during the last week of July 1997; Philip Davis, political reporter for National Public Radio, telephone discussion on Dec. 11, 1996; Edward Epstein, political reporter for the *San Francisco Chronicle*, discussions on several occasions before and after the election; Curtis Gans, director of the Committee for the Study of the Electorate, telephone discussion on May 28, 1996; Andrew Glass, Washington bureau chief for Cox News, telephone discussions in Mar. 1996 and on Dec. 4, 1996; Elaina Hadler, director of National Public Radio's *Talk of the Nation*, telephone discussion on Dec. 10, 1996; Marvin Kalb, former CBS newsman, now director of the Joan Shorenstein Center at Harvard, telephone discussion on Dec. 9, 1996; Mary Klette, director of politics and polling at NBC News, telephone discussion on Feb. 3, 1997; Charles Kuralt, former CBS newsman, telephone discussion on Mar. 5, 1997; Wesley Pippert, director of the Washington Reporting Program at the University of Missouri-Columbia and 30-year UPI veteran, telephone discussion on Dec. 7, 1996; Gordon Sabine, former professor of journalism and dean of the College of Communication Arts and Sciences at Michigan State University, telephone discussion on Apr. 14, 1997; Barbara Saffir, political researcher for the *Washington Post*, telephone discussion on Dec. 4, 1996.

8. Maybe campaigns that ignored their own Websites just didn't get it. They assembled pro forma sites with a few pictures and some text, and figured that fulfilled their obligations to the teckies. They didn't post press releases or campaign updates, or supply something fresh enough to keep reporters and constituents coming back. Of all the public media, the Web is the most time-sensitive, and its audiences simply will not tolerate stale information.

9. California's Proposition 215, in part, states the following (from "The Letter of the Law in California, Arizona," *USA Today*, Nov. 7, 1996, p. 3D).

(A) To ensure that seriously ill Californians have the right to obtain and use marijuana for medical purposes where that medical use is deemed appropriate and has been recommended by a physician who has determined that the person's health would benefit from the use of marijuana in the treatment of cancer, anorexia, AIDS, chronic pain, spasticity, glaucoma, arthritis, migraine, or any other illness for which marijuana provides relief.

(B) To ensure that patients and their primary caregivers who obtain and use marijuana for medical purposes upon the recommendation of a physician are not subject to criminal prosecution or sanction.

10. Letter dated Oct. 21, 1948, from Charles G. Ross, secretary to the president, to Herman Cohen, announcing supervisor, WSUI at the State University of Iowa.

11. Information taken from the Electric Library Web site: http://www2.elibrary.com. The site's notes that its rate for unlimited usage is $9.95 per month for individual subscribers.

12. Jon Swartz, "E-Mail Is Becoming Much More Than Just Text," *San Francisco Chronicle*, Nov. 12, 1996, p. C4.

13. A number of companies have developed programs that deliver graphic E-mail messages. They offer clip art, graphic designs for greeting cardlike messages, and animation. Some of the active players are General Magic, Prodigy, Hallmark Cards, and Media Synergy.

14. Yahoo began offering some 50 sites for discussions on sports, politics, business, and international news. The company planned to fund the service through advertising revenue earned from ads posted on the sites.

15. Alexander maintained an active Website, and also occasionally got on-line for chats with voters, but these were far and few between and were usually used to draw publicity from the other media.

16. In the case of television, people learned early that a visual medium is hardly ideal for long, droning speeches. Windy addresses might work on radio, but television audiences are geared for action and don't cotton to talking heads. In 1988, Bill Clinton forgot his home audience—and, it would seem, even his live audience—in his marathon address at the Democratic National Convention. This hour-long speech was a classic example of a misplaced message for television.

17. Quotation taken from R. Reddick, *News Backgrounder, A Briefing Paper for Journalists*. Reddick is the director of the Foundation for American Communications, an independent nonprofit educational institution for journalists. The *News Backgrounder* is part of a continuing series of briefing papers published by the organization. http://www.facsnet.org/report-tools/newsbackgrounders/main.html.

18. Pollard, *The Presidents and the Press*.

19. C. Kuralt, "The View from the Road," a speech at the Department of American Studies, Notre Dame, University, Aug. 1986.

20. Ibid.

21. From an interview on Mar. 5, 1997.

22. From an interview on Mar. 12, 1997.

23. James Reston, *Sketches in the Sand* (New York: Alfred A. Knopf, 1967), xi.

24. See G. Selnow, and R. Gilbert, *Society's Impact on Television: How the Viewing Public Shapes Television Programming* (Westport, CT: Praeger, 1993).

25. Bob Dole is credited with being the first presidential candidate to give his Website address on national television. He did so at the end of the last debate with Bill Clinton.

26. A. Sulzberger, address to the New York State Publishers Association, Aug. 30, 1948.

27. From an interview on Dec. 9, 1996.

28. Louis Harris and Associates released a survey in mid-December 1996 that

suggested there was considerable distrust of the press among Americans; 51 percent said the media usually "got the facts straight," and 44 percent said the news media are "often inaccurate." Harris also reported that 42 percent said news people are more arrogant, 31 percent said they are more cynical, 33 percent said they are less compassionate, 34 percent said they are more biased, and 24 percent said they are less honest than most people. The poll was reported in an Associated Press story by the *San Francisco Chronicle*, "Much Distrust of News Media, Poll Finds," Dec. 14, 1996, p. A6.

Chapter Seven

A Changing Public Agenda and Audience Fragmentation

It is traditionally American to fight hard before an election. It is equally traditional to close ranks as soon as the people have spoken. . . . That which unites us as American citizens is far grater than that which divides us as political parties. . . . We vote as many, but we pray as one. With a united people, with faith in democracy, with common concern for others less fortunate around the globe, we shall move forward with God's guidance.

—Adlai Stevenson
concession speech, November 5, 1952

THE CHILLING OF THE NATIONAL HEARTH

Eric Sevareid, the late CBS commentator and political analyst, once described American television as the national hearth. He was talking about the days of network dominance, when people gathered around the family television set to warm themselves by the evening newscasts and the prime-time lineups. The nation of some 250 million people, scattered across 3.5 million square miles, spanning the political spectrum, partitioned by ideology, race, and religion, found its locus in television. The symbolism is unmistakable. For nearly two decades, television was the community hearth. It delivered the news and told the stories that fed conversations around office coffeepots and dining room tables. For a brief period, television provided a common information currency that could be traded anywhere in the nation.

What technology giveth, technology taketh away. Until the mid-1970s, cable television was a sleepy service that brought signals into remote and mountainous areas. Then, in 1976, Home Box Office (HBO), bouncing a signal off Satcom I, started running full-length movies, mostly to see if American audiences would pay for a medium they had always used without charge. The results were legendary; in a matter of several years, cable companies were trenching neighborhoods throughout the country to lay the lines that over time would undermine the national hearth and fragment the viewers who had gathered around it.

Cable's conspicuous feature, of course, is its many channel offerings that give audiences not three but three dozen or more choices, and if the prophets are right, more than 500 channels when mature. Audiences revel in the options, but their pursuit of individual interests on the many channels fractionalizes the formerly common audiences and dismantle the national meeting place. Cable has so changed the industry that the networks, at one time able to muster 95 percent of the audience, today often can't scrape together even half of all viewers. Meanwhile, as cable struggles to bring most areas 35 channels, direct satellite TV races ahead with 200 or more.

Cable began a process that the Internet continues with a fury. This new, highly personal medium, even at the start, never reached out for large, blended audiences. From its earliest days, in all of its forms—E-mail, Gopher, the Web, chat rooms—the Internet laser-focused on the homogeneous, special interest groups that usually are small in their numbers but large in their loyalties. Despite great efforts by well-funded backers, the concept of a huge megasite has not caught on, nor is it likely to. You don't find network-size audiences anywhere on the Web, not even the key media sites that have the best chance to attract large numbers. Several Hollywood producers attempted to apply the "network model" to the Internet—to build a central site for wide-ranging audiences—and they quickly found that the "mass" concept didn't graft onto this targeted medium.[1]

The absence of big audiences on the Web has been a nagging frustration to many site operators, but what's wrong with a medium that subdivides and stratifies its audiences like the layers of a Dobosch torte and draws people away from conventional media? For many observers, not a thing.

From one point of view, the many sites and the many options suit individual users and the changing information marketplace. Marvin Kalb, who mostly sees trouble in the Web for journalists, acknowledges that "To some people, this medium is a wonderful thing. Those who run the big papers and networks and who controlled the agenda before, can't control it now. With cable and now the Internet, people have access to information from sources other than the powerful broadcasters and publishers."

Back in the 1970s, researchers said that we arrived at these issues through the agenda-setting function of the media. True, but we should remember that the underside of agenda-setting was reductive—it kept some political candidates and philosophies out of sight and out of mind. For so many years, office seekers who went unblessed by the media went unknown. Sadly, we'll never know the cost of their absence from the national debate.

The mainstream media's agenda-setting role remained in force during the 1996 election, but the Web had already demonstrated its capacity to pick the lock. As we have seen, Web searches that year turned up beefy lists of third-party candidates, little-known interest groups, and offbeat ideas. For many, it was the first time ever that they had had a public forum in which to express their views. It didn't amount to much in 1996, but Kalb's point is well taken. We are likely witnessing the last days where the big media control the national agenda.

Media researcher John Bane sees great promise in the Web's agenda-busting role because of what he believes is the corrupting "market-driven content" of the mainstream media. Newspapers pander by following the polls, then run stories that chase after these public perspectives: "Today, much of the reporting panders to the community under the guise of journalism." This sells newspapers and improves television ratings, but is it the kind of journalism that the country wants or needs? Public consumption may demonstrate that it's what the public wants, but Bane and others argue that it isn't what we need.

It has been a newspaper tradition to carry the banner for important issues. Look at the civil rights movement in the 1950s and 1960s. The papers went after this issue and kept it on the public agenda. Would they have done this if they were following the polls? Probably not, because the polls would have told them that most people didn't care much about civil rights.[2]

Bane argues that an eventual waning of the central power of the mainstream press, specifically in campaign reporting, is not much of a loss because of what the press itself has done to abdicate its moral and professional responsibility. Bane's observations on print media are even more apparent in broadcasting. The preoccupation of television news with trivia and trendy topics, at the expense of serious issues facing the country and the world, reflects the keen interest in exposing audiences to advertisers.

The author recalls an occasion when he was in Europe during a particularly volatile period. Countries budding from the former Yugoslavia were suffering wrenching street battles. The European Community was wrestling with mass immigration from the east and with economic and environmental problems from within. These events and issues had significance not only to Europeans but also to Americans, because they eventually would impact U.S. economic and military policies. Yet on at least one American network newscast (available by satellite) these stories were hardly mentioned.

All but ignoring these events would have been forgivable if it had been a busy news day and other weighty events filled the 22-minute news hole that night, but imagine the surprise when in that same newscast, the network ran several light features, including a three-minute piece on a street musician who played wine glasses. It's hard to understand the editorial judgment that placed such footage above coverage of developments in Europe, or God knows what other newsworthy events occurring on the planet that day. The problem is that events uncovered remain events unknown. Viewers never know what they're missing.

There was a time, roughly during the Brinkley and Cronkite years, when networks thought of the evening news as a sacred trust. Then it slowly faded into a headline service and finally resolved into a competitive money machine featuring star anchors whose job it was to be first in the ratings. Their approach to that goal, as Theodore White said, is to "color the flow of events with their personalities."[3]

You can't find a better example of conflicting values in news coverage than on February 4, 1997, when two compelling news events converged. The first was the jury verdict in the O. J. Simpson civil trial and the second, Clinton's State of the Union address.

The jury announced that it had reached its verdict at about the same time Clinton was starting his speech, and for the next hour, the court assembled in Santa Monica while the president's speech was under way. It was a race against the clock. Would Clinton finish his speech first, or would the jury open the envelope first? With cameras on the president, NBC scrolled at the bottom of the screen a promise that the instant the jury released its results, the network would break away from the State of the Union speech and cover the trial.

Granted, NBC actually aired the entire speech, but only because the verdict had not been announced. The network was spring-loaded to leave Washington the second the jury foreman rose from his chair in California. When push came to shove, the wildly popular preoccupation with the Simpson case would win out over the vastly more important dialogue between the president and the American people. Come the next morning, the Simpson decision would be inconsequential to all but a handful of players in the case, while the president's proposals would resound in national policy for years to come and affect us all. These newsworthiness factors, it seems, didn't play much of a role in the network's decision.

A colleague and coauthor of a book on television's influences, Richard Gilbert, who has worked for CBS, ABC, and NBC, demurs to some extent.[4] First, 24-hour news coverage by CNN has relieved the networks of their former responsibility as the only national TV news source, and second, the O. J. decision was arguably a more significant news event than the president's address. Why? Gilbert says the Clinton speech was 90 percent predictable and fully anticipated in papers, public TV, and evening network news. O. J., by contrast, was a breaking story of incredible interest to millions. Even the issues of race, celebrity, law and justice, and civil vs. criminal jurisprudence were of greater importance to most Americans than the rehashed clichés of the postelection period. His point: nobody will remember what Clinton said, but everyone will remember when a millionaire couldn't buy his way out of dishonor and financial ruin.

Gilbert's point is well taken. However, much of what he says reflects the trap of our current system of news as entertainment. Sure, CNN is a voice added to the chorus providing news to the American public, but we should remember that not all homes have access to cable, and those least able to afford it are left with the inane capsules on broadcast television. For them, CNN is not an option. Moreover, even if everyone had access, the addition of CNN no more relieves the Big Three of their obligation for responsible journalism than the presence of the *Washington Post* relieves Knight Ridder of its obligation to publish the truth.

Second, and more to the point, the O. J. story has become the domestic issue of the decade only because the media have made it so. Yes, as Gilbert says, it has inherent public interest. But why? To start with, O. J. is a product of the nation's two biggest entertainment machines— sports and Hollywood. They elevated his visibility and created his public persona. The celebrity Simpson then played nicely in another entertainment circus, the trial. The American people may recall the O. J. decision over Clinton's speech, but only because the media elevated this story over any other single issue. The media made O. J., then used him as an entertainment ace. Gilbert's observations are correct in every detail. However, he has fixed on the outcomes of a twisted infotainment process that itself is the corrupting influence.

The central media's control of the agenda, and their moves toward a journalism of the coin box, are poignant. From this view, the Internet's challenges are not only good but also necessary to open the public agenda and to fortify the substance of public debate. The Web can give voice to whispers rarely heard, and it can confront the powerful media, whose journalism often has come to reflect the concerns of accountants rather than editors.

The Internet's challenge to television is good for another reason. William Brock, who has worn many hats in Washington, including serving as head of the Republican National Committee,[5] said in an interview that television is a curse on the political process. "TV is now our primary mechanism for reaching the American people, and this medium has created huge problems for public communication. It forces us to deliver information in ways we might otherwise avoid."[6]

Brock says that television has made it easy to create a politics of wedge issues and attacks. The sound bites force political leaders to issue pithy one-liners because they know that little more can make it onto the evening news. Even if they were inclined to explain at length their views on the vital national issues, most of their words would wind up on the cutting room floor. Consequently, public figures, recognizing the need for public exposure, yield to the demands of this popular medium. In the process, they become unwitting participants in a dumbing down of the public debate.

What about newspapers for the details? It's true that a longer, more thoughtful treatment of the issues may make it into print, but the polls since 1965 have demonstrated that most voters get their news from television. Like Willie Sutton, who robbed banks because that's where the money is, pols turn to television because that's where the voters are.

Brock said that television thrives on negatives, violence, horror stories, inflammatory accusations, and the worst instincts of an audience. A calm discussion of the issues or an amicable political compromise will lose out every time to a nasty crack or a scuffle. This does two things. First, it overloads the public agenda with images from the dark side of politics. Ask people what they think goes on in Washington, and most, with disgust, will tell you about the fighting, back-stabbing, and corruption. Of course, such things occur in Washington, no denying that, but so do many productive and admirable accomplishments, which rarely make it in force to the evening news. The distortion occurs in the lopsided balance of the issues presented, which ultimately heightens public cynicism and reduces public interest in politics. We ask why half the eligible voters stay at home on Election Day. The answer, in part, might be the way politics is presented on the nation's most popular medium. It may be systematically demobilizing American voters.[7] Not that voters stormed the booths before TV, but the combination of nonissues on TV and our reliance on polls that tell us who won a week before the election make a mix lethal to civic duty.

Second, the preoccupation of television news with the negative elements of politics actually propagates these reactions. If they know that a political attack will make the evening newscast while a calmer response will not, public leaders, despite their better inclinations, too often yield to the temptation and give the medium what it wants. Moreover, fear that the opposition will make a sneak attack on the six o'clock news inspires preemptive attacks all around. Brock stressed that television's way of covering news engages the worst political instincts and contributes to the brand of attack politics that plays out every night in American living rooms.

"My hope," Brock said, "is that the Internet will give office seekers and political leaders a better way to offer their serious thinking on the key issues facing the country. Maybe this will offset the terrible condition that has evolved with television over the years." At least the more thoughtful views offered on the candidate's Website can complement television's glib treatments and give the serious voter a chance to learn more than the one-liners.

But do people really want more than they're getting on television? Do they care what a candidate really thinks, and would they take the time to chase down the candidates' views on the Web? People say they care and would investigate the facts.[8] Some of the news and information sites on the Web in 1996 claimed lots of traffic, and some of the major candidate sites also cited impressive hit rates, but the evidence is anecdotal and not very strong. Still, it isn't hard to believe that with proper promotion and presentation, the Web really can draw the attention of voters seeking a level of information that they are unable to find on television.

If nothing else, a growing public reliance on the Web for news and information will almost surely dilute television's power over political leaders and voters. The Web is likely to reshape the usage patterns for all the existing media. "We're talking fairly long-term, maybe in 5 to 10 years or even more. It will happen incrementally, and it won't happen overnight," Brock said. "The real impact of the Internet may be to relegate TV purely to entertainment. It's there now, really, but at least we'll recognize it for what it is and rely on the Internet—in whatever form it takes—as our principal source of news."

Indeed, if these promising views of the Internet evolve in time, the new medium—content-rich and audience-strong—has a good chance of breaking the iron grip of the central media. It may weaken TV's control of the public agenda, loosen its stranglehold on third-string candidates and philosophies, and impose an antidote to the sometimes toxic form of political communication. That would mark a redemption of the American political process of messianic proportions. The process may already be under way.

But there is more than one scenario, and some view this new medium with fewer hopes and larger fears. One of the great fears, based in no small part on media usage patterns already evident, is that the Internet's capacity to ultratarget runs the risk of fragmenting the population. It may divide the formerly common audiences into smaller and smaller groups, each forming around a narrow issue, a special interest, or a provincial philosophy that unites the members while separating them from outsiders. Carried to its end, a population driven by the pursuit of individual passions will become unwieldy and ungovernable. Self-interest will drive each group, and the competition among groups for scarce community resources ultimately will challenge the stability of the nation.

Orville Schell, professor and dean of Berkeley's Graduate School of Journalism, observes that the great irony of a populist medium so rich with information could be that it becomes the "great revenge of pluralism."[9]

That's a huge indictment of a medium just beginning. It's especially tough because present audiences are mostly regaling themselves with entertainment and interactive amusements, and not displaying the signs of a pernicious individualism. But the pieces are assembling, and the concerns are not far-fetched. If the fears are valid, we may long to push the genie back in the bottle.

Troubles may arise because the medium is designed to focus narrowly. Even the news media sites that started out looking for the same broad audiences on the Web that they reach in conventional print and broadcast forums, already are moving toward a narrowing of news delivery around the individual interests of their visitors. Services such as NewsTracker scan 300 Web periodicals for just the subjects you select, offering a deep but narrow examination of your pet concerns. Search engines operate by carving up the Web into parcels of similar topics. "Push" companies such as BackWeb and PointCast specialize in hand-delivering information about only the subjects that users have specified in advance. Sports fans, jazz buffs, and travel enthusiasts can indulge in their cravings all day and never lay eyes on news about anything else. That's where the problem lies; chasing after self-interest is the mark of this medium.

David Broncoccio, news anchor and senior editor for Public Radio International's *Marketplace* program, compared Website visits to video store visits. He said most people enter a video store and make a beeline to the section that most interests them. If you don't like foreign films, or documentaries, you probably avoid these shelves and select instead from your usual sci-fi or adventure options. He said most people seek information with which they are comfortable and don't go out of their way to sample something different or to be challenged by conflicting views.[10]

There was some evidence that voters in 1996 tracked down the sites of their favorite candidates and avoided the rest. The America's Voice election project offered some signs that voters may have looked to the sites that confirmed their ideological starting points. Even Randy Reddick's recommendations on writing news for the Web capitalize on the notion that visitors will follow their own interests (see Chapter 6). That's why he tells reporters to keep the core stories short and let readers follow their interests through hypertext. Don't ask everyone to read all the details, as we do in print. Let each reader pursue his or her own curiosity.[11] There's nothing startling about the concept.

Nor is there anything new. Cable and radio segment audiences. Magazines—once, like the networks, reaching huge, blended audiences—today, like cable television, have become quite targeted. So the movement toward audience fragmentation has been under way for years; the Web is only traveling down a well-trodden path.

Still, with the Web, it's a matter of degree. This is not a medium *adapting* to the targeted way of communication, it was *created* as a targeted medium. It doesn't offer 40 or 500 or a few thousand channels into which users can tuck away. This monster stockpiles well over a half million sites, and the number grows every day. Moreover, views can emerge on the Web that could never surface in conventional media. In 1996 you could spend hours on the Web reading about the philosophy of the Communist Party or the Libertarians, or the Natural Law Party. Where in the conventional media can you get regular installments of information about these parties? Add to this the chat rooms, bulletin boards, and other interactive resources that target users. Where else can you find such a thing? The Web is a medium of incomprehensible abundance and focus. It has so much information in so many places that it can appeal to the refined tastes of very small groups. Such ultratargeting leads to audience segmentation by siphoning users away from the common sites and distributing them into interest-bound bundles. The Internet's extraordinary capacity to target, compared with that of the other media, is the key to deepening concerns about the dangers of fragmentation.[12]

The dispersal of the audience—some call it atomization—runs several dangers in a political system built on a consensus of views among a popular majority of voters. People chasing down their own agendas are likely to limit their exposure to views at two levels.

First, they may miss issues that occur outside their routine surveillance of events. If they set up their news searches to snare stories about gun control, abortion, or privatization of schools, they'll get plenty about these topics, but nothing about a balanced budget, Medicare, welfare, and a spectrum of other issues also important to the national agenda. These audiences miss not only the other issues but also the essential latticework of issues facing political leaders and the nation. Abortion has implications for welfare, privatization of schools impacts the federal budget. Very few of the topics facing government today are isolated, and examining a select few subjects yields a spotty picture of the larger mosaic.

It's true that even now, people skimming the morning paper can skirt all these issues, but at least the information is there and incidental stories have a chance of grabbing the attention of readers in pursuit of their favorite topics. The likelihood of incidental exposure is even greater on a television or radio newscast. Their linear presentations force you to sit through each story, like it or not, and absorb information about matters that aren't on your list of key topics.

"Look at the scope of stories we cover on *Marketplace*," said David Broncuccio. "Every day, we provide stories from Wall Street and from

the economics-and finance-related agencies in Washington. Some people
tune in especially to hear us 'do the numbers,' which recaps the stock
market trading figures for the day. But, peppered in among these regular
items, we offer features and commentary that listeners did not specifically tune in to hear The broader exposure is a benefit to them personally
and to the larger society."

Broncoccio said the program gives listeners a broad view of subjects
that enriches their understanding of business in this country and around
the world. "George Lewinski, our foreign editor, recently aired a story
about child labor in Bangladesh. Do you think people would have tuned
in specifically for that feature? Probably not, but it held important information that helped explain the global labor market affecting some
American business operations."

Broncoccio talked about the importance of a wide-angle lens on the
news, and he said that the Web's capacity to winnow down exposure to
a limited range of stories can be dangerous to a population that needs
common references.

Second, people run the risk of an information blind spot within an
issue when they chase down sites given to partisan and ideological viewpoints. These sites typically emphasize one side of a debate, making little
pretense at evenhandedness. That is not their mission. Activist groups
design their sites to state a position—often as strongly as possible—in
order to reinforce the believers. They frequently overstate the urgency
of conditions and the strength of the adversaries, and at the same time
project a solidarity among supporters. These sites, furthermore, linked
to kindred sites, forming a daisy chain that is mutually reinforcing. A
visitor can spend all day immersed in sites that preach the same gospel.

It isn't hard to find examples. Search on environmental issues and
you'll arrive at a long list of sites fixing on pollution, deforestation, the
loss of animal habitats. Greenpeace, Earthwatch, the Nature Conser-
vancy, and hundreds of other organizations discuss the planetary threats,
urge action, and pass visitors along to like-minded sites. Rare among
these is mention of the legitimate concerns of chemical and timber companies, farmers and landowners. For these you must turn to the other
side of the ledger, where you'll find an equally lopsided discussion of
environmental policy and a distortion of the positions held by the environmentalists.

The Christian Coalition site pushes the right-wing agenda and pokes
a finger in the eye of the opposition. Factional jabs prevail on the pages
of the National Rifle Association, the Marijuana Policy Project, the John
Birch Society, the Workers of America, the F.E.A.R. (Forfeiture Endan-
gers America's Rights) Foundation, and many others. Issues-based organizations have always taken strong stands in brochures and
newsletters, and now they've taken to hard-hitting on the Internet. The

difference now is that the Internet gives them easy access to audiences that they could not have reached before. It also gives them unlimited space for their arguments and easy links with allies.

The problem with the ideological sites is that they blind the user to alternative arguments, and this sets several outcomes in motion. As Andy Glass noted, this flood of unbalanced information reinforces people's biases. If you start out believing that the government is planning to take away your property rights, then you aren't likely to have changed your mind after visiting the F.E.A.R. Foundation page and many similar sites. The polemics on these pages harden visitors' initial positions and inoculate them against alternative arguments.

Visitors loading up on these sites also are likely to form the impression that fringe ideologies are really mainstream. The essays and articles, E-mail correspondence and chat rooms create a sense that the idea is catching on, and that a movement is afoot. The impact of these sites accumulates to form the perception that a ripple is a tsunami.

We started with the thought that fragmentation can weaken a political system built on popular consensus. Political fortunes are made and lost on the ability of candidates and officeholders to find workable solutions that sit well with at least half the people. That challenge grows with the dispersion of beliefs within the population. A pluralistic society, by definition, is more difficult to satisfy than one in which the population has homogeneous views, all members pulling in the same general direction.

Pluralism has been our blessing and our curse since the Founding Fathers preferred the wisdom of a large, all-inclusive national government over the tighter, smaller, self-contained governments of the states. Madison saw an inherent strength in a larger collective, a belief that dominated his Federalist Number 10. Elkins and McKitrick comment: "A major premise of Madison's Federalist Number 10—is that a multiplicity of interests may function as a guarantee of political stability and against majority despotism."[13] A broad spectrum of views yields a kind of ballast effect, which Madison, at the time, saw as a counterweight to a party-dominated system.

In an interview, historian Stanley Elkins said that Madison had a shrewd sense of competing interests, creating a balance among the many participants. "But what happens if they don't talk to each other, I don't know." The system breaks down when communication comes to a halt. That is the curse of pluralism, at least of a system where the competing interests no longer talk, and worse, where they no longer share common reference points.[14]

The real trouble is with factions. They are "any group . . . actuated by some 'passion . . . or interest' adverse to the public good or to the rights of the whole."[15] Factions can form around "differences—of class, religion, property and what not—on which they might be based."[16] Elkins related Madison's fear of factions to the Internet's capacity to single out audiences and separate groups by individual concerns.

The interesting thing is that, in a curious way, we're getting back to an eighteenth-century concern. Factions were seen as bad because they were narrow and selfish. Now we're beginning to develop a fresh concern with factions. How do you get people to look at someone else's problems? The concern about factions is that you become so insulated against other points of view and you become so self-righteous that it can be very destructive for national purposes.

One thing clear about the centralized media is that they blanketed everyone, and even if they didn't bring about a common view—something impossible to imagine, and not very healthy, to boot—at least they provided common points of reference. The debate, could, therefore continue on universally familiar issues.

Bill Schneider, CNN's senior political analyst, said in an interview that throughout the twentieth century, the media have fed a mass public. "Before this century, people held the opinions of the political parties and distinctive subcultural views, but we now are more blended. You can see that in the polls." Schneider said that you can find factions on the fringes, but the national mainstream is undifferentiated in its focus on the primary national issues because of the centralized media's homogenization effects.[17] The mass media have provided the raw material for the focus—the endless argument and debate of the issues.

"Would the Internet encourage broad debate or encourage the factionalism that concerns us all? I'm not sure. I'm a bit frightened by it," Elkins said. The country has become large and diverse, and the media have been stabilizing. "I like national TV for what it does. You can argue that we need to get both sides of an argument. Will that come from the Internet? I'm not sure. I'm afraid that it might not."

If it doesn't, what happens in a system that isolates people into groups preoccupied with a restricted set of issues or points of view? Empathy got its definition when Native Americans suggested that you can't understand a fellow human "until you've walked a thousand steps in his moccasins." Traditional central media, for all their faults, at least offered the opportunity for people to observe the world from the perspectives of people unlike themselves. They let them see how legislation and policies impacted people, regions, and industries differently, and reminded them that in a perpetual climate of scarce resources, every gain has a matching cost—to someone.

Federal budget stories in newspapers and on the evening news, for instance, might show that the Pentagon's gain would be the National Science Foundation's loss. They would show how maintenance of the Social Security system might mean a partial dismantling of the welfare system. They would reveal how the coal used in the Midwest to fire the cauldrons of heavy industry kills forests in the Northeast that sustain tourism and the timber industry.

Moreover, these stories, in print and broadcast, often would show the human side of the equation and remind people that there was more at stake than the polemics of a political debate or two sides of a ledger sheet. Sometimes the human elements were played too strongly and the anecdotes overran the logic of a rational discussion. But the opportunity to examine issues from more than one perspective made an important contribution to the larger political debate.

What a fearful prospect it is that ultratargeting on the Internet could tuck people away into isolated chat rooms and ensconce them in a family of Websites that never explore the national themes from more than a single or limited perspective. Using the earlier examples, would people preoccupied with the purchase of military hardware understand, over time, the impact of losses to the National Science Foundation? Would chat rooms and Websites fixing on Social Security allow people to elude the images of hungry kids whose living assistance had to be sacrificed? If the Web limits and isolates users to the extent that some observers fear, it may rob people of the information—the images—that allows them to empathize with people whose fates rest on the other side of the balance.

The lack of empathy, moreover, makes it easier to draw up sides because it exaggerates the differences among people. It fixes on contrasts and misses shared concerns. This makes it easier to discount the holders of opposing values because rejecting their views comes with little challenge to personal beliefs. Our convictions are seen as separate and distinct. What affects me has nothing to do with you. More significant is the reverse: what affects you has nothing to do with me.

Further, a failure at empathy makes it easier to demonize the other person. It's an old trick of propagandists and others quite certain of their own virtues. They draw clear distinctions between them and us, making it easier to believe that "they" are not worthy of human respect. Some anti-abortion groups have preached this gospel, and so have racists and militia groups. For instance, late in 1995, an Army private shot and killed a black couple walking down a street in Fayetteville, North Carolina. The accused soldier said that he had done a community service and was quite surprised that "they put me in jail for it."[18] His white supremacist coaches taught him that blacks were not human, and for the soldier, that made the shooting easy. He later was convicted of murder and sentenced to life in prison.

Empathy is an antidote to such thinking, but fragmented audiences are not known for it—and that's the problem. The dangers of targeted media lie along the road, not just at the end of the journey. In other words, you don't have to accept an absolute view—that the targeted media will lay waste to all common meeting places—to see trouble with audience segmentation. A slow retreat from those meeting places where ideas can collide should be enough to cause concern.

It should be a concern because the sense of common purpose and shared interests breaks down long before we become a nation of isolationists holed up in private bunkers. Factionalism is a danger in any pluralistic society, and already we have our troubles with race, class, and ideological differences formed around religion, the right to life, the right to community resources. These and other cracks in society only deepen as people lose touch with the common text that provides the shared focus of the national community.

Andrew Glass made a frightening observation about the vulnerabilities of a population divided into information channels: "Good times are not always going to be here. What about in bad times, when the people are ripe for demagoguery?" The job of a demagogue is that much easier when a population is already divided and he can more easily drive wedges with individual seductions. Problems now evident can only grow when the nation faces a crisis.

THE TOWN SQUARE

The outcomes of widespread public use of the targeted Internet are uncertain. So early is the life of this medium, no one knows for sure how it will evolve. Will it continue to add targeted sites that appeal to special appetites, or will the trend moderate and maybe reverse? We may see a growing dominance of central sites, perhaps controlled by the major media, or the entertainment or software industry. They may never reach "network" size, but they may be big and powerful, compared with the others.

That's a thought expressed by NPR's Philip Davis: "The trends may swing the other way, who knows? People may think the Web is a lot of junk—surfing without substance. This may drive them back toward the trusted sources—on the Web or in traditional formats." None of this is implausible.

But Davis raises a bigger question: Will the Internet even be around in a dozen years? Maybe this thing is a flash in the pan. Lots of early adopters may have dropped cash on a trendy new toy that runs its course and eventually fizzles once the truth is out that nobody can turn a profit on the thing. In the end, it may prove to be a great research tool—a place to pull up census data and historical archives—but not someplace to visit every day for news and information. If this is the Internet's future, we'll continue with our media habits of the past 20 years.

Even if Websites remain targeted and the popularity of the Internet continues to grow, there is no certainty that it will bring about fragmentation and the other outcomes. These may be the unwarranted concerns of alarmists. There is much disagreement about these matters among professional journalists, academics, and historians, and not much consensus over the impact of this medium on individuals and the country. From this early view, and with so much unknown, we can probe into the future just so far and with little certainty. Still, there are signs we cannot ignore.

The medium continues to grow, and most significantly, it grows among the young, who will carry the habit into their adulthood. This argues that the medium *will* be around in a dozen years. Judging from time spent, grade school kids today are more comfortable in front of a computer than they are with a newspaper. That's no surprise. But research shows that Web usage has cut into television time, if only a little, and that *is* a surprise.[19] With increasing speeds of the video stream (downloading video images), the Web may seriously stiffen competition for the once-national pastime.

University students en route to the computer lab these days are passing by the library. They are finding the Web to be a richer, faster, more up-to-date research resource than what the library can offer. This generation is developing a dependence on the new medium, and it is not likely to be a tool they will soon abandon.

It's naive to think that anyone could alter the evolutionary course of the Internet. Nor could anyone affect how the population uses it or ultimately is changed by it. Dan Boltz, a political reporter for the *Washington Post*, compares the manipulation of the Internet to the stock market: "How these change is the result of millions of people doing things individually. For the Internet, it's a matter of the interaction between commercial investment and personal use."[20] The medium is resistant to change or manipulation by any central power. Its design was engineered so that the Internet was decentralized to withstand the forces of an atomic blast. Now, those very safeguards may serve to protect it from more benign attempts at control.

A growing dominance of the Internet puts us in a bind. If it continues to encroach on the audiences of the central media, we will find ourselves contending with a fragmentation probem that could be immensely destructive to the democracy. The most conspicuous remedy is to maintain, somehow, a handful of big, centralized media that continue to reach large enough portions of the population, even while that population is darting frenetically among the cable television stations and Internet sites. No doubt, this media-based solution is best for this media-generated problem.

POLITICAL LEADERS NEED TO PROVIDE FOCUS

The job of providing a national focus, however, cannot be left entirely to the media. Much of it will fall to the political leaders. Orville Schell would put the onus on the president and other key political leaders to stake out the town square for the people.[21] He said it is their responsibility, abandoned of late, "to provide the central point of political gravity, to teach and to lead," and thereby to offer a coherent view of the world, one that imbues the entire society with a way of looking at things. "They may not agree with each other, but they will be looking at the same things, and that's exactly what we need now."

One of the great dangers of a "politics of the polls," discussed earlier by John Bane, is that leaders get it backward. They don't offer the central texts that Schell calls for or that unifying vision for the direction of the country. Instead, they see what each subgroup wants—the religious right, the environmentalists, the isolationists—then cobble a patchwork of policies that please the most and offend the least. This is a flawed political philosophy that sees no gap between public opinion and the public interest.[22] Where is the center in this thinking, and where is the unifying structure among the policies that result? It's the difference between a home designed by Frank Lloyd Wright and a handmade house built in the 1960s by hippies. Wright planned his structures from the inside out; the hippies added a plywood room whenever another person settled in.

Big money accounts for many of these sins. Powerful political donors become like puppeteers, making many politicians so beholden that they don't take a step unless they feel the tug of a donor's string. Big money provokes decisions that send the policy makers in a hundred directions, each of which favors the special interest of one well-heeled group or another.

You are unlikely to find a more conspicuous example of this than the 1997 tax legislation, which built in scores of tax breaks for narrow interests. There is no evidence of a guiding philosophy among the seemingly random collection of cuts.[23] As Brookings Institution's guest scholar Bill Frenzel put it on NPR's *All Things Considered*, "This is the tax cut that has no soul, no principle behind it."[24]

The obvious by-product is the abandonment of policy that arises from central goals. Here, too, like the hippies' houses, policies are tacked on to please the latest arrival—only in Washington, the arrivals must come with bulging pockets, or they are soon sent packing.

Many American political leaders may have what it takes to set the direction needed for the central focus of the nation. The system itself, however—the polls, the political cash, the many hours spent on fundraising—may keep them from their work. Schell asks, Where are the American versions of Nelson Mandela and Vaclav Havel? Their texts, writings, and speeches have become the navigation points for their people. They are the thinkers who have had the courage to think out loud. Why are these models sadly absent from the American political scene? People looking to the White House and congressional leadership often come away disillusioned.

Indeed, our system of public and political communication may conspire against the emergence of such political figures. Washington is a place where every private sneeze is made public. Policies often are killed in utero by the press, which sells more papers and airtime when faults can be found. Reporters-commentators-analysts leap quickly and harshly on victims, and their pounding hurts public images and personal spirits.

Politics is so savage that political gains often can best be made not by proposing something new and inventive but by sinking the ideas of others. The debilitating effects of attack politics last well beyond the elections and are felt far beyond the Beltway. Strong ideas, of course, must stand up to challenges, but how can they be born in an attack environment that is abortive? The running feud between press and pols makes it difficult, if not impossible, for our system to give birth to another Jefferson, Madison, Lincoln, or Roosevelt. Short of a complete system overhaul, how realistic is it, then, to look to political leaders to tackle the challenge of audience fragmentation that the Internet may hasten?

CONCLUSION

Readers may well expect that this book, being about the Internet, might end with a suggestion that our electronic hero somehow come to the rescue. It's tempting. But this is a hero without a halo.

The Internet will cause trouble, let's get that up front. There's a good chance that its many attractions will lure people away from the central places and balkanize the population. It won't happen all at once, but it will cut into the shared experiences and it will add another weight to the pressures already at work on the fissures in the society. No one can judge the severity of these rifts any more than geologists can predict action along the San Andreas Fault. But we know for sure that the tectonic plates of mass communication are shifting because of the Web.·

The Internet, even in its infancy, is cutting into the dominance of the established press. Ironically, this challenge to the centralized media is not coming at the hands of tyrants, as it has in other countries so many time before, but from the changing habits of people brandishing the First Amendment. They are not taking ideas off the table, but piling the table high with new ones. As the Internet cuts into the press, however, it also cuts into the very instruments that have given the population focus and a common agenda. That's the rub. Pluralist democracies need focus. When we lose it, we lose our direction.

If the past is any guide, the mainstream media will stay around in their present form while developing a presence on the Internet. That's the ideal. We can sustain central media—a town square for all to visit—while enjoying the tiny information strip malls for the special inventories you can't find anyplace else. We'll get our facts and keep our focus.

The Internet will give political leaders direct access to the people. The primitive top-down Websites seen in 1996 will adopt sophisticated interactive formats making them more of a force in political communication. Officeholders will communicate regularly with their constituents, not just when they run for office, and they'll hold more interactive sessions. A dialogue between pols and people will be possible without the help of big press or big money. Free of the 10-second sound bite and 30-second spots, political leaders could lay out their thinking more fully and obtain public views more directly. This strips away a crusty layer that has formed since the big media became central to political communication.

Finally, the voters will be able to talk among themselves and form a nucleus of opinion that was not possible before. One of the big problems voters in this century have faced is the inability to reach a critical mass. Town hall meetings once served the purpose, sometimes union halls did, but not anymore. We have lost the chances to form groups of sufficient size and heft to get Washington to listen, short of million-man marches and the like, which are usually no more than a flash in the pan. Maybe that will be simpler with the Internet. Maybe.

There you have it, the best-case scenario: the political leaders get immediate access to the people; that opens up channels of communication that are personal and direct, which in turn allows voters to talk among themselves and make up their minds about the goings-on in their name; money will be less critical because this is an inexpensive medium. All of this triggers a three-star jackpot—the routing of the affluent pullers of political strings.

Call it the politics of proximity, where political leaders and voters stand cheek by jowl. It's a paradox of technology that through this twenty-first-century medium our system of electoral politics could end up where it began: retail politicking with a passion for personal conversions.

The Net may elbow out the meddlers who, in the past 200 years, have inserted themselves between the pols and the people and robbed this participatory democracy of its spirit. Dependency on wholesale media will diminish, and with it the extravagant need for cash that has put the purse above principle and moneyed interests above the public good.

That's as rosy as it comes. It's anybody's bet that the Internet will have such an extraordinary effect, because nobody knows just where this interactive thing will take us or how the information it bears will nourish the hungry roots of this democracy.

Only one thing is certain. We need powerful measures to repair the growing separation between the politicians and the people who put them in office. The Internet comes with a huge risk, but in the end, it may be our greatest, best hope.

NOTES

1. The author examined the possibility of a network-type family of sites with two groups preparing to fund such a large undertaking. One examined a youth network—which was somewhat targeted, like Fox TV—and the other, a general, one-size-fits-all network like the Big Three. After extensive audience research and careful examination of the Web, both concluded that audiences would never be large enough to underwrite such an expensive venture. They also concluded that a general site could offer nothing that visitors would pay to access. Both groups dropped the idea.

2. From an interview on Apr. 30, 1996.

3. T. H. White, *America in Search of Itself: The Making of the President, 1956–1980* (New York: Harper & Row, 1982), 186.

4. G. Selnow and R. Gilbert, *Society's Impact on Television: How the Viewing Public Shapes Television Programming* (Westport, CT: Praeger, 1993).

5. William Brock served as U.S. senator from Kentucky (1971–1977), chairman of the Republican National Committee (1977–1981), U.S. trade representative (1981–1985), and secretary of labor (1985–1987).

6. From an interview on Feb. 2, 1997.

7. This is a position maintained in S. Ansolabehere and S. Iyengar, *Going Negative: How Campaign Advertising Shrinks and Polarizes the Electorate* (New York: Free Press, 1995).

8. MSNBC's America's Voice poll reported that 32 percent of people said they visited a Website for the express purpose of obtaining political information.

9. From an interview on Jan. 29, 1997.

10. From an interview on Feb. 4, 1997.

11. R. Reddick, *News Backgrounder: Promises and Pitfalls for Journalists on the Information Highway* newsletter published by the Foundation for American Communications.

12. But will people chase down only the things that interest them? That's an open question. Much of the evidence is anecdotal, and any empirical research is pre-Internet. William Crano, a leading social psychologist and specialist in human communication, says that in task-driven settings, people pursue information that is useful and supportive. Their behaviors are less certain when faced with more ambiguous situations, such as surfing the Web for enjoyment and general information-gathering. "Other than the real saintly people, most will say 'I'm going after the information I like.' "

In the laboratory, Crano said, subjects often display balance in their selection of information: "But don't forget, these are students usually under the gun to look at both sides of an issue. There are usually considerable 'demand effects' in the lab that drive subjects to display such evenhandedness. I'm not so sure in the real world, free of such expectations, people won't go after whatever pleases them. In fact, it's a pretty good bet."

13. Madison later helped organize the Jeffersonian Republican Party even though earlier the notion of party was not respectable. Elkins and McKitrick state that "there was no neutral vocabulary for talking about [party]" (*The Age of Federalism* [New York: Oxford University Press, 1993], p. 286). Stanley Elkins said in an interview, "If you pick up the Madison of the Federalist Papers, you miss the fact that he will change once he organizes the Jeffersonian Republic an Party. And then he convinces himself that he and Jefferson represent virtue and that the Federalists are monarchists. This is rather unfair if you're John Adams."

14. From an interview on Feb. 14, 1997.

15. Elkins and McKitrick, *The Age of Federalism*, p. 87

16. Ibid.

17. From an interview on Feb. 14, 1997.

18. Reuters story printed in the *San Francisco Chronicle*, "Soldier Shot Black Couple, Ex-Paratrooper Testifies," Feb. 15, 1997, p. A2.

19. *Yankelovich Cybercitizen II Report*, August 1996.

20. From an interview on Feb. 10, 1997.

21. From an interview on Jan. 29, 1997.

22. Theodore Sorensen describes how John F. Kennedy saw a great difference between public opinion and the public interest. In Kennedy's first State of the Union message, he described his responsibility to "lead, inform, correct and sometimes even ignore constituent opinion, if we are to exercise full that judgment for which we were elected." Quoted in T. C. Sorensen, *Kennedy* (New York: Harper & Row, 1965), 310.

23. See Clay Chandler, "Small Interests Targeted for Big Tax Breaks," *Washington Post*, June 19, 1997, p. A1. Downloaded from http://www.washingtonpost.com on June 30, 1997.

24. Statement by Bill Frenzel, guest scholar in the department of government studies at the Brookings Institution, on National Public Radio's *All Things Considered*, June 30, 1997.

Appendix: The Public's Acceptance of the Internet

RELUCTANCE TO USE A NEW MEDIUM

Stand on the craggy bluffs at Bodega Bay in northern California, and you can see the muddy waters of the Russian River flow into the Pacific Ocean. It's remarkable to observe that the confluence is not immediate; rather, the opaque river flows unchallenged far offshore before its dark brown waters are absorbed by the ocean.

The scene at Bodega Bay is something like the image one gets looking at the flow of information from a new medium. In the 1920s the makers and users of news, who had known only print, didn't know what to make of information delivered by radio. It was fast and ephemeral, the news stories were prepared differently and consumed differently from print news. A decade would pass before radio's information output would merge fully with the larger flow of the national news. Television, too, took years to blend in with the information habits of the public. It wasn't until 1956 that both parties used television in political campaigns, fully eight years after the technology was in place. Networks stayed with 15-minute newscasts until 1962, a dozen years after the medium's commercial debut.

The Internet is being adopted more quickly than its two predecessors, but it isn't integrating immediately into the information mainstream. Most people don't browse the Web for news the way they read the morning paper, watch the *Today* show, or listen to National Public Radio's *Morning Edition*. For most audiences, the Internet has not yet become part of the daily routine. It's too early for that. Maybe like radio, to which a very few listened obsessively and the mass audience thought it a curiosity until *The Green Hornet* came along, the Web—so compulsively used by its fans—will grab its masses just as soon as irresistible programming bursts forth.

We can attribute some of this relatively slow start to long loadtimes of the sites, thin news coverage, and the audience's need to be interactive after almost 80 years of playing a passive role. Perhaps more to the point, though, is "natural resistance." We all settle into rigid patterns: some people read the front section of the *Chicago Tribune* with the first cup of coffee, then the sports with the second cup, and for them that doesn't vary. A colleague once complained that she missed the news on the way to work because the NPR transmitter was knocked off-line. When asked why she didn't change stations, she said that she *always* listened to *Morning Edition* and never thought of changing. She just shut off the radio. The Web is no exception to the rule that old habits die hard.

Another problem comes from the operational end. Like the rest of us, news operators haven't figured out the Web yet. They aren't sure how to present on-line news. Accordingly, while some journalists are using Randy Reddick's "onion approach" to writing for the Web, many are still using the old models.

This practice isn't new. Early radio copy was extracted from newspaper stories. Early television newscasts were sclerotic shots of reporters reading radio copy.[1] Today, the layouts on media sites look more like *USA Today* than the *New York Times*, so at least Web news media push trendy graphics; but for the other items, they aren't all that much different from conventional newspapers. Typically they post headlines in order of importance; they divide the news into national, international, business, sports, and entertainment; they drop in a few pictures, sometimes the same shots used in sister newspapers; offer advice columns; run classifieds and display ads.

As we have discussed elsewhere, the media sites have experimented with such Web features as two-stage writing, hypertext, search engines, feedback, audio and video clips, each in search of the holy grail—a format specific, appropriate, and exclusive for the Web. The mainstream media are exploring ways to tell a Web news story that's a "specialty of the house," hoping thereby to attract a loyal audience and create real revenue. Unfortunately, audiences have been small and profits have been illusory for most vendors.

The experts are still squabbling over the statistics, but it's safe to say that around 40 million people had access, and nobody knows how many of these were active users.[2] The sales of computers continue to be brisk, and the adoption of Web technology has been remarkable. The early adopters were younger, more educated, and more affluent. The second wave, middle-aged and middle-income users, will increase gradually—but increase it will.

According to the Pew Research Center, "About 21 million (12% of the voting age population) obtained political or policy news from online services . . . and of them about 7 million (4%) used the Internet and/or commercial services for information about the Presidential election."[3] The difference between those who *could* and those who *did* explore the information sites is due, in part, to a lack of interest in politics or news, but also to confusion and uncertainty over the technology. We can't expect people to adopt the medium into their routines when so many continue to wrestle with the mechanics of the thing.[4]

Many newcomers had difficulty understanding the concept of the Internet, which at times affected how they applied the procedures. For instance, some people got hung up on the differences between the Web and proprietary service providers such as AOL, and they couldn't grasp the function of hypertext or realize that sites linked together were not necessarily constructed by the same developers. This sometimes led to trouble.

Adelaide Elm, spokeswoman for Project Vote Smart, tells how visitors often failed to understand that some PVS links connected to partisan sites. These users complained bitterly when they thought this neutral organization was playing an advocacy role.

Even Bob Dole seemed confused. In 1996, he charged the White House with doing the work of foreign governments because its home page linked to a site touting Japanese markets. Dole was referring to a link to a Japanese trade office site run by the Japanese government. The White House posted it to help American exporters market their products abroad. News accounts suggested that Dole thought the White House didn't merely link to the Japanese trade site, but was somehow involved in its development.[5]

Average users were sometimes confused by all the http addresses, bookmarks, search engines, feedback options, and other abstractions that were new to this medium, to say nothing of hardware snags. The stories have been well circulated about a gent who thought the CD-ROM drive was a cup holder, and the woman who, thinking she had a microphone, shouted commands into her mouse.

Confusions over hardware and software and the failure to grasp the basic concept of the Internet will continue to slow its adoption. Sadly, these hurdles will impede the integration of Website information into the mix of conventional knowledge assembled through newspaper articles and newscasts. There is a natural inertia to the adoption of anything radically new and technically demanding. When you realize that most parents and grandparents rely on eight-year-olds to program their VCRs, you see it will take time for the Web to share equal space with the other media.

How do we hasten this process? Andy Glass, Washington bureau chief of Cox News Service, says two developments must take place. First, the industry needs to simplify Internet access. Everything—hardware, software, marketing—must be made easier.

Start with the purchase of equipment. Early radio and television offered only a few product models, and that simplified choices for audiences still new to the technology. By contrast, computer vendors offer a vast range of choices that confuse and intimidate many customers who haven't yet mastered their VCRs or programmable microwaves. Computer-illiterate people are forced to decide chip speeds, disk sizes, RAM capacities, and modem speeds that affect the operation of the equipment and the cost by thousands of dollars. "Complete packages" sometimes don't include CD-ROM drives to input programs or monitors to see them. To the initiated, the details are simple, but to the unschooled they are frightening.

In all fairness, Apple Computers has gone a long way toward simplifying the process. The company's market research has picked up on the confusion and anxiety associated with the adoption of equipment, and accordingly it has made a point of selling complete, ready-to-run systems—at least up to the Internet access phase. Apple's advertisements stress the simplicity. For instance, in full-page newspaper ads, Apple says that getting into computer technology is great, "Unless you're sitting in front of a computer trying to make it all work . . . Windows PCs often treat . . . hardware as extras. Macintosh computers, on the other hand, come multimedia ready, right from the box."[6]

Apple may ease up-front decisions that get computers up and running quickly, but getting a system home and wired up is only half the struggle. There's more to getting on-line, and Apple doesn't help much here.

People must choose a service or access provider, often without really understanding what these terms mean. Then, loading the communication software requires more uninformed decisions, this time about communication ports, modems, account names, and passwords. The judgments often are random. so the outcomes are a roll of the dice.

Essentially, the multistep process required to get on-line obliges average people, dumbstruck by this technology, to act as general contractors. It forces them into a job where they don't know the subcontractors by name, or even what they do. People don't have blueprints or a good sense for the appearance of the final product. And, if that's not enough, they foot the entire bill themselves, with little awareness of the raw material costs. The complex process is intimidating, expensive, fraught with error, and, in the end, sometimes fruitless. Stories surface now and then about people who fail, and return the computer to the box. Not many people ever packed off their radio or television set because they couldn't figure out how to work it. Even though early television sets weren't always plug 'n' play, getting them up and running was a lot simpler than rigging a computer for the Internet.

Apart from the need to simplify the setup, Andrew Glass stresses the need to simplify the software. He observed that most browsers are not easy to use, especially for people used to operating their television sets with point-and-click technology. Programmers will need to make site changes as simple as channel changes, E-mail access as simple as telephone access. In 1996 that was not the case.

Glass said there also must be better user education. Simplifying setup and software is essential, but it must be tied to information about how to join the hardware and software into a functional system. It's like improving an athlete's pole-vaulting skills and lowering the bar at the same time. The end result will be an easy jump.

The education does not have to involve formal classes or intimidating manuals. Bring education into the public forums and make it accessible. How? Videotapes could help. They use a familiar medium and can demonstrate the lessons visually. Simple guides can ramp people into the technology, but they'll have to be more basic than even the *Internet for Dummies* series.

For-profit companies could take the cue and bundle the information along with access to telephone advice. Newspapers and magazines that run Websites could provide periodic inserts that explain the process and promote access to their online ventures. It's self-serving, sure, but it also serves customers very much in need of such information. The point is, public education, which so far has been scattered and inadequate, should become focused and more available. The media, computer companies, and third-party jobbers might find a rich market in public education and derive a second payoff from a new, opened-up medium.

The simplicity of setup, access, and use will speed that second wave onto the

Internet and substantially increase the role of this medium in political communication.

Andy Glass, at Cox News, tells about a seminar he conducted at Harvard, a few months before the election, where the discussion turned to the likelihood that the Internet would someday play a significant role in the dissemination of news. Glass said the discussion reminded him of meetings at the Reform Club in London in 1842, where members debated the future of the railroad in Britain. The railroad, of course, not only endured, it became a decisive element in the second phase of the industrial revolution.

The Internet, Glass predicted, will become an indispensable tool in the delivery of public information, joining print and broadcast as a full-fledged national organ, common as the morning paper, familiar as the movies. When that happens, he said, the Internet will have a significant impact on political communication. In order for *that* to happen, however, turning to a Website has to be as easy as turning on the morning news.

NOTES

1. See F. L. Smith, *Perspectives on Radio and Television: Telecommunications in the United States, 2nd ed.* (New York: Harper & Row, 1985).

2. Measures of on-line users vary considerably among research firms. Yankelovich in August 1996 counted 42 million U.S. users 18+ years of age who had been on-line within the previous 12 months. Nielsen found, in a study conducted during the same month, that 48 million people age 16+ in the United States and Canada had access. IntellQuest found 35 million people 16+ years of age who used an on-line service or the Internet in the first three months of 1996. These statistics are reported by CyberAtlas on the company's site, downloaded on Feb. 25, 1997. URL: http://www.cyberatlas.com/market.html.

3. The Pew Research Center, "News Attracts Most Internet Users." URL: http://www.people-press.org/tec96sum.htm.

4. On Jan. 17, 1997, NPR's *Science Friday* devoted an entire program to figuring out the Internet. Ira Flato, the host, noted that getting on the Web had a "very steep learning curve," and many people were unable to assemble all the components necessary to complete the setup—the computer, software, and the service or access provider. Newspaper and magazine articles and television shows have addressed the difficulties of accessing the medium.

5. The *Washington Post* reported that Dole said, "After three and one-half years of stewardship by Bill Clinton and his advisers, . . . it is the Japanese who are writing the trade policy papers for the Clinton White House." The *Post* noted that White House spokeswoman Mary Ellen Glynn said, in response, "I'm not sure that Senator Dole understands exactly how the Web works, that links are a way to jump from one site to another. . . . We set up links with lots of different things." P. Blustein, and C. Chandler, "White House Defends Its Web Links to Japanese: Dole Lashes Out at Clinton for Allowing Home Page Access to Foreign Ministry's Document," *Washington Post*, Apr. 30, 1996, p. D1.

6. From a full-page ad in the *San Francisco Chronicle*, Feb. 15, 1997, p. A17.

Further Reading

Aberbach, David. *Charisma in Politics, Religion and the Media: Private Trauma, Public Ideals*. New York: New York University Press, 1996.

Alger, Dean E. *The Media and Politics*. San Diego: Harcourt Brace and Company, 1995.

Ansolabehere, Stephen, Roy Behr, and Shannto Iyengar. *The Media Game: American Politics in the Television Age*. Englewood Cliffs, NJ: Prentice Hall, 1992.

Barber, James D. *The Pulse of Politics: Electing Presidents in the Media Age*. New Brunswick, NJ: Transaction Publishers, 1992.

Blumler, Jay, and Michael Gurevitch. *Political Communication*. New York: Routledge, 1995.

Buchanan, Bruce. *Renewing Presidential Politics: Campaigns, Media and the Public Interest*. Lanham, MD: Rowman and Littlefield Publishers, 1996.

Cavanaugh, John W. *Media Effects on Voters: A Panel Study of the 1992 Presidential Election*. Lanham: University Press of America, 1995.

Crigler, Ann N., ed. *The Psychology of Political Communication*. Ann Arbor, MI: University of Michigan Press, 1996.

Croteau, David, and William Hoynes. *By Invitation Only: How the Media Limit Political Debate*. Monroe, ME: Common Courage Press, 1994.

Cunningham, Liz. *Talking Politics: Choosing the President in the Television Age*. Westport, CT: Greenwood Publishing, 1995.

Davies, Andrew C. *Telecommunications and Policy: The Decentralised Alternative*. New York: St. Martin's Press, 1994.

Davis, Richard. *The Press and American Politics: The New Mediator*. Englewood Cliffs, NJ: Prentice Hall, 1995.

Davis, Richard, ed. *Politics and the Media*. Englewood Cliffs, NJ: Prentice Hall, 1993.

Diamond, Edwin, and Robert A. Silverman. *White House to Your House: Media and Politics in Virtual America*. Cambridge, MA: M.I.T. Press, 1995.

Exoo, Calvin F. *The Politics of the Mass Media*. Saint Paul, MN: West Publishing Company College and School Division, 1993.

Fallows, James. *Breaking the News: How the Media Undermines American Democracy*. New York: Random House, 1997.

Garrison, Jasper. *The Invisible Warriors*. Detroit: Smartfellows Press, 1995.

Gibbons, Arnold. *Race, Politics and the White Media: The Jesse Jackson Campaigns*. Lanham, MD: University Press of America, 1993.

Graber, Doris A., ed. *Media Power in Politics*. Washington, DC: Congressional Quarterly, 1993.

Hamamoto, Darrell Y. *Nervous Laughter: Television Situation Comedy and Liberal Democratic Ideology*. Westport, CT: Greenwood Publishing, 1989.

Harvey, Jack B., and Cayle Martinez. *Self Righteous, Arrogant and Untouchable*. Nevada City, CA: Crystal Lake Publishing, 1996.

Harvey, Lisa S. *Stolen Thunder: The Cultural Roots of Political Communication*, Vol. 4. New York: Peter Lang Publishing, 1994.

Hughes, Elizabeth M. *The Logical Choice: How Political Commercials Use Logic to Win Votes*. Lanham, MD: University Press of America, 1994.

Iyengar, Shanto, and Richard Reeves. *Does the Media Govern?: Politicians, Voters and Reporters in America*. Thousand Oaks, CA: Sage Publications, 1996.

Jacobsen, John K. *Dead Reckonings: Ideas, Interests, and Politics in the "Information Age."* Atlantic Highlands, NJ: Humanities Press International, 1997.

Jamieson, Kathleen H., and Karlyn K. Campbell. *The Interplay of Influence: News, Advertising, Politics, and the Mass Media*. Belmont, CA: Wadsworth Publishing Company, 1992.

Jamieson, Kathleen H., and Joseph N. Cappella. *Spiral of Cynicism: The Press and the Public Good*. New York: Oxford University Press, 1997.

Just, Marion R. *Crosstalk: Citizens, Candidates, and the Media in Presidential Campaign*. Chicago: University of Chicago Press, 1996.

Kellner, Douglas. *Media Culture: Cultural Studies, Identity and Politics Between the Modern and the Postmodern*. New York: Routledge, 1995.

Kennamer, J. David, ed. *Public Opinion, the Press, and Public Policy*, Westport, CT: Greenwood Publishing, 1992.

Kerbel, Matthew R. *Remote and Controlled: Media Politics in a Cynical Age*. Boulder, CO: Westview Press, 1995.

Kraus, Sidney. *Televised Presidential Debates and Public Policy*. Hillsdale, NJ: Lawrence Erlbaum Associates, 1988.

Kraus, Sidney, and Dennis Davis. *The Effects of Mass Communication on Political Behavior*. University Park: Pennsylvania State University Press, 1976.

Lanoue, David J., and Peter R. Schrott. *The Joint Press Conference: The History, Impact, and Prospects of American Presidential Debates*. Westport, CT: Greenwood Publishing, 1991.

Lenart, Silvo. *Shaping Political Attitudes: The Impact of Interpersonal Communication and Mass Media*. Thousand Oaks, CA: Sage Publications, 1994.

Malek, Abbas, ed. *News Media and Foreign Relations: A Multifaceted Perspective*. Greenwich, CT: Ablex Publishing Corporation, 1996.

Mann, Thomas E., and Gary R. Orren, eds. *Media Polls in American Politics*. Washington, DC: Brookings Institution, Oct. 1992.

Naureckas, Jim, and Janine Jackson, eds. *The FAIR Reader: An Extra! Review of Press and Politics in the '90s.* Boulder, CO: Westview Press, 1996.

Nimmo, Dan D., and Chevelle Newsome. *Political Commentators in the United States: A Biocritical Sourcebook, 1930 to the Present.* Westport, CT: Greenwood Publishing, 1997.

Norris, Pippa, ed. *Politics and the Press: The News Media and Its Influences.* Boulder, CO: Lynne Rienner Publishers, 1997.

Page, Benjamin I. *Who Deliberates?: Mass Media in Modern Democracy.* Chicago: University of Chicago Press, 1996.

Popkin, Jeremy D., ed. *Media and Revolution.* Lexington, KY: University Press of Kentucky, 1995.

Robbins, Bruce, ed. *The Phantom Public Sphere.* Minneapolis, MN: University of Minnesota Press, 1993.

Rosenstiel, Tom. *The Beat Goes On: President Clinton's First Year with the Media.* New York: Twentieth Century Fund Press/Priority Press Publications, 1994.

Rubin, Bernard. *Media, Politics, and Democracy.* New York: Oxford University Press, 1977.

Sabato, Larry J. *Feedingy: How Attack Journalism Has Transformed American Politics.* New York: Free Press, 1993.

Savage, Robert L., Dan Nimmo, and Lee Thayer, eds. *Politics in Familiar Contexts: Projecting Politics Through Popular Media.* Greenwich, CT: Ablex Publishing Corporation, 1990.

Schmuhl, Robert. *Demanding Democracy.* Notre Dame: University of Notre Dame Press, 1994.

Selnow, Gary. *High-Tech Campaigns: Computer Technology in Political Communication.* Westport, CT: Praeger, 1994.

Spitzer, Robert J., Ed. *Media and Public Policy.* Westport, CT: Greenwood Publishing, 1992.

Swanson, David L., and Mancini Paolo eds. *Politics, Media, and Modern Democracy: An International Study of Innovations in Electoral Campaigning and Their Consequences.* Westport, CT: Greenwood Publishing, 1996.

Trend, David. *Cultural Democracy: Politics, Media, New Technology.* Albany, NY: State University of New York Press, 1997.

Warshaw, Shirley A., and Gerald R. Ford, eds. *The Eisenhower Legacy: Discussions of Presidential Leadership.* Silver Spring, MD: Bartleby Press, 1992.

Wheeler, Mark C. *Politics and the Mass Media.* Malden, MA: Blackwell Publishers, 1997.

Winograd, Morley, and Dudley Buffa. *Taking Control: Politics in the Information Age.* New York: Henry Holt and Company, 1996.

Wolfsfeld, Gadi. *Media and Political Conflict: Contests in the Central Arena.* New York: Cambridge University Press, 1997.

Woodward, Gary C. *Perspectives on American Political Media.* Needham Heights, MA: Allyn and Bacon, 1996.

Index

About the Author

GARY W. SELNOW is a Professor of Communication at San Francisco State University and the developer of *America's Voice*, a nationwide program using television and the Internet to air the political views of American voters. He is the author or editor of five books, including *Society's Impact on Television* and *High-Tech Campaigns*.